CLAIMING HISTORY

CLAIMING HISTORY

Colonialism, Ethnography, and the Novel

Eleni Coundouriotis

COLUMBIA UNIVERSITY PRESS / NEW YORK

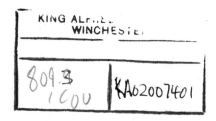
Columbia University Press
Publishers Since 1893
New York   Chichester, West Sussex
Copyright © 1999 Columbia University Press

Cover: Appliqué cloth showing Dokpowe (work-cooperative) at work.
Melville Herskovits, *Dahomey: An Ancient West African Kingdom,* Plate 15.
New York: J. J. Augustin, 1938. Reproduced by permission.
The Research Foundation at the University of Connecticut
generously provided funds for the book's color cover.

Library of Congress Cataloging-in-Publication Data
Coundouriotis, Eleni.
    Claiming history : colonialism, ethnography, and the novel / Eleni
Coundouriotis.
        p.   cm.
    Includes bibliographical references (p.   ) and index.
    ISBN 0-231-11350-1 (alk. paper). — ISBN 0-231-11351-X (pbk. :
(alk. paper)
    1. European fiction—History and criticism. 2. African fiction
(French)—History and criticism. 3. African fiction (English)—
History and criticism. 4. Africa—In literature. 5. History in
literature. 6. Imperialism in literature. I. Title.
PN3491.C67   1998
                                                98-34458
809.9'9358—dc21

For my parents

CONTENTS

■■

Acknowledgments *ix*

Introduction *1*

1. The Traditional Cultures of René Maran and
Chinua Achebe *21*

2. History, Human Sacrifices, and the Victorian Travelers
to Dahomey *45*

3. Contesting Authenticity: Paul Hazoumé, Ethnography,
and Negritude *73*

4. Resistant History in Paul Hazoumé's *Doguicimi* *97*

5. History as Transgression in *Le Devoir de violence* *116*

6. Temporality and the Geographies of the Nation: "The Future
Present" in *The Famished Road* *141*

Afterword *165*

Notes *173*
Works Cited *193*
Index *205*

ACKNOWLEDGMENTS

I began working on this book following a Whiting Foundation fellowship and while I was a lecturer for the Committee on Degrees in Literature at Harvard. Both were crucial supports. Although this book was a new project conceived after the dissertation, I owe a major debt to my dissertation advisers, Jonathan Arac and Edward Said. The example of Jonathan Arac's scholarship has been sustaining, and his encouragement to pursue this study several years after I finished my degree was crucial. Edward Said has been a constant inspiration. The freedom and rigor of his thinking, his courage, and love of conversation have stayed with me as constant reminders of what is possible.

A fellowship from the chancellor's office of the University of Connecticut in the fall of 1997 allowed me to complete this study. The staff at the interlibrary loan office of the Homer Babbidge Library at the University of Connecticut was invaluable. Tara Hurt of the Thomas J. Dodd Research Center at the University of Connecticut assisted me with the illustrations. I would also like to thank Geneviève Brassard, who helped put together the English translations at the last minute, and Ellen O'Brien for help with the index.

For her valuable insights on the draft of the manuscript, I would like to thank Margaret Higonnet. Not only did Jennifer Crewe provide intelligent guidance, but I was constantly reassured by Ron Harris's careful oversight of the production of the book, and my readers at Columbia University Press were conscientious, sensitive, and very supportive—my work could not have fallen into better hands. I benefited greatly from their suggestions.

All translations are my own except where indicated otherwise. The illustration from Dalzel, *A History of Dahomy*, is reprinted with permission of the British Library. Quotations from *Doguicimi: The First Dahomean Novel*, by Paul Hazoumé, translated by Richard Bjornson, are reprinted with permission of Lynne Rienner Publishers.

The most special thanks of all I owe to Thomas Recchio for being a most amazing reader—insightful, patient, sympathetic, imaginative—and for his warm love and support that carried me through.

CLAIMING HISTORY

Introduction

The Inaugural Gesture

When Yambo Ouologuem's *Le Devoir de violence* appeared in 1968, the reviewer for *Le Monde* hailed the novel as "the first African novel worthy of the name" (quoted in Miller, *Blank Darkness* 219). Nineteen sixty-eight seems a rather late date to be making such a claim, yet Ouologuem's reviewer was reflecting a pervasive attitude in the reception of African literature. It has become a critical commonplace to inaugurate the African novel repeatedly as a means of identifying the "authentically" African.

A more recent example is Ben Okri's *The Famished Road* (1991). The novel first received mixed reviews. Charles Johnson, writing for the *Times Literary Supplement*, complained about a novel "padded out with descriptive passages that slow it down" (*TLS*, April 19, 1991). However, when *The Famished Road* emerged as the surprise winner of the Booker Prize in 1991 (the London *Times* byline on October 23, 1991, read "Prize for Outsider"), the novel's visionary style was perceived as innovative. A fuller discussion of the novel's Africanness emerged across the Atlantic, where, for example, the reviewer for the *Boston Globe* noted that Okri created "a sense of reality unlike anything known in the West" (Parini 103). In a much more nuanced review for the *Nation*, Anthony Appiah compared the novel to *Le Devoir de violence* and Ahmadou Kourouma's *Les Soleils des indépendances*, francophone works of "rhetorical complexity" of the kind not yet found in the anglophone novel, according to Appiah, until *The Famished Road*. Proclaiming the relative youth of the "black African novel in English," Henry Louis Gates situates *The Famished Road* within a larger inaugural movement where Okri's work signals the abandonment of realism (an imitative form) for a return to Yoruba "mythic narrative." Gates relies on the notion of an African authenticity (his labeling of Okri as a Yoruba writer) to inaugurate a new stylistic maturity in anglophone fiction.

Every gesture to inaugurate anew is profoundly revisionist. In the cases of Ouologuem and Okri, the inaugural gesture creates the opportunity to reinvent the authentically African and cast a pall of inauthenticity on the writers that preceded them. The impression that past works are inauthentic emerges as their historicity—their entanglement in their historical moment and worldly situation—becomes evident through hindsight. An awareness of historicity spoils authenticity. Therefore, the pall of inauthenticity cast on precursors through the inaugural gesture masks a denial of history.

Authenticity may be deployed as a critical measure of value, yet the novels themselves speak against any concept of the authentic. Belated as they would be as inaugurators, Ouologuem and Okri demonstrate, ironically at times, that they belong to a worldly, cosmopolitan tradition of the novel. Soon after the enthusiastic reception of his novel, Ouologuem was charged with plagiarizing a number of Western novels (including Graham Greene's *It's a Battlefield* and André Schwartz-Bart's *Le Dernier des justes*). Even more provocatively, the novel's themes of political violence are intrinsically connected to its subversive textual borrowings. As Christopher Miller's extensive analysis of the plagiarism controversy has shown, the claims of Africa as a lost origin in the novel are based on theft and violence. Ouologuem depicts the African past as "a purloined, kidnapped and usurped origin, as an originary violence" (*Blank Darkness* 233). The authenticity discovered by the reviewers betrays an attitude toward Africa lampooned in the novel. The novel prefigures its own reception, and its studied intertextuality subverts the premise of its reception as authentic.

To attribute authenticity is to mask a particular history by an act of violent repression. It is not surprising that the concept of authenticity has been thoroughly problematized in literary theory. By returning to the site of one of these attacks, Derrida's critique of Lévi-Strauss, we are reminded that all cultures are inauthentic, that there is no "society without writing," and implicitly therefore that all cultures have history (*Of Grammatology* 109). In *Tristes Tropiques* Lévi-Strauss derives the value of authenticity in a moment of essayistic self-discovery where he compensates for a failure of vision in confronting others. Authenticity evolves as the logical consequence of his written, retrospective account of an unsettling personal experience. "Completely virgin landscapes," he tells us,

> have a monotony which deprives their wildness of any significant value. They withhold themselves from man; instead of challenging him, they disintegrate under his gaze. But in this scrubland, which stretches endlessly into the distance, the incision of the *picada*, the contorted silhouettes of the poles and the arcs of wire linking them one to another seem like incongruous objects floating in space, such as can be seen in Yves Tanguy's paintings. Being evidence of man's former presence and of the futility of his efforts, they mark the extreme limit he has tried to exceed, making it more obvious than it would have been without them. The erratic nature of his enterprise and the failure by which it has been punished confirm the authenticity of the surrounding wilderness. *(272)*

A completely virgin landscape is invisible without the traces of man's (Western man's, of course) attempts to mar this landscape. It is by opposition to the line that the authentic wilderness becomes visible. Dissolution and extreme limits are overcome by the repeat visitor who has an affirming experience of recognition (the wilderness as authenticity). Lévi-Strauss, returning to a site that has been already marked, therefore, proposes *authenticity* as the compensatory term to cover up the failures of previous encounters and other histories. By extension the people who live in this wilderness are "among the most primitive to be found anywhere in the world" (272). Moreover, Lévi-Strauss's allusion to an Yves Tanguy painting extends James Clifford's affiliation of ethnography to surrealism in the 1930s (in *Predicament* 117–51). By the 1950s we do not find surrealism borrowing displaced ethnographic facts or imitating the ethnographic tendency toward fragmented realities; instead we see surrealism making a wild landscape readable, surrealism providing the schemata of perception. This reversal is significant because it emphasizes not only the derivative nature of the authentic (in this case, it is borrowed from surrealism) but also authenticity's dependence on the erasure of context, of background. The landscape with the *picada* running through it is like an Yves Tanguy painting because the wires and the poles are like "incongruous objects floating in space"—the space is the flat color, the featureless, blank background of the canvas on which are displayed the defamiliarized objects of the surrealistic imagination. The *picada* divides and shapes the background, making its contours visible.

To turn back to the novel, we find the same decontextualization when critics read a novel as authentically African. Context is divorced from narrative and then recast as a catalog of scenes of African life without historical specificity. A reinvented background emerges that is informed by the dividing line separating the authentic from the modern. *Claiming History* examines a few novels—not a canon, or a particular tradition, but a few paradigmatic works that share the common feature of having been received as inaugural works—in which their authors lay claim to and explain a particular history against various covert or overt acts of narrative repression. The book documents how history is claimed through fiction, a hybrid discourse in Bakhtin's terms, where narrative explanation delineates new authorial positions and undercuts established perspectives. Fiction can then interfere with the prefiguration of narratives by defining the field of prefiguration as its field of representation.

Le Devoir de violence and *The Famished Road* are relatively recent examples of a long-standing habit of inaugurating the African novel anew by proclaiming the authentic Africanness of a particular work. Not all important works of African fiction have been greeted in this manner, however.[1] It is those novels that engage history in ambitious and resistant ways that elicit the accolade of authenticity and are perceived as inaugural. The effect (and unstated purpose) of this manner of reception is to diminish the historical ambitions of these novels and distract their readers by highlighting instead the novels' description of everyday life in an African community. Therefore historical fictions were repeatedly received as ethnographic fictions and their authors' historical questioning obscured.

The reception of the novels I examine in this book (works by Maran, Achebe, Hazoumé, Ouologuem, and Okri) demonstrates that Africans also participated in the tendency to diminish the historical by praising African authenticity. There was a lot at stake in repressing the discourse of internal critique at a time of anticolonial struggle. A case in point is the African reception of *Batouala*, René Maran's 1921 novel. The preface to the novel was an extended attack on colonialism, but the novel itself posed some serious questions about the role of Africans in the colonial situation. Consequently, there has been much discussion of Maran's anticolonialism (the preface led to the novel's censorship in all French colonies) and praise for his style, but little serious analysis of his story. The novel was recognized as authentic by both Parisians and Africans. Léopold Senghor declared in 1965 that Maran had been "the precursor of negritude in francophone culture" (*Hommage* 9), and Abiola Irele, following Senghor's lead, anointed Maran as "the creator of the modern African novel" (132).

Maran's prominence as an inaugural figure was enhanced when *Batouala* won the Prix Goncourt and Maran became the first black writer to be so distinguished. Despite the award and Senghor's sanction, however, Maran's status as the inventor of African fiction is incongruous since, for one thing, he was not African. Maran was born in Martinique of Guyanese parents. He was educated in France, where he lived from the age of four. He worked in Africa for the French colonial service from 1910 until 1923, and it was during these years that he wrote *Batouala*. After 1923 he never again returned to either Africa or the Caribbean and resided continuously in France. Irele does not ignore Maran's origins and treats him along with Césaire and Fanon as a Martinican writer who was able to do "something far in advance of exoticism, something more than a mere outside representation of a foreign atmosphere, but an evocation that goes a long way towards *restituting* the inner quality of life in a specific human universe" (132, emphasis added). Irele deploys what Clifford has called the language of "salvage ethnography" ("Ethnographic Allegory" 112–3), although he acknowledges implicitly Maran's emphasis on historical specificity.

At the time of *Batouala*'s publication there had been only one fran-cophone prose fiction published by an African author. Ahmadou Mapaté Diagne's twenty-eight-page story *Les Trois volontés de Malic* had been pub-lished by Larose in Paris the previous year. A Senegalese teacher (who was also at one time secretary to the head of the Ecole Coloniale, Georges Hardy), Diagne addressed his story to an audience of schoolchildren as an argument for French literacy. Although the theme of French education be-came pivotal to the francophone novel after 1945, the excessive didacticism of *Les Trois volontés de Malic* made it unnovelistic (Midiohouan 61).[2]

Looking to mark the beginning of francophone African fiction, Senghor turned to Maran as the inventor of an authentic discourse about Africa. For Senghor, Maran's importance is purely aesthetic:

> After *Batouala* one can no longer make Africans live, work, love, cry, laugh or talk like whites. It is no longer even a matter of making them speak "petit nègre," but wolof, malinké, éwondo in French. Because it is René Maran who first gave expression to the black soul, in a negro style, in French.   *(Hommage 13)*

Implicitly Senghor claims that language can attain a large measure of trans-parency and echo the salient elements of any culture. Senghor's assump-tions about the function of style echo Bakhtin, who argued that, in prose, considerations of style can divorce themselves from convention and render language flexible enough to reflect distinguishing features of the reality being represented ("Discourse in the Novel" in *Dialogic* 378). Senghor ad-dresses this same capacity for assimilation articulated by Bakhtin: Maran successfully shaped his medium (the French language) to the reality he was describing. This amounts to praising Maran for his documentary capacity and his translation of an African culture into French, both of which are ethnographic gestures. Moreover, this reinvented French language symbol-izes a cultural marriage, a resolution of unproductive conflicts into creative expression. Senghor derived from *Batouala* the stylistics of the African hu-manism he was to propose as the cornerstone of his negritudinist project.

Senghor's placement of Maran's work within the ethnographic para-digm is not surprising. Christopher Miller used Senghor's affiliation with the project of ethnography as the starting point of *Theories of Africans* (1990). Miller's rationale for reading francophone literature in the context of anthropology is that francophone fiction emerged in tandem with anthropology and thus, Miller argues, anthropology, from Leo Frobenius onwards, forms the most powerful discursive context for this literature.

Although undeniably, ethnography is a crucial context for reading francophone fiction from the colonial period, the exact dynamics of this exchange are particularly complex (as in the case of Maran and Hazoumé) precisely because of the contemporaneity of the emergence of these discourses. Miller can make a good case for a reading of Camara Laye's *L'Enfant noir* (1953) in terms of its anthropological context, but the same cannot be said of *Batouala*, which was published in 1921. Indeed it is the reception of *Batouala* (by Senghor, for example, in 1965) that registers the kind of appropriative and defining relationship between anthropology and African realist fiction that Miller describes. After all, Frobenius's work on African art (which is Miller's starting point) appeared in German in 1931 and then in translation in France in 1936.[3] Moreover, it is the historiographical ambitions of Maran (and even more so of Hazoumé) that complicate their relationship to the emergent discourse of ethnography.

An anecdote will serve to show the degree to which reception defined the discussion and future readings of the novel. *Batouala* was published with the subtitle *un véritable roman nègre* (a true negro novel) added by the publisher, who obviously must have thought that the novel's commercial value rested on its appeal as a symbol of authentic African culture. But notions of authenticity are not universal: what the French considered authentically African was not necessarily what the English considered authentically African. Within a year of its original publication, an English translation was published by Jonathan Cape in London. Entire sections of the novel were deleted from the English translation to make it conform to a different set of expectations about the authentically African. For example, the sexual orgy that follows the ritual dance in the original is deleted from the translation. Such interferences mark the narrative set in motion by the inaugural gesture. But they are also a matter of reception and do not reflect the author's intent.[4]

Batouala may be said to argue for its inaugural position by the type of story that it is, a story that anglophone readers are familiar with through the later work of Chinua Achebe. In *Batouala* Maran tells the story of the disintegration of a traditional village community under French colonial rule. But tradition is valorized by the novel just as it recounts the historical passing of traditional mores. Maran licenses a new sense of Africanness, articulated in opposition to Western influences, which is then disseminated by the novel as tradition. Given *Batouala*'s plot, therefore, it is clear why Maran should be considered as an important precursor of Achebe. As Simon Gikandi has noted, the perception that Achebe's work inaugurates the anglophone canon has limited comparative studies with his precursors (2). But Achebe's precursors are not only his Nigerian compatriots, such as Tutuola, but the francophone authors of negritude. The degree to which a response to negritude shaped the budding literature in English in Nigeria in the late 1950s is made clear by the important thematic surveys of the two pioneer Nigerian literary publications, *The Horn* and *Black Orpheus*, conducted by W. H. Stevenson and Bernth Lindfors, respectively (in Gérard 2:659–668 and 2:669–679). Soyinka's well-known attack on negritude ("The Future of West African Writing"), which appeared in *The Horn* (1960, 4:1), made the Nigerian rejection of negritude official (Stevenson in Gérard 2:664). The primary goal of *Black Orpheus* as a publication (founded in Nigeria in 1957 by two pioneer, European scholars) was to introduce anglophone Africans to French-, Portuguese-, and Spanish-speaking writers from Africa and the Caribbean.

Achebe's fiction consistently marks a starting point for anglophone readers, in large measure because of the type of story he presents rather than because he was first. Achebe, not Tutuola, whose work preceded Achebe's, is the inaugural figure. The recent biography of Achebe by Ezenwa-Ohaeto makes Achebe's standing as an inaugural figure amply clear and ties it explicitly to the system of colonial education that distinguished the young, bright Achebe as a future leader from very early on. Achebe, along with other educated men of his generation, was raised to be the inaugurator of a new Nigeria, and the success of his fiction fulfilled this expectation. The story of *Things Fall Apart*, the progressive incursion of a European presence on a traditional African community, became the canonical starting point of a new literature just as it became the justification for a new nation.

To know, however, that this type of story had already been rehearsed in a widely disseminated French novel provides important grounds for comparison and shifts our attention to how Achebe handled the conjunction of the ethnographic, the fictional, and the historical differently from Maran.

The difference in tone between *Things Fall Apart* (1958) and Achebe's third novel *Arrow of God* (1964) charts Achebe's increased commitment to history and active dissociation from ethnography. In *Things Fall Apart* he maintains an orientation toward his Western reader, explaining ethnographic detail in order to get it right even while he aims pointedly at diminishing his reader's authority. In *Arrow of God* we are left guessing about such culturally specific details as, for example, the significance of the *ikenga*. The reader does not learn the full meaning of the sacrilege committed by splitting the *ikenga* in two until Winterbottom explains it to Clarke fourteen pages after the original incident (23, 37). Ethnographic fact originates from a British authority. A non-Ibo reader is dependent on Winterbottom and is complicit with Clarke in his ignorance, affiliations that the reader needs to examine critically in order to read historically.

History and the Sacrificial

If Achebe's fiction can be read productively against the background of René Maran, it is also useful to compare both Achebe and Maran to an author who followed an entirely different model of historical fiction and left aside the local realities of village life to focus instead on the traditions of an African monarchy and precolonial statehood. Paul Hazoumé never acquired a large African audience, but retrospectively his fiction appears as an important challenge to the restrictions of the ethnographic. Writing about a subject matter that had been thoroughly sensationalized by European writers beginning in the eighteenth century—the human sacrifices of Dahomey (now Benin)—Hazoumé undertook to evaluate historically the dynamics of a culture that grew out of the slave trade and thus was a product of a shared Afro-European history. His only novel, *Doguicimi* (1938), is usually identified as the first work of historical fiction from francophone Africa. In typical fashion *Doguicimi* garnered awards in Paris for being ethnographically accurate. Praise for the novel recast the historical as the ethnographic, and although Hazoumé was recounting the events during the reign of King Guezo (1818–1858), his account was read as a description of present-day Dahomey.

When compared to the standard ethnographic work on Dahomey, Melville Herskovits's *Dahomey: An Ancient West African Kingdom*, this recasting of the historical *Doguicimi* as ethnographic is not surprising. Herskovits's work, also published in 1938, creates a portrait of Dahomey that is a mixture of contemporary detail acquired from his own travels to Dahomey and information gathered from previous travelers there. Herskovits recognizes that the Dahomey he is describing does not exist anymore, but it is questionable whether it ever existed since much of what he uses to describe the ancient (in fact, nineteenth-century) kingdom he has garnered through his observation. Dahomey is reinvented as a collage of past and present flattened into one chronotope.

The conjunction here of two competing texts—a historical novel by an African and an ethnographic monograph by a prominent American anthropologist—published in the same year and treating the same subject matter (Dahomean human sacrifices) forms a pivotal moment in the dialogue between Africa and the West. A dialogue between "uneven interlocutors," in Edward Said's terms, the historical evaluation of the human sacrifices is a moment of literary history from which we can set in motion once again a sidelined and misread African historicism, whose repression reverberates through the work of later African writers—as, for example, in the negative historicism of Yambo Ouologuem and the visionary critique of the nation in Ben Okri. Herskovits's work is still considered a classic of its kind. It established Herskovits as the leading Africanist among American anthropologists and advanced his influential method of cultural relativism. On the other hand, Hazoumé's historical fiction has been largely ignored by other African writers (who have turned to alternative models such as Maran and Achebe) and is occasionally used as a source of material for historical reemplotment by academic historians of Dahomey.

Both Herskovits and Hazoumé have in common a large literature of travelogues to Dahomey (beginning in the eighteenth century) over the course of which there is a progressive diminishment of narrative in the accounts of human sacrifices. Narrative explanation is increasingly supplanted in this literature by a rigorous convention of cataloguing that enacts rhetorically the progressive inroads of first British and then French control over the area. This tendency to appropriate through the act of cataloging culminates in Henri Hubert's *Mission scientifique au Dahomey* (1908).[5] Hubert, a metereologist and geologist by training, undertakes to assess the value of the newly acquired colony of Dahomey by cataloguing its assets, including its people. Ethnology becomes subsumed to the objective and quantifying description of the physical sciences. A progressive diminishment of the narrative treatment of Dahomean culture in the works of Western travelers manifests itself in the trajectory that spans Archibald Dalzel's *The History of Dahomy: An Inland Kingdom of Africa* (1793) to Hubert's 1908 catalogue. Both Herskovits and Hazoumé redress this trend. Herskovits fully elaborated context by adhering to his notions of cultural relativism. Moreover, he gained added influence by riding the crest of ethnographic authority in the 1930s. Hazoumé turned to the narrative amplitude of the historical novel. Although trained as an ethnographer (he published his own critically acclaimed monograph on Dahomey's ritual of the blood oath, a study that won him an appointment to the Musée de l'Homme in 1938), Hazoumé was committed to explaining the political realities that led to these Dahomean practices and to exposing the accountability of both Africans and Europeans in these practices.

Contemporary to Hazoumé and Herskovits, Georges Bataille, Michel Leiris, and the rest of the Collège de Sociologie thought extensively on the sacrificial and even planned to conduct a human sacrifice.[6] In his writings Bataille draws from the Aztec practice of human sacrifice and the abstractions of Marcel Mauss (and his collaborator Henri Hubert, the sociologist).[7] He demonstrates that it was not the historical specificity of particular practices of sacrifice that intrigued him but the sacrificial as a generalized human impulse. Hazoumé's work adds an important dimension to the theories of the Collège de Sociologie because it historicizes the Europeans' fascination with sacrifice as a part of a repressed history of Afro-European collaboration in the slave trade. Narrative, and historical explanation in particular, get lost somewhere between the abstractions of theory and the concrete description of Dahomey's material resources of Hubert's *Mission scientifique*. History has become an invisible discursive space now occupied by the native writer, with the result (as I will show) that the invisibility of history is maintained.

Despite his historiographical ambitions, Hazoumé was praised as an ethnographer, not a historian, because to a European audience Africa did not have a history.[8] The reception of Hazoumé's work in the late 1930s gives ample evidence of Johannes Fabian's charge that ethnography created an allochronic discourse according to which the other never occupies the same historical time as the Western observer. Cast as travelogue, the ethnographic monograph diminishes the distance between self and other by the observer's travel to the space occupied by the observed. In the written account, the distance traveled is metaphorically converted into temporal distance. The West and Africa, for example, are elements in an "ideological relation" mapped along a "temporal slope." The "temporal slope" denies the actual *coevalness* of the elements arranged along it (104). The allochronic discourse that results reveals that "the absence of the Other from our Time has been his mode of presence in our discourse" (*Time and the Other* 154). This paradox (presence determined through absence) holds because ethnographic discourse is generated from the reinvention of temporal relations to suppress coevalness. Fabian's thesis lays bare the effects of praising a historical novel such as Hazoumé's as ethnographic. The historical as a narrative of becoming is suppressed, and the only glimpse of the historical that is allowed is the recuperation of an origin through evidence of its continued and unchanging existence.

In later years, when scholars of African literature began to take stock of the literary output of the colonial period, the historical character of Hazoumé's work was perceptible; it led, however, to the work's marginalization. In her pioneer literary history *Black Writers in French* (1963), Lilyan Kesteloot dismissed Hazoumé because he was too historical. She deemed his work "not sufficiently literary" (10). Hazoumé's marginalization was compounded by the fact that his other works were an ethnography and a book of essays on anti-Nazi propaganda. He wrote no other works of fiction, and therefore his career was not easily recognizable as literary. Later Abiola Irele reinforced Kesteloot's judgment of Hazoumé and dismissed *Doguicimi* as a failure, although he acknowledges that *Doguicimi* follows logically in the footsteps of *Batouala* (147). For Irele, Hazoumé's work fails because it is too hybrid, too generically impure, whereas *Batouala* appears to be more genuine. This difference in reception, however, had a political origin. Whereas Maran wrote a controversial attack against colonialism in the preface to *Batouala*, Hazoumé's reputation was marred by accusations of procolonialism that have prevented his appropriation as an authentic figure.

James Clifford has placed a corrective emphasis on the narrative elements of ethnographic works, but his definition of ethnography (for example, "a characteristic attitude of participant observation among the artifacts of a defamiliarized cultural reality" [*Predicament* 121]) harbors its own potential repression of narrative as historical explanation. How, when, and where does defamiliarization take place? Fabian has called ethnography an "ideology of relations" (104). If ethnography is an "attitude," in Clifford's terms, then its discourse is prefigured in the gesture of defamiliarization that is left outside of the purview of the ethnographic. Such a defamiliarization took place progressively in the turn away from narrative and to cataloguing in the accounts of human sacrifices. Narrative inevitably recorded the observers' involvement in the ritual acts; cataloguing suppresses this involvement and erases the elements of contact from which a historical account can be articulated.

The Argument for History

Narrative authority has been very heavily contested in African literature. It has been contested both in the reception of works of African literature in their primary commercial market, the West, and in colonial and postindependence Africa amongst Africans themselves. The political implications of occupying a position of narrative privilege from which to explain history have been so explosive that this position has been occupied more often than not surreptitiously. The novels I examine lay claim to and explain particular histories against various covert or overt acts of narrative repression.

Although the novel presented African writers with an opportunity to elaborate their own description of African culture, it denied them scientific authority over their descriptive domain. The literary conventions of the novel have always functioned for African writers as a site of contest where the limits of literariness are constantly challenged in order to initiate an alternative discourse of knowledge. As V. Y. Mudimbe has argued, the discourse of knowledge about Africa has been largely a "discourse of competence," either of "geographical or anthropological" competence. Those with knowledge produced texts "about unknown societies without their own texts" (*Invention* 175–6). These discourses of competence, however, were based on false premises, as Mudimbe and others have relentlessly shown. Since this book's chronological beginning is the nineteenth-century description of Dahomean culture by European travelers, it is apt to note Philip Curtin's assessment that the nineteenth century saw a decline of historical knowledge about Africa. The populist sensationalism that governed all discourses about Africa disseminated so much misinformation and skewed perceptions so radically that any attempts at objective knowledge were subverted (*Image* 413).

In the late 1950s the attitude toward African historicism began to change. The establishment of the newly independent nations of Africa coincided with the emergence of African history as a distinct academic field that challenged the construction of Africa in the discourses of competence and turned its attention to the heretofore ignored ancient texts and oral histories of the continent (*Invention* 181). Although, as Steven Feierman has pointed out, there were hardly any academic historians who identified themselves as Africanists in the 1950s, by the late 1970s there were several hundred in the United States (*Africa and the Disciplines* 168). For Mudimbe and others this academic historical discourse has presented its own dangers since it still seems too closely affiliated to Western paradigms of historical narrative.

Opposed to this narrative of the emergence of an academic discourse of history we find a competing development, an Africanist historical discourse that has largely taken place in the literary field of the novel. In the field of postcolonial studies, the tendency has been to see cultural production as central to the anticolonial struggle and to draw from this fact confirmation of the pivotal importance of culture to politics. Aimé Césaire's negritude is a project that fits this order of things: culture is the primary scene of historical transformation. Political change follows as a result of transformative cultural expression. Though the path from culture to politics may represent accurately the trajectory of the anticolonial struggle as it unfolded, it obscures the fact that the only avenue of publication consistently available for African writers was literature. Thus, not all, but some writers—those preoccupied with history—wrote literature while aiming at creating the possibility of a new African gnosis. One of the shaping impulses behind their fiction was to counter the authority of European social "scientists" who studied Africa and Europe's relation to Africa. The ambitions behind the cultural production of Africans in European languages are directed at the totalizing discourses of the ethnographic description of African peoples and a European historiography into which Africa had been incorporated as a blank space, a void. As David Spurr has argued, the negation of space that unfolded in European descriptions of Africa as darkness extended into a total negation of African histories. In Africa there is no de-velopment but "a continual state of self-presence" available as the foil to European historical destiny (Spurr 99). Assimilationist education directed colonial subjects to adopt European national histories in the deletion of their own histories. By writing novels, Africans sought to constitute them-selves discursively as historical subjects.

If there is a process of retrieval here, it is not a matter of resurrecting a lost authenticity but of reestablishing points of contact not only with the West but within the national communities. Even Paul Hazoumé's *Doguicimi*, which seeks to revise the West's understanding of its history by insisting on the African remembrance of a shared historical involvement, addresses the political divisions amongst Africans in colonial Dahomey foremost; its his-torical retrospective is meant to serve the cause of creating a blueprint for a postcolonial national identity.

In chapter 1, "The Traditional Cultures of René Maran and Chinua Achebe," I investigate the generic ambiguities of three novels frequently de-scribed as ethnographic: *Batouala, Things Fall Apart*, and *Arrow of God*. The in-terplay among history, fiction, and ethnography is recorded by showing how the features of each discourse establish the necessity for the others. History requires realistic description that evokes the ethnographic. Narrativity emerges in resistance to the ethnographic. Fiction becomes the grounds for a double history: the history of the demise of intact traditional societies and the history of the invention of the myth of tradition (in which the novels themselves participate) as a strategy of cultural survival during colonialism.

Out of this doubleness we glimpse the critical consciousness of both Maran and Achebe. They produce inevitably incomplete portraits of whole communities, but, more important, they treat cultural wholeness as a construct. Their works diverge in the degree to which they historicize their critical awareness. Here Maran's unironic implication in an ethno-graphic project contrasts with Achebe's more self-conscious treatment of ethnographic discourses. Both authors, however, participate in, as well as criticize, the invention of African traditions as a response to the denigrat-ing ideologies of colonialism.

The next three chapters share a common focus on Dahomey and sacrifice that posits an entirely different configuration of tradition, authenticity, and narrative. The relevant questions here are: what is the importance of the sacrificial to history, of authenticity in relation to the sacrificial, of narrative as a response to undo the notions of authenticity invented by the sacrificial?

One narrative convention against which twentieth-century African novelists have had to write back is that generated by nineteenth-century travelers to Africa and identified by Patrick Brantlinger as the narrative of atrocity. Chapter 2, "History, Human Sacrifices, and the Victorian Travelers to Dahomey," is a literary history of the Victorians' travelogues about Dahomey, in which is recorded an implicit and, in the case of Richard Burton, an explicit denial and repression of the Dahomeans' point of view in history. Burton recounts a debate between himself and the king of Dahomey over the origin of ritual human sacrifices where he censors the king's explanation that implicates the Europeans in the narrative of atrocity. While the notion of a "native point of view" is highly problematic, as I show in later chapters of the book, it provides a point of reference for what must be repressed by the authors of the travelogues. Moreover, these texts in which the "native point of view" is silenced are the background of the "scientific" texts about Dahomey that were produced in the 1920s and 1930s. The link here is direct: the travelogues are frequently cited in Western scientific texts.

Chapter 2 functions as an archaeology for a "scientific" discourse of human sacrifice. This discourse was generated out of an eagerness to testify to atrocity despite the refusal to witness it. The travelers invariably considered watching the ritual a form of participation they had to forego, but they exploited the possibilities of that "not seen" as a means of sensationalizing their narratives. Although the human sacrifices are historical fact, the descriptions of them by Europeans were based often on suggestion and their own imagination. They require, therefore, a counterhistory.

Chapter 3, "Contesting Authenticity: Paul Hazoumé, Ethnography, and Negritude," examines a little-known work of autoethnography, Paul Hazoumé's *Le Pacte de sang au Dahomey* (1937). Largely misread by the ethnographic establishment in Paris as a critique of a traditional practice, the study explained a ritual that created ties of allegiance among members of a community not linked through kinship. The French outlawed the blood oath when they conquered Dahomey because it challenged allegiance to the empire and was socially disruptive. Hazoumé's study was well received because it played into the hands of the French colonial government. What Hazoumé's contemporaries were blind to, however, was that Hazoumé's explanation was not of a stable, unchanging ritual but of a practice that had been adapted to changing historical circumstance and had survived by going underground amongst the criminal element in colonial Dahomey. Hazoumé records the resilience of local culture against the colonizer's "civilizing" influence. In a later essay (published in the inaugural issue of *Présence africaine* in 1957), Hazoumé situates his thought in terms of his African contemporaries, especially Senghor, and exposes his argument for a historical ethnography. In this 1957 essay Hazoumé picks apart the errors in ethnographic works about Dahomey and argues that these errors arise out of an ignorance of history. Read alongside his own ethnographic work, the essay helps explain why Hazoumé remained on the fringes of negritude, a dissident voice against a romanticized notion of authenticity.

"Resistant History," the last of the three chapters on Dahomey and sacrifice, provides a reading of *Doguicimi* (1938), Hazoumé's monumental historical novel about the nineteenth-century reign of King Guezo. Although *Doguicimi* garnered several awards in Paris and has been consistently recognized as the first historical novel from francophone Africa, it has been neglected in recent years despite the intense interest in African literature. Hazoumé's reputation as an establishment ethnographer and his ambivalent politics make readers wary of him. Read as a counterhistory from the "contact zone," *Doguicimi* takes on its full significance as a very provocative work. The Victorian travelogues operate as background to Hazoumé's novel, where they are lampooned. A British delegation comes to visit King Guezo in the novel and retreats in horror. But other equally important texts inform Hazoumé's counterhistory: Flaubert's *Salammbô* and Jules Michelet's *Histoire de la Révolution française*. Hazoumé draws from Flaubert for his realistic technique, especially in the description of violence. He uses Michelet to remind the French public of the unfinished work of the French Revolution and to suggest a rival narrative of the birth of a nation.

Read as a reinscription of the uses of history by French colonial ideology, *Doguicimi* uncovers the falsification of the ideals of the Revolution of 1789 in their deployment for the advance of empire. Two tropes gain prominence here: the human sacrifices as the reign of terror, and Doguicimi, the heroine, as a Joan of Arc figure, mother to the emergent nation through her martyrdom. Hazoumé draws from Michelet's treatment of Joan of Arc, especially Michelet's argument that the awakening of the people in the march to the

Bastille prison is a reincarnation of the spirit of Joan of Arc. She is the prophetic, first manifestation of the people's will that becomes fully realized in the glorious moment of July 14, 1789. Cast in the terms of this reinscription, Doguicimi becomes a symbol of Dahomean national becoming. Michelet figures as the dialogic background of the novel, although this background gains resonance against the appropriation of the descriptions of the Revolution (especially the terror) in the discourse of French colonial policy.

The radical nature of Hazoumé's book becomes patent if we set it next to Melville Herskovits's *Dahomey: An Ancient West African Kingdom*, the ethnographic study that became the authoritative text on Dahomey. Published in 1938, the same year as *Doguicimi*, Herskovits's study displays all the features of "allochronic" discourse: it creates a timeless Dahomey through a stitching together of anecdotal accounts from nineteenth-century travelogues, as well as Herskovits's observation of an "authentic" culture already prefigured and thus "ancient" in 1938.

Chapters 3 and 4, therefore, historicize the "scientific" discourse on Dahomey by juxtaposing the "scientific," "objective" texts on Dahomean culture by westerners next to the resistant, historicist work of the Dahomean, Paul Hazoumé.

Said uses the term *reinscription* in *Culture and Imperialism* as part of a spatial metaphor of "overlapping territories" in which the resistant culture must "recover forms already established . . . by the culture of empire," but, as Said sees it, this process is not necessarily tragic (*Culture and Imperialism* 210, 216). In the instances where the object is to create a comprehensive historical narrative, reinscription posits an incursion of the subaltern's speech in the discursive territory of the colonizer. If this incursion repeatedly defines the subaltern in the terms of the colonizer's discourse, it also erodes the coherence of that discourse to a breaking point where it must be reinvented and the parties of the dialogue (colonizer and subaltern) must reengage with new identities. Such experiments at reinventing historical discourse are to be found in the novels examined in my last two chapters, *Le Devoir de violence* and *The Famished Road*.

Yambo Ouologuem's *Le Devoir de violence*, the focus of chapter 5, "History as Transgression," links violence explicitly to the project of historiography, setting up its characters either as sacrificial victims or as perpetrators of sacrifice. Continuing along the lines of the discussion of the transgressive pleasures in the narratives of sacrifice, I suggest that the transgressive sexual acts and political violence of the novel are important not only for what they represent realistically (ethnographically) but for the narratological situation of the reader in these experiences. Postcoloniality is a space of becoming into which one has no access other than by transgressing beyond the boundaries of a Manichaean discussion divided between native and westerner. Ouologuem demonstrates an active rejection of a nativist point of view as a means of emergence into postcoloniality, an act of historical becoming as of yet unrealized in his estimation.

The final chapter, "Temporality and the Geographies of Nation: 'The Future Present' in *The Famished Road*," focuses on place and memory. I turn to the problem of the nation for the writing of African history with Ben Okri's phantasmagoric mapping of the nation in *The Famished Road*. Nigeria becomes the focus of my discussion of the postcolonial nation, extending the earlier discussion of Nigerian history in the work of Achebe. Okri's historical retrospection unmasks the confusions of colonial divisions and tests the degree to which the boundaries of local culture coincide with those of the nation. I read *The Famished Road* as a critique of the nationalist paradigm for political liberation. Homi Bhabha's analysis of the nation as chronotope attempts to rehabilitate a liberationist nationalism through concepts of duplicity: a "double time" and a "spatial disjunction." Okri's novel is a rejection of the kind of liminality that Bhabha endorses in favor of a practice of transgression narrated through Azaro's travels in and out of the fantastic. Place, not time, becomes the narrative paradigm in *The Famished Road*. There is a need to think some more about the narrative problem of nation, not only diachronically as emergence, progress, and development but synchronically as place. Okri's contribution in his reinvented realism is to address the nation as a problem of place, treating the synchronicity through which we experience place historically.

Claiming History addresses what I perceive as an urgent need to theorize a practice of history within postcolonial studies. The place of history in the book is twofold: first, the works under examination are historical novels that propose a particular practice of history, and, second, the study itself theorizes the role of historical criticism in postcolonial studies.

By looking at historical novels by African writers from the colonial and postcolonial periods, I describe a struggle for empowerment by native peoples. Historical narration not only "answers back" to Europe but has consistently over several decades addressed a legacy of violence of Africans against Africans. *Claiming History* traces this discussion among Africans, often mediated and projected through the European colonial presence but consistently claiming an African audience. It is my contention that these voices of historical argumentation have either been silenced or co-opted as ahistorical voices speaking ethnographically for an "authentic" other. In what is undeniably an extremely politicized area of speech, Africans who criticized fellow Africans during the struggle for independence from colonial rule were repeatedly condemned as sympathetic to the colonizers. In the postcolonial period those opposed to national projects continue to be persecuted. Ironically, it has been in the interest of both the colonial powers and the nationalists, before and after colonial rule, to maintain an oppositional dialogue. Opposition gives coherence by forcing conformity on each side. *Claiming History* attempts to explode this conformity, to highlight the voices of those who defied it.

Resistance, which has been a dominant paradigm in postcolonial studies, often provides a useful entry into the historicity of texts. However, resistance has been theorized mostly in terms of the opposition between Europe and its others. Edward Said's work (in *Culture and Imperialism* especially) goes a long way in this direction. Said expands the notion of resistance to the scholarly work of third world intellectuals. Resistance spills out over the boundaries of literary production that has kept the relationship between West and non-West in recent years one between critics of culture and producers of culture. In *Claiming History* I suggest a different paradigm, one of dissidence rather than resistance. Dissidence proclaims difference from within. It shatters the cohesion of a national community. Dissident speech poses different challenges for historical criticism because it is often successfully co-opted and requires rediscovery through a historical lens that can properly contextualize it. This type of historical work is a new challenge to postcolonial studies, which have so far theorized declarative (or *performative*, to use Homi Bhabha's term) forms of resistance. Dissidence subverts from within. It orients our attention toward the internal dynamics of a community where it is most difficult to look.

■■

CHAPTER ONE

The Traditional Cultures of René Maran
and Chinua Achebe

Traditionalism emerged with particular force in the context of anticolonial struggle. But although traditionalism was a way to oppose the "civilizing mission" of colonialism, the rigorous uniformity it required created dissent. René Maran and Chinua Achebe have both described traditional culture in ways that have helped romanticize it in the light of anticolonial struggle. Because both authors orient themselves historically, they also explain the reasons for dissent from traditionalism. In their novels traditionalism emerges out of the characters' efforts to make sense of their historical moment; it implies an essentially dichotomized historical experience, divided between then and now. The authors' account of the shaping of anticolonial consciousness examines critically the characters' understanding of the past and seeks to link the then and now.

The story that inaugurates African fiction in French and English is that of the demise of a traditional village community under the repressive influence of a colonial regime—the plot of both Maran's *Batouala* (1921) and Achebe's *Things Fall Apart* (1958). The appeal of this plot is that it sets in motion notions of tradition usable for anticolonial resistance. In part Maran and Achebe attempt to wrest control of the invention of African tradition by the European colonial powers who used the codification of indigenous traditions as a means of control over the colonial subject. As Terence Ranger has argued, "The invented traditions of African societies—whether invented by the Europeans or the Africans themselves in response—distorted the past but became in themselves realities through which a good deal of colonial encounter was expressed" (212). The historical narratives embedded in these novels address the uses of the past in the lived reality of colonialism. These are the narratives that we need to recover.

Achebe's later novel, *Arrow of God* (1964), heralds a new postcolonial literature of critical self-examination. Although traditional culture and the West are still opposed to each other, the opposition no longer lends coherence to tradition. The African community turns in on itself, imploding from its own contradiction. Here the novelist's historical narrative explores the effects of invented tradition. Thus whereas *Batouala* and *Things Fall Apart* are engaged in inventing traditional culture in a manner parallel, if resistant, to the invention of African traditions by the colonial powers, *Arrow of God* demonstrates that these processes do not take place separately. Tradition is never pure or distinct, and Achebe deconstructs its appeal for the reader.

Although authenticity is an ideology of colonialism that seeks to dehistoricize native culture, in the hands of Maran and Achebe the idea is transformed into a claim enunciated as resistance to colonialism. Ranger's discussion of invented traditions dramatizes quite effectively the situation of writers such as Maran and Achebe who claim authenticity for themselves. Giving a history of the pressures that impelled the invention of tradition, Ranger explains:

> The assertion by whites that African society was profoundly conservative—living within age-old rules which did not change; living within a framework of clearly defined hierarchical status—was by no means always intended as an indictment of African backwardness or reluctance to modernize. Often it was intended as a compliment to the admirable quali-

ties of tradition . . . This attitude towards "traditional" Africa became more marked as whites came to realize in the 1920s and 1930s that rapid economic transformation was just not to take place in Africa . . . or as some whites came to dislike the consequences of the changes which *had* taken place. The African collaborators, playing their role within one or other of the introduced European traditions, then came to seem less admirable than "real" Africans, still presumed to be inhabiting their own, appropriate universe of tradition.   *(247)*

One can easily see why as a response to these circumstances African writers such as Maran and Achebe would want to wrest control of what authentic Africa is. Though this reappropriation of authenticity is an act of resistance, especially by an African writer who does not fit in either category offered (as "collaborator" or "'real' African," i.e., peasant), it is also a confining situation in which the African writer inescapably (because he lives the reality of colonialism) speaks from between dual oppositions. Thus the need for a further resistance evolves out of these circumstances, and the dissenting voice that enunciates the limitations of tradition emerges in works such as *Arrow of God*.

Both Maran and Achebe adopt a realist aesthetic that combines the ethnographic and the historical. These discourses, however, frequently work at cross-purposes. Ethnographic description has often repressed historical context in the effort to re-create whole cultures. Historical consciousness, on the other hand, seeks to recover repressed narratives of cultural loss and fragmentation. Both authors had to confront what I call the "ethnographic impulse," the desire to restore the local cultures under their observation and to revise the mastering descriptions of Western ethnography. The "ethnographic impulse" reflects actual historical circumstances. As a response to a sense of injustice aroused by the representation of Africa in the West, the ethnographic impulse expresses itself first in an effort to describe with impartiality a particular African culture. For the colonial subject aware of his historical moment, this task of description entails elaborating a narrative of causality whereby the author implicates his Western reader in a history of African denigration. It is in the way in which Maran and Achebe each transform the restorative discourse of the ethnographic impulse into history that their dissenting voices take shape.

Maran, Ethnography, and the Anticolonial Novel

Maran is much more implicated in the ethnographic discourse of his times than has been acknowledged so far. Although the links between negritude and anthropology (especially via the aesthetics of Leo Frobenius) have been studied at length (see, for example, Christopher Miller's *Theories of Africans*), the negritudinist reception of Maran's work has not been scrutinized with the same attention. The precursor of negritude who heralded a new, "authentic" African discourse in French, as Senghor claimed, was esteemed by criteria shaped through the ethnographic eye. Moreover, Maran's irregular position as a black man doing ethnography (not autoethnography) merits more attention as it scrambles the usual paths of power and authority that define the relation among author, audience, and the observed in an ethnographic text. Although early in his career Maran tried self-consciously to write ethnographically, he was not concerned with authenticity in the abstract, decontextualized way in which his work was received. *Batouala* is a work of anticolonial protest where the authentic gains legitimacy from the justice of its cause.

What is the relation between *Batouala* and French ethnography in the 1920s? Published in 1921, *Batouala* stands at the threshold of both a new fiction and a new ethnography. The first writer of African descent to win the Prix Goncourt, Maran announces the arrival of the francophone African novel. At the same time, however, *Batouala* is a transitional work in French ethnography, resting at the margins of the discipline but also somewhere in between the methods of two of its towering figures: Maurice Delafosse and Marcel Mauss. Delafosse was the reigning ethnographic authority in France in the early 1920s; he had also been Maran's boss while they both served in Oubangi-Chari (now the Central African Republic)—Maran from 1910–1923, Delafosse as governor from 1918–1919. His best work is a dictionary of the Fon language of Dahomey. When he returned to Paris after his years of service in Africa, he became the first professor of Black African Languages at the Ecole des Langues Orientales (Clifford in *Predicament* 61). Delafosse's death in 1926 coincided with the inauguration of courses offered by the Institut d'Ethnologie, which he helped found along with Mauss, Lévy-Bruhl, and Rivet.

In his teaching at the Institut d'Ethnologie beginning in 1926, Mauss stressed the concept of a "descriptive ethnography," encouraging his students to see themselves as both "statisticians" and "novelists": "Sociology and descriptive ethnology demand that one be at once a chartist, a historian, and a statistician . . . as well as a novelist able to evoke the life of an entire society" (*Manuel d'ethnographie* 8). Though not a "statistician," Maran had been warned about being a kind of "chartist." His adviser on the manuscript of *Batouala*, Manoel Gahisto (to whom, in fact, he dedicated the novel), warned him about producing a "mummified catalog" of rituals and customs (*Hommage* 132).[1] As for representing an "entire society," Maran's realism incorporated an aesthetic of totality. Thus *Batouala* anticipated some of Mauss's lessons, while it became the target of Delafosse's scathing critique.

Delafosse set out to diminish the ethnographic authority of Maran's novel by adding a lengthy attack on *Batouala* to the second edition of *Broussard: L'Etat d'âme d'un colonial* (1923). *Broussard* is a curious work. Delafosse sets out to do an ethnographic study of the French colonial official as *broussard* (bushman), a figure like himself whom he treats nostalgically as a type about to become obsolete: "The type is near extinction," he warns (2). The book is what James Clifford has characterized as "salvage ethnography," but the object of study is the ethnographer himself.[2] Delafosse implicitly recognizes that ethnography is a discourse that authenticates, and in authenticating the *broussard* he can discredit Maran's pretensions. According to Delafosse, Maran was not a convincing realist (a skill necessary for an ethnographer) because he kept his distance from the natives.[3] Charging that, "From the verandah where, spread out on his lawn chair, M. René Maran listened to the conversations of the subjects under his administration . . . he must have heard these only imperfectly" (171), Delafosse aimed to show that the natives were inaccessible to Maran. Delafosse concludes, "*Batouala* is neither really a novel nor really negro [*ni véritablement nègre*]." Maran's "ethnographic impulse" is denigrated as the failure of his artistic enterprise. His critical insights were dismissed as a caricature ("*un portrait caricatural*") (*Broussard* 171–2).

Delafosse and Mauss offer radically different models of ethnographic authority. Delafosse held up the *broussard*'s experience of assimilating into the bush as scientific authority; for Mauss, dispassionate objectivity and sympathetic imagination were more important. Delafosse had trained as a linguist and had traveled extensively in the African bush as part of the international commission charged to map the border between French and British territory in the Volta. He reinvented himself as a kind of "bushman." One of his students remembered Delafosse as someone who "embodied for us the great ancestors and the most authentic Africa [*la plus profonde Afrique*]" (Deschamps 97).[4] The ethnographers Mauss trained for the field (he himself never traveled anywhere) were taught to remain detached observers and to bring back to the metropolitan center unprocessed facts for interpretation and explanation.[5] Ethnographic authority stayed back home in the university setting. Students of Mauss, such as Michel Leiris, may have been attracted to primitivism, but their experience in the field is of its failure.[6]

Unlike Delafosse, who thought he had fulfilled his own expectations of seeing Africa, Maran struggled hopelessly to reconcile himself to a disappointing reality. Having left his native Martinique for Bordeaux at age four, Maran had been thoroughly assimilated. He entered the French colonial service in search of a steady job because he was in dire financial straights. From Maran's personal writings about his experience in Africa we learn that he felt fairly alienated from African realities. Although he may not compare to the *broussard* type that Delafosse invented, there are striking similarities in his personal writings to Michel Leiris's *L'Afrique fantôme* (1934), a record of disillusionment. Leiris complains repeatedly about the diminishing sense of exoticism in his own experience of Africa during the Dakar-Djibouti expedition: "Increasingly the level of exoticism diminishes. . . . I must look at the pictures that have just been developed to imagine that I am in something that resembles Africa" (*L'Afrique fantôme* 171). Africa here means an imagined construct visible only in the expedition's staged photos and not palpable in the day-to-day reality of traveling across the continent.

Maran's sojourn in Africa was similarly disillusioning. Alienated from both the natives and the corrupt colonial administration, Maran complained frequently about his isolation. His milieu was not conducive to intellectual engagement; it rendered him sluggish and depressed. Africa, he declared, is a place for dreams, whereas Europe alone can stimulate the mind: "I write little or not at all. Out of fear of tiring my injured eyes, I neglect my reading. I dream. I am a fakir of dream [*un fakir de rêve*]. There. To awaken me, France would be necessary. [*Pour me réveiller, il faudrait la France*]." (*Hommage* 124). Like Leiris, who obsessively recorded his dreams (Clifford, in fact, calls *L'Afrique fantôme* an "oneirography" [*Predicament* 165]), Maran is in a constant state of dream. The African bush appeared inert, and he could not connect with it; his only stimuli were letters that came from France: "In this inert bush where nothing connects us to life, it is moving to meditate on these departures that make us melancholy and desperate for weeks. Empty bush; bush with no name!" (*Hommage* 124). Life is elsewhere; here is numbness, inertia, dream.[7]

Maran's construction of Africa, however, is contradictory. In his personal writings there is a day view, associated with realist representation akin to Leiris's photographs, and a night view, more ambience than picture, associated with darkness and the auditory rather than the visual. The day landscape distanced through observation is teeming with wildlife. However, it requires a *magician*'s powers to be rendered into language, a common disclaimer in realist description. The result, however unreal it may seem to the French reader, is not exoticism, Maran claims, but realism (*Hommage* 103). At night, Maran abandons his intellectual pursuits and succumbs to the sensations of his surroundings, producing an oneirography not unlike Leiris's:

> And I dream, that is to say I listen carefully to the distant and diminishing rumors, the drums and the songs. The fireflies fly around. I listen and I breathe. And here are fragrances, seemingly making the croaking of numerous toads more exotic. And the night, evoking dreams, becomes voluptuous, like the favorite's caress.   (*Hommage 109*)

The inertia, in fact, is in Maran, not out there in the bush. Like Leiris, dream is a metaphor for a state in which sexual arousal is possible. The ambience suggests sexual thoughts to which, however, both authors have difficulty surrendering. The sounds of the drums turn into a longing for France, figuratively the beloved that Maran has left behind and to whom he must be faithful: "Why do these perfumes of wild mint and balm-mint transform themselves to the extent that my sense of smell confuses them with the delicate aroma of damp thyme and wet lavender? Why does this noise of the drums—oh! so far away—mimic the discreet arpeggio of the piano in the evening?" (*Hommage* 109).

Frantz Fanon gave Maran a pivotal place in his analysis of the psychopathology of assimilationism and interpreted Maran's longing for France as the symptom of an abandonment neurosis. Maran's career as a writer and intellectual was shaped by the pivotal experience of his mother's—his cultural mother's, France's—abandonment.[8] Maran challenges the *broussard*'s easy confidence. For him, just as it is later for Leiris, the ethnographer is a more ambiguous, dislocated, unmastering observer.

In his correspondence with Manoel Gahisto (a translator of Brazilian novels into French who facilitated the publication of Maran's work), Maran had explicitly disavowed the literary: "This is not literature," he wrote. "It is not invented exoticism [*de l'exotisme imaginé*]. It's veneer [*du plaqué*], a snapshot, the real thing" (*Hommage* 103). Although rejecting the literary and imagined in favor of the real and objective, Maran acknowledged the artificiality of all representation by characterizing his work as "veneer." He wants to represent surfaces, the "snapshot" appearance of things, so that the impression seems irrefutable, "real."

Gahisto advised instead that Maran should fictionalize his account in order to make it publishable. *Batouala* needed a plot, and Maran should avoid "a meticulous knowledge" (*un savoir minutieux*) (*Hommage* 132).[9] At issue here is once again a problem of authority. Gahisto signaled to Maran that only literature was within his reach; Maran resisted the literary because he wanted his descriptions to be read as real. The novel was inspired by a pressing political situation that required a discourse of the real. Under pressure to emplot his ethnographic description, the problem of representation for Maran becomes a problem of narrative, of *histoire* as both story and history.

Although he was doubtful about the feasibility of his project, Maran resisted Gahisto's pressures as much as possible, insisting that, "in this novel, there will be no plot, or so little!" (*Hommage* 136). He destroyed and restarted the draft many times over, but instead of adding action, he added more descriptive detail. Fearful that he was not creating as complete a picture of native life as possible, Maran tore up his drafts to rewrite them because, "I found in them a series of imperfections that worry me; the oversights, involuntary of course, would yet add to the local color" (*Hommage* 144).

Maran's dissenting voice comes across most clearly in the preface to *Batouala*, where he explains ethnography as a tool of dissent. For Maran, the novel had to be objective (nothing but facts, as he explains) so as to support the polemic of his openly anticolonial preface. Indeed, the novel was banned in the colonies soon after publication precisely because of its preface, where Maran expresses his indignation at the injustices of French colonialism. In the preface he also describes the conditions under which his own authorial voice was shaped, clarifying for the reader the severe constraints on his ability to represent the natives, limitations that stem from his position as a French-educated Martinican writing about Africa. The preface is not only a political critique but an exploration of his own displacement. He begins by declaring that his novel is objective: "This novel is therefore entirely objective. It doesn't even attempt to explain: it takes stock. It doesn't protest: it records" (10).

In this posture of objectivity, Maran claims to keep his discourse within acceptable limits. Objectivity—a voiceless narration—holds the black author within the boundaries of appropriate speech. These boundaries (marked by the repression of indignation and explanation) are active pressures that constrain his freedom of expression. He presents the novel, therefore, as a censored text, an instance of repressed speech. He disavows explanation; the novel, he claims, merely states. But, since explanation establishes causality, its absence inhibits the elaboration of a historical narrative. The problem for Maran is how to elicit from his reader the insights gained through his indignation and not mar the appearance of objectivity.

In order to demarcate the discursive territory to be opened up by the novel, Maran stages a contest of points of view in the preface, disorienting the reader until he establishes his location in the attack against colonialism more precisely. Maran acknowledges that the impression of objectivity results from the repression of his own point of view:

> In the course of those six years, never once did I succumb to the temptation to utter a word. I urged an objective conscience to the point of repressing thoughts that could have been attributed to me. The negroes of Equatorial Africa are not self-reflective. Deprived of a critical mind, they never had nor will they ever have any kind of intelligence. Or at least, that is what one pretends. Mistakenly, without a doubt. Because if non-intelligence was a negro characteristic, there would be very few Europeans in Africa.   *(9–10)*

The second sentence here is extremely ambiguous because Maran does not identify the constituency of those who could have attributed thoughts to him. What is the source of the interference? Is Maran speaking of the colonial authorities? Or is he referring to the subjects that he is observing? Maran's sense here is not immediately evident.

As the passage continues, Maran first adopts a colonialist's perspective and then unmasks it. He owns and then disavows the colonialists' belief that the African is unreflecting and unintelligent. The thoughts that threaten to interfere with Maran's efforts to be objective must doubtless be the thoughts of the natives since these are the thoughts owned but not represented in the passage. To be objective, Maran represses speech from the perspective of the natives' discontent with their impoverished lives. Speaking forcefully in his own voice, however, he marks the instances of repression. These reminders of repression then condition our reading of the scenes that follow in the novel.

He charges that colonial officials are decadent drunks who do not have the will to resist the influence ("*de résister à l'ambiance*") of their surroundings (14). While the officials lead a life of decadence, the natives starve. Their traditions are sacrificed for the ideals of progress and development. But these ideals do not make sense because the conditions of native life are continuously worsening (10). In a tone that anticipates Césaire's attack on the pretenses of the "civilizing mission" in "Discours sur le colonialisme" (1955), Maran charges that civilization is built on a pile of corpses:

> Civilization, civilization, pride of the Europeans. . . . You build your kingdom on corpses. Whatever you wish, whatever you do, you act in deceit. Tears gush forth and pain cries out at your sight. You are the force that exceeds justice. You are not a torch but a raging fire. Whatever you touch, you consume. *(11)*

The imperative of civilization is the rule of might over right. Colonialism is violent. It exercises its powers by consuming its object (a consumption that becomes literal in the accounts of the human sacrifices in Dahomey).

But Maran's position as a black man and as a French colonial official could make sense only within the framework of an ideal nation: France as a multiracial nation in which all share the humanist ideals of the French Revolution. But the French Empire was not such a nation. As an assimilated Frenchman, Maran had a profound desire to belong to France's intellectual community. He appeals to intellectuals as his allies; writers, his "brothers in spirit," are the "keepers" (*les mainteneurs*) of the nation (*Batouala* 13). If literature is the means through which a nation maintains its integrity, then it is imperative that French intellectuals decry colonialism. He locates his own discourse in French national discourse. At the same time, Maran is not agitating for the abolition of colonialism but for its reform. Indeed he is dissenting from within French nationalism and not proposing an African nationalism. The ideal of a multiethnic, multiracial French nation is opposed to the harsh realities of a repressive empire, an opposition that Paul Hazoumé also articulated pointedly in *Doguicimi*.

Maran's diatribe against colonialism got him into political trouble. Although he attained instant celebrity with the Prix Goncourt for *Batouala*, the award soon created a sizable scandal.[10] Soon after the prize had been given, the novel was banned in all the colonies. Although his employers at the French colonial service promoted him for winning the Prix Goncourt, Maran was soon forced to resign (Egonu 539, Ojo-Ade 18). He began a second career as a literary critic for various newspapers but complained that he was given only material relating to colonialist literature to review because he had been classified as a colonial by his editors (Midiohouan 64). Nonetheless, Maran emerged as a pivotal figure for the African diaspora, hosting black intellectuals in his home in Paris. And, as a reviewer of black literature, he exercised a significant influence (Fabre in *From Harlem to Paris* 70–3).

Maran's problems with authority and authorship are reflected in the troubles of his protagonist, the chief Batouala, who faces a war of attrition against his authority mounted by his own people. The French colonial officials remain on the margins; the process of cultural denigration is silent and underhanded, its mechanisms having been internalized to such an extent that the people of Oubangi-Chari are destroying the fabric of their own culture. Maran represents an "authentic," traditional African culture by suggestion, projecting it onto the emptiness registered by what is no longer there.[11]

As a modernist novel of disillusionment and loss, *Batouala* exemplifies very well Lukacs's description in *The Theory of the Novel* (1920). Much like Lukacs's notion of a "created totality," tradition in *Batouala* is a construct implied by what is there only imperfectly. Realism works through indirection more often than not, suggesting through absence, or through the other, the whole represented. The concept of totality comes into play not as an idea about surface truths, or the appearance of things, but as a hidden, subterranean, deep structure of relations that reveal themselves only in fragments, and are constantly transforming under historical pressures.[12] As Lukacs suggests, it is through the hero's experience, his sense of dissonance, that the absent totality of life is suggested to the reader (*Theory* 53, 71).

Batouala is such a Lukacsian hero of modernity, and the mood of lazy malaise that opens the novel indicates the unease of his soul. As the novel begins, it is morning and Batouala is having difficulty waking. He has lost his sense of purpose and wonders what there is to wake for (21–2). The narrator signals the chief's diminishment when he makes the chief's consciousness interchangeable with that of his mangy dog, Djouma. Demoralized and lacking in motivation, Djouma, the narrator tells us, wonders in despair whether he is "less than nothing" (27).

The tribe itself, the Banda, is conscious of its own decline. The natives are demoralized, their culture is in decay, their beliefs and value systems are in a crisis all because they have been devalued and exploited in their contact with Europeans. Oddly enough, Senghor let these aspects of the novel pass without comment, applying instead an authenticating discourse and proclaiming an aesthetic unity (the unity of style of Maran's language) that obscured the historicity of the novel. As attitudes toward negritude have become more critical in recent years, the reception of Maran's novel has also suffered. His tendency to ethnographic description has been deemed embarrassing, an indication of his assimilation.

But Maran's novel is an act of writing back, an attempt to criticize colonialism by using ethnographic description—realistic, scientifically objective description, as he claimed in the preface—to make the injustices of colonialism transparently evident. Maran conveys the degradation of rituals under the colonial gaze, and this I would highlight as his historicizing gesture. It distinguishes Maran's ethnography, since so much ethnographic writing was aimed at reconstructing pure or whole rituals, often deliberately correcting the ritual actually observed by the ethnographer.

In *Batouala* the action is organized around the extended description of two rituals: the circumcision ceremonies and the annual hunt. During the love dance that follows the circumcision ceremonies, Batouala is humiliated by losing his favorite wife, Yassiguindja, to his best friend, Bissibingui, a younger, stronger man who threatens Batouala's authority in the village. During the hunt Batouala is injured and dies. Both rituals set the stage for the chief's demise.

The description of the love dance makes especially clear the ways in which Maran novelizes ethnography. Yassiguindja is cast in the role of the male partner in the dance. Since this is a scene that belongs to Maran's ethnographic description of native custom, he could have described the scene just as he did the circumcisions, using anonymous characters. In fact, Yassiguindja's partner in the dance remains anonymous. Yet Maran deliberately names Yassiguindja in the role of the man. Acting out the traditional role, Yassiguindja assumes the male genitalia and dances the sexual conquest of the female partner. A moment of authenticating cultural retrieval is disrupted by the pressures of the added context of novelistic story (the love triangle of Bissibingui, Batouala, and Yassiguindja); the significance of the ceremony changes. The reader cannot fail to read Yassiguindja's assumption of male genitalia in the ritual dance as a challenge to Batouala's authority even though this interpretation has nothing to do with the traditional, ritualistic meaning of the dance. Reading the text as a novel in which the characters' psychology and motivation are crucial structuring elements, we see that Yassiguindja exercises symbolically her choice of sexual partner because she is in a position of strength. Yassiguindja as the male dancer intimidates the woman into submission, a course of events that bears meaningfully on Batouala's loss of sexual prowess and authority. His culture has been emasculated. The set scene of native ritual in the novel says less about the authenticity of the ritual than about the historical consciousness of its participants.

Batouala, who as hereditary chief is responsible for transmitting tradition, talks about customary beliefs without conviction. To instruct his people about their identity is to tell them about what they have forgotten. When he speaks, he constantly remarks on the difference between now and then:

> In the past, women who wanted to become mothers, and all desired motherhood then—could not eat kid [young goat] or turtle. We knew then [*Nous savions alors*] that those who ate kid would be struck with barrenness. . . . We also knew [*Nous savions aussi*] that our ancestors could create rain at will. They could do it, but they only used their gift judiciously, when the seeding season approached.   *(143–44)*

Batouala's remarks are cast not as a discourse of belief but as a discourse of knowledge (*savoir*) which, however, has lost its relevance because, transmitted to those who are not knowledgeable of tradition, it has no authority.

Moreover, in this particular instance, Batouala is violating tradition by revealing to Bissibingui secrets those in his station in life are not supposed to know. In Batouala's explanation, the ancestors' powers are exaggerated, mythical. What is important here is that Batouala remembers the past as a whole world, as a time, for example, when man had a direct, unmediated relationship with nature and the gods, when the meaningfulness of things was easily apparent.

Batouala's malaise, however, has a more concrete cause than a generalized sense of discontent. It is articulated explicitly as a dread of imminent economic changes and specifically, a dread of alienated labor:

> Work did not scare him.
>
> In the white man's language, however, this word took on a surprising meaning. It meant getting tired without seeing any immediate or concrete result; it meant worry, sorrow, pain, diminished health, the pursuit of imaginary goals.
>
> Oh! The white men. They would do better to return home, all of them. They would do better to focus their ambitions on domestic affairs or the cultivation of their land, instead of channeling them to the conquest of money that is stupid.   *(21)*

Having not yet succumbed to the necessity of alienating his labor in a capitalist mode of employment, Batouala finds himself at a historical threshold where he can see the economic and cultural changes the Europeans are effecting. Cultural loss is perceived here as a change in the conditions of work: work in a capitalist economy is emptied of personal meaning, and as a result it becomes fatiguing. Batouala goes on to distinguish between *fainéantisme* (idleness) and *paresse* (laziness); disputing the myth of the "lazy native," Maran claims that it is not laziness to live from day to day.[13] Batouala is grieving the imminent loss of a particular way of life. Maran locates the sensibility of loss in the consciousness of the native and not in the consciousness of the European who "discovers" the primitive as the loss of his own innocence. The predicament of the native is in essence the predicament of modernity: alienation from nature and belief, increased social atomization, despair, homelessness. Batouala's grief renders him the quintessential novelistic hero of disillusionment.

Maran makes his point most powerfully at the very end of the novel, when an injured and ailing Batouala succumbs to the ultimate humiliation of seeing Yassiguindja and Bissibingui making love. Immediately preceding their union, Maran illustrates the devaluation of tradition and of Batouala's authority in an exchange between the French authorities and the natives. At a loss as to how to cure Batouala of his injuries (he was attacked by a panther during the hunt), the natives turn to the French commandant, whose answer to the natives' plea for help is "Batouala might as well die, and all the m'bis with him" (185). The most shocking aspect of this response is that the natives then use it to authorize their own defiance and disrespect of Batouala. The reader understands at the end of the novel that the supremacy of French authority had already been established for some time. When reviewed from this new perspective, the display of traditional ritual that has unfolded during the course of the novel seems forced, more performative than genuine. It is not necessary for the French to interfere. Their authority is evident to everyone, and its currency is marked by the ease with which the commandant marks Batouala's irrelevance.

There is another moment of such ironic revision in the novel, which is once again linked to what appears as the accidental, casual presence of the French authorities on the scene. In the sexual orgy that follows the circumcision ceremonies, Batouala is prevented from reaching Bissibingui and Yassiguindja (who are trying once again to be alone together) by the sudden appearance of the French authorities. Acting out their disciplinary role, the French impose fines on the natives for creating unrest. The orgy has a double nuance: it is putatively a description of custom that belongs to Maran's ethnographic project, but it is also evidence of how the contents of the novel are shaped by a discourse that precedes the novel: Africa as a place where excesses are realizable. "Sexual rapture [*ivresse sexuelle*], doubled with drunkenness [*ivresse alcoolique*], it was an immense joy of savages, exempt from any restraint," we are told (93). But it is important to note that the lack of dignity and the excessiveness found here are facilitated by a European influence: drunkenness.

The orgy (which follows the ritual performance of the "love dance" that enacts sex) exemplifies Fanon's interpretation of the psychopathology of ritual dancing in *The Wretched of the Earth*. According to Fanon, the acting out in the "permissive circle" of the dance purges the violence internalized by the native through the experience of colonialism. Those acts that seem to give evidence of the brutality of the native register the detrimental effect of colonialism on the native (*Wretched* 56–7). In *Batouala* the intrusion of the colonial police to disrupt the orgy guarantees a reimposition of order after the indulgence in excess. The intrusion of the police is also narratologically the intrusion of plot (of "sjuzet") into the serially accumulating details of the orgy—elements of story (or "fabula") that make up the ethnographic account. As the pornographic details (deleted from the first English translation) are aligned with the ethnographic discourse, Maran suggests that ethnography without historical perspective (gained here by the disruptive effect of the police presence that reorders the scene) is like pornography: a fantasy of escape for the reader into a primitivism that is otherwise inaccessible. The intrusion of the police brings things into perspective: the excesses of the orgy are not in opposition to the disciplinary presence of the police but a product of it.

The casualness with which the French impose their authority and exact punishment reveals the extent of their penetration of the native setting. Unimpeded and with unquestioned authority, they invade the space of the ceremonies. Should the reader have been under the illusion of participating in an authentic African ritual, s/he is quickly reminded that as authentic as circumcisions, love dances, and uninhibited sex may appear, in the existing order of things the customs shown to the reader are already corrupted. Indeed, it is only through the prism of this devaluation (the indignity of drunkenness, for example) that native customs become available to the reader. With their space easily violated and their rituals interrupted, the natives occupy a clearly diminished position.

Despite Maran's extensive efforts to re-create what Senghor called the style and rhythm of African life, the narrative representation of traditional practices acts dramatically in the text to show their historical obsolescence. This is, in fact, the historical content of Maran's novel: the change of values as a loss of "native" authority. Grief at the loss of authenticity and the invention of authenticity are two aspects of the same emplotting gesture, and they are anchored in a consciousness of colonialism's humiliating rule.

Undercutting the Ethnographic:
Achebe's Representation of Tradition

Things Fall Apart (1958) and *Arrow of God* (1964) have been described as ethnographic and even as parodies of ethnography.[14] Both novels recount the ways in which rigid notions of tradition are established through particular historical circumstances. Achebe redefines and makes newly relevant those same values whose passing he records in these novels. Indeed, often the historical insight that Achebe brings to his fiction works against the stories he tells and the ethnographies he provides. History, as a means of writing back, teaches something different from the stories (the Ibo do not fall apart, the empire does). It also demonstrates that timeless, ethnographically complete traditional cultures frozen in time never existed. Thus, for example, Okonkwo's notion that his society was more orderly and stable in the recent past reflects his yearning for order, not a historical fact. By this Achebe does not mean to diminish the disruptive effect of colonialism but to shift attention to a longer span of history. Before the events recounted in *Things Fall Apart* at the turn of the century, there was plenty of disruption; the Atlantic slave trade, for example, would have been one cause of such disruption.

Although published only six years apart, *Things Fall Apart* and *Arrow of God* reflect different historical moments. *Things Fall Apart* belongs to the independence struggle and *Arrow of God* to the years immediately following independence, anticipating Nigeria's impending crisis of civil war. Both novels are set in traditional Ibo communities, but their action is separated by a period of twenty years.

In *Things Fall Apart* Achebe sought to invalidate the empty claims of British cultural supremacy in view of the violence of their colonization and their inability to recognize the complexity of the Ibo civilization. The discrepancy between the meaning of Okonkwo's death to his people and the District Commissioner's facile treatment of Okonkwo highlights Okonkwo's tragedy. The Commissioner looks forward to treating Okonkwo as a curious detail, "one reasonable paragraph" in his projected work, *The Pacification of the Primitive Tribes of the Lower Niger* (209). The Commissioner's response, however, powerfully reinforces the uses of the novel itself as an alternative to the presumptions about "pacification" and "primitive tribes" (209). *Things Fall Apart* takes its place as the counter-oeuvre to works such as the Commissioner's through which European readers have claimed to know Africa.[15]

Like Yeats's poem "Second Coming" from which Achebe borrows his title, *Things Fall Apart* announces the coming of a new era amidst the danger of cultural disintegration. Edward Said has argued for the poem's immediate relevance to the colonial situation of African writers ("Yeats and Decolonization" 90). Colonialism manifests itself as a period of cultural disintegration and not of the achievement of a higher culture (*Culture and Imperialism* 235). Achebe's title, however, may also make a different comment on the colonial situation if we see Okonkwo's death as the moment that crystallizes resistance. Then, reading against the grain, we may surmise that the warning about an impending (violent) disintegration potentially bears on the colonial order itself and not on the dissolution of the native culture.

A novel of resistance, *Things Fall Apart* powerfully addressed the aspirations of the independence movements sweeping through Africa in the late 1950s.[16] It reflects, therefore, the ethnographic impulse to reconstruct a whole culture. From the outset of his literary career, the operative concepts in Achebe's thought have been the experience of colonialism as what Abdul JanMohamed has called cultural "denigration," and the perception that the African intellectual's duty is to envision a cultural "restitution" (JanMohamed 153–4). However, unlike the "salvage ethnography" of European ethnographers who sought, as Clifford has explained, to preserve what was already lost, Achebe's autoethnography aims at affirming the contemporaneity of native cultures with those of the West. Ibo culture is decidedly not a finished thing looked at nostalgically at the moment of the novel's composition but the very perspective from which an Ibo writer of the late 1950s is looking at his own continuous history. Achebe shows the persistence of African ways of life during the colonial period and the incomplete, gradual, and painstaking inroads of European culture.

Although Okonkwo commits suicide because he despairs at his own people's failure to take up arms against the British, the result of his suicide is not to pit him against his community but to reveal to the reader the absolute divide between Umuofia and the British. The novel ends with a definite hardening of positions as Achebe unambiguously energizes the reader into an anti-British position and uses the recent past (the first decade of the twentieth century) to address his own situation during the independence effort. We cannot but correlate the indignity of the District Commissioner's paragraph on Okonkwo to the racist assumptions from which any perpetuation of colonialism stems. The witnesses to Okonkwo's despair (including the reader) respond by channeling their sense of tragedy into resistance to the legacy of racism and colonialism. In *Things Fall Apart* Okonkwo's suicide is a defining moment that makes clear where the conflict lies and resolves the ambiguities presented during the course of the novel.

The historical sensibility of *Arrow of God* is quite different, however, from that of *Things Fall Apart*. At the end of *Arrow of God* Achebe's narrator explains Ezeulu's tragedy in terms of his son's (Obika's) death, an event that obstructs an opportunity for clarification:

> It looked as though the gods and the powers of event finding Winterbottom handy had used him and left him again in order as they found him.
>
> So in the end only Umuaro and its leaders saw the final outcome. To them the issue was simple. Their god had taken sides with them against his headstrong and ambitious priest and thus upheld the wisdom of their ancestors—that no man however great was greater than his people; that no man ever won judgment against his clan.
>
> If this was so then Ulu had chosen a dangerous time to uphold this wisdom. In destroying his priest he had also brought disaster on himself, like the lizard in the fable who ruined his mother's funeral by his own hand. For a deity who chose a time such as this to destroy his priest or abandon him to his enemies was inciting people to take liberties; and Umuaro was just ripe to do so. The Christian harvest which took place a few days after Obika's death saw more people than even Goodcountry could have dreamed. In this extremity many a man sent his son with a yam or two to offer to the new religion and to bring back the promised immunity. Thereafter any yam harvested in his fields was harvested in the name of the son. *(229–30)*

These last paragraphs of *Arrow of God* provide the reader with what Gary Saul Morson and Caryl Emerson have described in their work on Bakhtin as a moment of "authorial discovery." (For Morson and Emerson this is a formula devised to explain Bakhtin's notion of hybridization. See *Creation of a Prosaics* 335). Here the author's discovery (the final paragraph of this quotation in particular) is opposed to common opinion and the characters' use of common opinion. We know that the community of Umuaro lacks clarity because the narrator explains to the reader the implications of their judgment. The importance of this authorial discovery becomes evident when we look back at the ending of *Things Fall Apart*, which concludes with the ironic undercutting of ethnographic discourse—the title of the ethnographic text, *The Pacification of the Primitive Tribes of the Lower Niger* comprises the novel's last words. *Arrow of God* by contrast, therefore, provides a lot more explicit explanation. It sets in motion a historical consciousness that records how factors internal to the Ibo community contributed to a course of events that led to an assimilation and adaptation of Western values by Africans. So, although the story details a degree of cultural loss, it also treats the Ibo as historical agents who continue to shape their own culture. Achebe claims the position of historian from his perspective in 1964, anticipating the catastrophic divisions of the postcolonial nation.

Arrow of God, and not *Things Fall Apart*, is the novel in which Achebe analyzes historically the tendency of the native culture to dissolution and resists the ethnographic impulse to construct a coherent whole. The ominous warning in the title of the first novel seems in retrospect to have been premature. In *Arrow of God* (set twenty years later) we find a familiar Ibo community that does not seem to have fallen apart but is arguably once more on the verge of falling apart. While in *Things Fall Apart* the British and the community of Umuofia collide, *Arrow of God* demonstrates how the Ibo community had continued to exist side by side with the British administration throughout the period of colonialism.

Despite the redoubled effort by the narrator to record and systematize Ibo culture in *Arrow of God*, the critical juncture in the story is a moment of unraveling that demonstrates the incapacity of tradition to serve the community. Ezeulu's downfall at the sudden and seemingly arbitrary death of his son confuses the relationship among the various factions in the novel and leads to a false resolution whereby those who stand to gain by the priest's demise come to power while the real problem of the British remains unresolved. The narrative point of view makes clear that the community's judgment and Ezeulu's acceptance of it are misguided and inadequate in face of the greater historical changes taking place.

In contrast to *Things Fall Apart*, the truth revealed ironically at the end of *Arrow of God* is a criticism of the community (an attitude similar to Maran's) and not a reinforcement of the values that it embodies. This criticism of the community contrasts with *Things Fall Apart*, where Okonkwo's failure is reinvested by the novel into a positive symbol for his community. The story acts as a corrective to what Umuofia has become resigned to as its defeat, and Achebe's tragic sensibility allows for the privileging of Okonkwo despite the strict moral of the story that tells us that suicide for the Ibo is an act of shame.[17] Okonkwo's friend, Obierika, recognizes that Okonkwo's suicide attains new meaning in these particular circumstances, revising the customary view that suicides are disgraceful. Obierika, therefore, demonstrates a responsiveness to the historical situation that redresses the denigration of the present. Obierika's speech to the British signifies against its literal meaning. He tells them in an accusatory tone: "That man was one of the greatest men in Umuofia. You drove him to kill himself; and now he will be buried like a dog" (208). Here Obierika acknowledges the fall of a great man. But since Okonkwo was not considered one of the greatest men in Umuofia until this very moment when his friend's tribute revises Okonkwo's image, Obierika has effectively monumentalized Okonkwo. The fact that he cannot be buried with proper honors makes him a martyr, a new type of hero.

Whereas the tragic treatment of Okonkwo elevates him out of the realm of his personal failure and into the historically significant realm of anticolonial resistance (if only symbolically), in *Arrow of God* tragedy detracts from the characters' claims to be actors in their own fate. The narrator shows that despite the conviction of Umuaro's leaders that they are saving their community by overriding the priest's authority, the community disintegrates even further. Ezeulu is the victim of the community. He struggles with the meaning of his changing role while the forces that directly undercut him are opportunistic. Achebe interposes the narrator's insight of the tragic potential of the circumstances to disrupt the impression of the community's self-satisfaction.

In *Arrow of God* Achebe examines the difficulty faced by the Ibo community in coming to a consensus about the impact of the British presence. The British call Ezeulu to their administrative quarters and detain him at the time when he is needed by his community to call the beginning of the harvest. This precipitates the crisis of the novel. Yet the main conflict pits African against African in an assessment of the efficacy of the traditional ways of life—a test of their artificiality. Tradition has clearly become rigid. Ultimately the onus to forge a viable solution to the crisis facing the community falls on the Ibo. As an added indication that the audience addressed here is not a European audience, Ibo culture and history are not explained for the European reader but, rather, are documented for an Ibo reader who needs to take stock of them.[18]

The most distinct difference between Achebe's treatment of the two communities of Umuofia and Umuaro is the way in which he contextualizes each one in terms of its more remote past. Umuofia's origins are unspecified: "Its most potent medicine was as old as the clan itself. Nobody knew how old" (11). By contrast, in *Arrow of God* we learn that Umuaro was formed as an alliance against the slave raiders (16–7); its origin as a community is linked to the European presence in Africa. Another way by which Achebe historicizes the two portraits of traditional Ibo society is in relation to the actual historical massacre at Abame.[19] In *Things Fall Apart* the massacre takes place during Okonkwo's exile (127–130). In *Arrow of God* it resonates from the beginning as the founding act of violence that established the authority of the British.

Furthermore, the generational clash between Winterbottom and Clarke in *Arrow of God* marks the continuously evolving history of imperialism itself. We can surmise that Winterbottom and the District Commissioner in *Things Fall Apart* are of the same generation. In fact, Winterbottom lends Clarke a book by the title of *The Pacification of the Primitive Tribes of the Lower Niger*. Winterbottom is by now an old-timer, in disagreement with the present policies and not respected by his authorities. Imperialism has an "old" and a "new," an evolving history.

By contextualizing Umuaro in this manner, Achebe also shows how the British in Africa and the Ibo community in Umuaro have a shared past. The vague, mythic origins of Umuofia, on the other hand, are problematic. It is as if, before coming into contact with the British, Umuofia existed outside of history, in an idyllic, perfectly ordered, and static world—a characterization typical of the European discourse of allochrony. But this impression is given by the ethnographer-narrator who is addressing a European audience that bears responsibility for inventing the myth of such an idyllic place. The idyllic past defines a point of view; it does not articulate a history. It is the point of view that generates Okonkwo's tragedy: both his suicide and the crystallization of resistance. Resistance derives from an absolute opposition of two cultures, and thus paradoxically it is articulated most clearly through the ethnographic impulse of cultural restitution. By contrast, the ending of

Arrow of God marks anticlimactically the conversion of some Ibo to the other side, in a manner that results in a compromised integration of cultures that sets in place the elements of a continuing history of contact.

The kind of authorial explanation we find at the end of *Arrow of God*, evidence of what Bakhtin has called hybridization, is the type of authorial interference in the text that Maran disallowed himself in *Batouala* in order to maintain the appearance of objectivity. Written in free indirect discourse, *Batouala* presents reality through multiple points of view belonging to the characters. Christopher Miller has read *Batouala* as an example of how free indirect discourse can be used to politicize narrative by dispersing the central authority of the narrative voice over multiple points of view. Miller (who uses Kourouma's *Les Soleils des indépendances* as his primary example) explains the use of free indirect discourse by African writers as Bakhtinian dialogizing and reminds us that for Bakhtin, "reported speech is one of the main devices of dialogism, a 'hybrid construction' constitutive of the novel as a genre; free indirect discourse is one way in which the 'borders' between speakers can be infiltrated and polyphony heightened" (Miller in *Theories* 220–2; he cites from Todorov 73).

The dialogic and the hybrid are not equivalents in Bakhtin's thought, however. As critical devices, the dialogic and the hybrid have different functions. The dialogic addresses the point of contact and interaction among various discourses found in the same text. The hybrid, which Bakhtin considers to be a distinguishing and thus necessary feature of literary discourse, identifies different discursive spaces that are contiguous with each other.[20] In other words, although the dialogic and the hybrid both describe the dynamics of heteroglossia, they function differently as analytical tools. The dialogic addresses the dynamic at the point of contact; hybridization enables us to delineate distinct discursive spaces that are working simultaneously in a text. The dialogic forges together; the hybrid separates. As a critical device, the hybrid enables the reader to map the text as a multiplicity of contiguous discourses that are distinguishable from each other. It lays out the text as a mosaic. More important, hybridization is the feature of literary uses of language that displays most clearly the explicatory nature of literary (and especially novelistic) projects.

Such moments of explication (or "authorial discovery" as Morson and Emerson have called them) are lacking in *Batouala*. Maran has repressed all explanation; he has refused to separate the competing claims of the many voices in his text and has therefore only held up a mirror to a confused situation. After all, Bissibingui (Batouala's challenger) remains an appealing figure despite his injustice to Batouala. On the one hand, Bissibingui represents the new and, by implication, the "progress" that Maran views as inevitable. On the other, the appeal of Bissibingui rests in his being a surrogate for the failing Batouala, so we are left with the impression that the qualities Bissibingui has must have once been Batouala's. The two figures remain conflated, and Maran does not explicitly prevent us from prolonging our romance with an idealized Batouala. There is no critical clarity here of the sort suggested by hybridization and that is to be found in *Arrow of God*. Maran ends the preface by quoting Verlaine, " 'Now go, my book, wherever chance will take you' " (18). He throws up to chance the reception of his book because the truth ought to tell itself. If Maran is ultimately forward-looking in *Batouala*, asking what is to be done, he also leaves too much ground to the reader, disavowing his own voice.

Senghor praised Maran for his ability to evoke the values of a precolonial Africa—to reinvent these in his fiction. More to the point, however, Maran exposes the obsolescence of these values and the vacuum created by a new civilization that has no moral core. Missing from the novel is the history, an explanation, of how the obsolescence came about. The meticulousness with which Maran elaborates the setting (the time and the place of the action) is evidence of the historicity of the novel. But the mechanisms of change have no explanation, and thus they remain alienating, overpowering, and out of reach, reflecting Maran's own placelessness. African writers, on the other hand, were able to lay claim to place, as Achebe did in his commitment, for example, to the Biafran cause, the Ibo separatist movement that led to the Nigerian civil war of 1967–1970. So the historical discourse of Africans emanates from a sense of place, more often than not refracted through the complicated politics of the postindependence African nations. African places and nations had already been described exhaustively by Europeans when most African nations were gaining independence around 1960. Historical narration entailed the reinscription not only of narratives of development but of descriptions of place, a reclaiming of time and place.

⁛

CHAPTER TWO

History, Human Sacrifices, and the Victorian Travelers to Dahomey

If tradition in *Batouala* and *Things Fall Apart* appeals to an ideal of a well-regulated, intimate society with clearly defined boundaries, the accounts of sacrifice in nineteenth-century Dahomey problematize these boundaries radically. In *Revolution in Poetic Language* Julia Kristeva understands sacrifice as the regulatory principle in society, from which emerges the symbolic and thus signification and history, in the sense of communal memory or a shared narrative of the past. Following the lead of Marcel Mauss and Henri Hubert in their classic study of sacrifice, Kristeva contends that "far from unleashing violence, sacrifice shows how representing that violence is enough to stop it and concatenate an order." Kristeva then links representation to violence: "[sacrifice] indicates that all order is based on representation: what is violent is the irruption of the symbol, killing substance to make it signify" (75).

Nineteenth-century Dahomey presents us then with a paradox: a literal killing of substance, the actual "sacrifice" of human beings, at a scene that is fundamental to the emergence of Africanist history. It leads us to ask what happens when sacrifice is an actual, historical violence legitimated by "tradition," and "tradition" a product of a shared Afro-European history. Europeans emptied Dahomey of its own historical meaning by representing it as a place of spectacular violence. It is this process of representation, a violence in itself, as well as the Africans' response to it that I seek to historicize. Sacrifice may be "found at the extreme end of the social code," at the "limit," as Kristeva explains (78), but this limit is also a contentious place for the historical subjects that emerge at the scene of sacrifice.

Dahomey was heavily implicated in the slave trade; thus from the state's inception in the seventeenth century, the ruling class of Dahomey participated in the systematic victimization of African peoples.[1] However, Dahomean culture, like all cultures, was multifaceted. The exclusive identification of Dahomey as the place of human sacrifice is a product of the Afro-European encounter. This chapter investigates the ways in which the Victorian travelers to Dahomey managed their role as witnesses to atrocities at a time when Britain had a heightened imperialist interest in Dahomey. The next two chapters look at the shaping of an alternative historical narrative by the Dahomean writer Paul Hazoumé.

Narrative Conventions of Testimony

Few places had been as completely demonized by European travelers as Dahomey. When Richard F. Burton arrived there in 1863, he was prepared to find a "lake of blood big enough to paddle a canoe in" (Brodie 212).[2] For Dahomey had acquired by the middle of the nineteenth century the most "sinister" reputation as a place of savagery where purportedly ritual killings ("sacrifices") of thousands were annual events.[3] There was, by this time, a sizable literature on Dahomey, which could be distinguished as a subgenre of travel writing concerned with testimonial accounts of "native" atrocities.[4] Descriptions of the ritual of human sacrifices were repeated often enough that they acquired their own narrative conventions. Like all conventional narratives, they became predictable and included certain set pieces: the erection of the sacrificial platforms, the bondage of the victims and their transportation to the top of the platform, the king's distribution

FIGURE 2.1   From Dalzel, plate 5

of cowries to the crowd followed by the dismemberment of bodies, the exhibition of mutilated corpses and skulls, and finally the parade of the king's wealth.

The British efforts to bring Dahomey under their sphere of influence in the nineteenth century charts a history of failure. Dahomey eventually became a French colony after a series of sustained military attacks in the early 1890s. During the height of the transatlantic slave trade in the eighteenth century, however, the British had been very much implicated in Dahomey's culture of violence. This complicity, moreover, had seemed unproblematic. The illustrations that appeared in Archibald Dalzel's *History of Dahomy* (1793), for example, document the presence of British naval officers at the scene of the ritual sacrifices in a celebratory fashion (see figure 2.1). The British officers are at the center of the illustration (elevated on the platform), looking at a scene of execution at the lower right-hand corner and

FIGURE 2.2   From Forbes (2:52), "The Human Sacrifices"

smiling with pleasure at various slaves standing below offering them treasures (jewelry, cowries, etc.). The picture is arranged in such a fashion as to
place the execution in the margin (although our attention is drawn to it by
the gaze of one of the officers) and the economic exchange at the center.
This arrangement establishes the proper order of things: the contact between Africans and the British is a commercial one in which the British are
the dominant party. Yet the illustration insidiously suggests an alternative
narrative: the British officer looks at the scene of the execution with unambiguous pleasure, pleasure purchased through the economic transaction
that has ordered the center of the illustration.

What happens later in the narratives of the Victorians can in part be
summarized by looking at illustrations from two travel accounts subsequent
to Dalzel's history. The illustration of the scene of sacrifice in Frederick
Forbes's book (showing the sacrificial platform and a throng of naked men
waiting eagerly for the bodies to start falling [figure 2.2]) displays no Europeans, but there are two Union Jacks flying prominently at the center of the
illustration. British complicity is registered here through this official symbol
of their presence, even though Forbes or any other member of his delegation are absent from the scene. The illustration correlates closely with
Forbes's narrative in which a refusal to witness the human sacrifices out of

FIGURE 2.3   From Skertchly, "The So-sin [human sacrifices] Victims"

moral compunction is subverted by the need to report the details, creating, therefore, the paradox of an absent witness. The absent witness is the major figure of testimony in these narratives. Gone is the unproblematic amusement of Dalzel's officers—to be replaced, however, with a more surreptitious pleasure evident in the illustration from Skertchly's account (figure 2.3). This illustration erases any trace of the British presence but at the same time heightens the visibility of the violence. The bodies of victims are drawn in a geometric fashion, creating an aesthetics of horror. Mutilated bodies form an architectural motif, shaping an arcade over a road, on which we also see some natives occupied in everyday activities. Correlating closely with Skertchly's narrative, the illustration reflects the transformation of Dahomey into a landscape of sacrifice. This reinvention of the sacrificial scene complicates the figure of the absent witness.

The progressive sensationalization of Dahomey as a place of horrors in Victorian travel writing, therefore, records two sequential gestures on the part of the Victorians: a deliberate distancing from Dahomey through its aggressive othering, and then a renewed engagement with a reinvented Dahomey toward which the Victorians adopt an ambivalent attitude of pleasure and repulsion. The problem of the testimonial figure in these texts arises from the tendency to avoid a narrative account of the atrocities. The six Victorians who wrote accounts of their visits to Dahomey (John Duncan, F. E. Forbes, Peter W. Bernasko, A. P. Wilmot, Richard Francis Burton, and J. A. Skertchly) are obsessed with the sacrifices, but Forbes, Burton, and Skertchly refused to see the sacrifices. To give credibility to his account, Burton used Wilmot's and Bernasko's accounts as appendices to his text; they saw and he explains. Burton's distance from the sacrifices gives him greater authority to explain Dahomean culture. Indeed, he goes a long way toward inventing what Paulin Hountondji has called an *ethnophilosophy* (Hountondji 20–1, 38): explaining Dahomean culture (and, by extension, all African culture) according to one axiom. For Burton this axiom was that Dahomean culture is fundamentally religious, and thus by implication not historical.

Although human sacrifices were also associated with other West African states (Ashanti and Benin, for example), in the accounts of Dahomey they are a central aspect of the narrative, not one among many reported practices but the main event. The writers and readers of these accounts assumed what Burton pointed out explicitly: that Dahomey was synonymous with human sacrifice (Burton 2:17). To pick up a book on Dahomey, therefore, represented a conscious choice to read about human sacrifices.[5] The question then becomes whether the "true" tales produced by travelers to Dahomey are acts of testimony. Or are they instead allegories for a variety of fantasies that engaged what Christopher Lane has identified as the negative drives of colonialism (such as the "failure of self-mastery," the "death drive," etc. [2]).

The preoccupation with Dahomey was far from arbitrary; rather, it enacted a very particular historical project: to suppress a record of cultural approchement between Britain and Dahomey in the eighteenth century. Because of its extensive relationship with the British during the height of the transatlantic slave trade in the eighteenth century, Dahomey had been accessible. It had been a place where it was possible to view native African customs, and participation was even encouraged by the natives in charge. After their abolition of the slave trade in 1807 and the 1833 emancipation of slaves, the British tried to dissociate themselves from slavery by casting it as an African problem. By 1865 the British had accomplished a reevaluation of the history of slavery so that slavery was widely regarded as part of African tribal history (Brantlinger 179). The literature by British travelers to Dahomey participates in this cultural project of othering slavery. In mid-century, British travelers began diminishing instead of aggrandizing Dahomey until it was eventually reinvented as pure savagery. From this new distance, the Victorians produced narratives of increasingly imaginary realms where atrocities proliferated out of control.[6]

Dahomey reached the height of its military power during the reign of King Guezo (1818–1858), a period that coincided with the accelerated missionary efforts of Europeans and their attempt to move inland. The Europeans, however, did not achieve anything resembling direct control of West African states until after 1880. Dahomey's intransigence fits a pattern of successful resistance by West African states and of failed, costly efforts by Britain and France to penetrate beyond the ports on the coast where they had been a presence for two hundred years (Ajayi and Oloruntimehin 209). Moreover, Dahomey's relationship with the British in particular was unique among West African states in this period. Secure in its impenetrability, Dahomey received the British delegations with a marked degree of openness and refused compromises from a position of strength.[7]

The first of the Victorians to travel to Dahomey, John Duncan arrived there in 1845 sponsored by the Royal Geographical Society. He traveled through Dahomey because he had been refused passage through Ashanti. Duncan's commission by the Royal Geographical Society had been awarded in recognition of his efforts in the Niger Expedition of 1841, where he was one of five survivors out of three hundred participants in this missionary expedition that ended in miserable failure. His feat was not only to visit Abomey, the inland capital that had become a sort of geographical limit for travelers, but to travel beyond it and reach the Kong Mountains to the north.[8] He passed through Abomey again on his return from the Kong Mountains and remained for a second visit. Duncan did all this traveling despite suffering from a gangrened leg, which he was ready to amputate himself if necessary (2:chap. 12).

Duncan is in many respects atypical of this group of Victorian travelers. He was an adventurer and neither a missionary nor an antislavery crusader. Of modest background and with little education, he had begun his career by enlisting in the First Regiment of the Life Guards in 1822. After sixteen years of service, he "was anxious for a field of greater enterprise" (Duncan vi). Ambitious, physically strong, and courageous, he was patriotic but not motivated by Christian idealism (Temperley 71). *Travels in West Africa* conveys a participatory attitude, a sense of being in the fray rather than a bird's-eye view. Duncan's description of the sacrifices is intimate, close-up. Moreover, by identifying with those in authority rather than the captive slaves, Duncan rendered the European as the ally for the African slave master. Later writers on Dahomey reacted with alarm to Duncan's complicitous narration (which they cited obsessively), as they sought to dissociate themselves from the culture of slavery. In trying to stamp out the traces of Duncan's complicity, these writers create a cohesive body of texts. Their narratives stall and turn into static compositions of tableaux in some instances, or mindless catalogs of material things in others. The refusal to narrate represses any traces of causality that might have linked Europeans to the practices of the Dahomeans.

Travel writing generally has a very vexed relation to the notion of presence. Usually composed after the return home, travel narratives reconstruct presence awkwardly, wrestling constantly with their own textuality. The distinction between "narrative time" and "story time" evoked by Gérard Genette at the beginning of *Narrative Discourse* is always a pressing concern in travel literature (33). Which is the present that counts? The time of the narration, or the time in which the experience being narrated unfolded? The depiction of extreme violence makes this difficulty even more pressing. The anxiety over the loss of self-mastery, or even of mastery *tout simple*, is worked out in the supplemental, and deferred, terrain of writing.

A naive storyteller, Duncan sets out to explain the sacrifices as precisely as possible.[9] His narrator is full of bravado, and his tone is consistently light. Moreover, he places himself literally in the scene; he is an actor, not an observer.[10] The executioner, who is the protagonist, is rendered as a fumbling, inept killer. Duncan's humor is at the expense of the victims whose executions are botched. The author's presence in the action functions as a barrier between his own readership and the native "mob." After only a passing reference to the mob that is at the scene to witness the executions, Duncan ignores it completely. This deletion of the native spectators creates the aura of a private viewing to the executions.[11] The intimacy of the scene enhances the private pleasure of reading, which enables the safe and unembarrassed consumption of the excessive narrative that follows:

> Poor old Mayho, who is an excellent man, was the proper executioner. He held the knife or bill-hook to me, but I again declined the honor; then the old man, at one blow at the back of the neck divided the head from the body of the first culprit, with the exception of a small portion of the skin, which was separated by passing the knife underneath. Unfortunately, the second man was dreadfully mangled, for the poor fellow, at the moment the blow was struck having raised his head, the knife struck in a slanting direction, and only made a large wound; the next blow caught him on the back of the neck, when the brain protruded. The poor fellow struggled violently. The third stroke caught him across the shoulders, inflicting a dreadful gash. The next caught him on the neck, which was twice repeated. The officer steadying the criminal now lost his hold on account of the blood which rushed from the blood-vessels on all who were near. Poor old Mayho, now quite palsied, took hold of the head, and after twisting it several times around, separated it from the still convulsed and struggling trunk. *(250–1)*

The violence of Duncan's own ordering of the narrative is palpable in the relentless linearity of his transcription of events, which culminates in the final severing of the semidetached head. Moreover, Duncan represses what must have been the second victim's defiance: the victim, we are told, raised his head and then, the "poor fellow struggled violently." Oddly, the victim becomes responsible for the bungling of his execution and contributes to the spectacularization of his body's dismemberment.

This displacement of responsibility onto the victim enables an identification between the narrator and the executioner. The executioner's incompetence drives the cumulative logic of this extensive description: he can't do it right, so the narrative is extended until the action is accomplished. A surrogate, textual pleasure is derived from the willful prolongation of the narrative, the deferment of the severing of the head. Duncan may have refused to do the actual killing, but he can prolong the time of action by giving his reader more or less detail, as he pleases. Instead of one clean action, the execution produces a segmented action that requires sustained attention by the narrator to be recounted completely. The narrator becomes a sort of executioner who duplicates the event with greater control.

Duncan has created a written account whose supplemental relation to the real event seeks to displace the real event in significance. As supplement (in the Derridean sense), Duncan's narrative is not only a substitute for the action recounted but something in excess to it, a surplus (*Of Grammatology* 144). Supplementarity also entails the ambition to master. Derrida's elaboration of the idea of supplementarity derives from Rousseau's discussion of autoeroticism. In the *Confessions* autoeroticism is the "dangerous supplement" to the inaccessibility of the desired person. For Derrida, "The supplement has not only the power of *procuring* an absent presence through its image; procuring it for us through the proxy [*procuration*] of the sign, it holds it at a distance and masters it" (*Of Grammatology* 155). Autoeroticism becomes for Derrida a "model of reading"; textual pleasures are autoerotic pleasures and thus economical. The notion of mastery implicit in autoeroticism posits the possibility of a fantasy that is an improvement over the real because it does not waste energy. In Derridean terms, the supplement conserves energy and safeguards against dissipation while procuring the pleasures denied in actual experience.

The desire for mastery motivates Duncan's narrative.[12] This mastery, however, cannot be accomplished without a fantasy of the consummation of its object. The pleasure denied in the real action (Duncan refuses to carry out the executions himself and thus "holds [himself] at a distance") is retrieved as a narrative consummation, at once safer and more satisfying. Duncan's account reveals what other accounts later struggle to disguise: that the participation solicited by the narration provides a surrogate for the performance of violence.[13]

The text invents its own logic of expenditure, a linear parataxis of detail upon detail linked by the simplest form of causality. The supplementary status of the text enables this fiction of expenditure that does not threaten to consume and destroy the self.[14] Moreover, because the threat of self-consumption is neutralized, expenditure does not detract from mastery but confirms it. Duncan conquers his own anxieties through his narrative; his attitude was unsettling to those who followed him to Dahomey. Forbes, Wilmot, Burton, and Skertchly all sought to disclaim Duncan's pleasures.

Forbes and Wilmot, both naval officers who served in the antislavery blockades off the coast of West Africa, took on their role as witnesses to atrocity defensively. As commander of the *Bonetta*, Forbes successfully interdicted six slave ships off the coast of West Africa in 1848, an accomplishment that is noted in William Laird Clowes's history of the Royal Navy (6:366–7).[15] He followed up his service at sea with two successive antislavery missions inland to the king of Dahomey in 1849 and 1850. On the first he accompanied Duncan, who had returned to Africa as vice-consul at Whydah in 1849. Duncan thought that the presence of a naval officer on an antislavery mission would be a good thing.[16] The trip in 1849, however, was cut short because of Duncan's ill health (Forbes 1:94). Forbes and Duncan reached Abomey but returned after a short stay. Then Forbes traveled again to Abomey on his own in 1850 and witnessed the annual sacrifices. His narrative solution to the problem of complicity was to describe not the action but the place of sacrifice.

In Forbes's *Dahomey and the Dahomans* (1851), it is possible to correlate the account of human sacrifices with the heroic narrative of discovery. He configures the site of the sacrifices as an alternative landscape to the mountains and lakes of the African interior revealed to the explorers. Human sacrifice is transformed into a landscape that is circumscribed by the narrative point of view. Thus the starting point of Forbes's account is that "The king insisted on our viewing the place of sacrifice" (2:51).

Mary Louise Pratt has described the masterful "verbal paintings" (usually promontory descriptions) that are the most privileged rhetorical moments of the narratives of discovery. Pratt unmasks the discoverer's empty posture of triumph; she argues, obviously enough, that the discovery is fanciful since one cannot discover a place known to so many others. Using Burton as her primary example, Pratt shows that the climactic moments in the narratives of discovery entail an erasure of the native's presence from his land and the "deistic" reordering of the landscape as a "verbal painting" composed by the European viewer (*Imperial Eyes* 204–5).

In a rhetorical gesture that is analogous to those described by Pratt, Forbes "discovers" and thus invents the sacrifices as a landscape by reordering the scene he witnesses as a series of tableaux. Instead of narrating a meaningful and continuous action, Forbes gives us disjunected pictures. The description of place transvalues action into landscape; restoring history to this represented landscape, moreover, surfaces as a preoccupation of postcolonial writers, as in the case of Okri's *The Famished Road* (see chapter 6). For Forbes, sacrifice is a topos rather than a story. The topos can generate stories, but these stories are always implicit, never explicit in the travelogue itself. Forbes's refusal to duplicate the sacrifices as actions in the manner of Duncan's account invites a different type of engagement from his reader, the contemplation of a site of horrors, not the explanation of how the horrors occurred.

Forbes accomplishes this change of emphasis from action to environment by declaring himself an unwilling witness. He is coerced by the king to be present at the scene of the sacrifices, but once the ritual is under way, he successfully evades seeing the killings. The recounting of the sacrifices begins with Forbes's assumption of the equivalent of a promontory position. He climbs to the top of the king's platform from where he should be accorded a privileged view of the proceedings (2:46). But, once on top, Forbes does not look below; he describes the scene on the platform: the king (whose demeanor is noble and whose skin practically white) and the ceremony of distributing cowries to the crowd below.[17] He does not see the crowd below, he smells it: "The naked multitude emitted an effluvium only to be compared to the fetid atmosphere of a slave ship; and as the mass oscillated there arose a vapour like the miasma of a swamp" (2:47). The mob is described indirectly, by analogy only. Each of the two analogies refers to a particular place: the slave ship and the swamp. In these rhetorical gestures, Forbes refuses the view his promontory position affords him: he is at the scene of sacrifice but also absent from it because it happens down by the mob and not up at the platform.

When the sacrifices begin, Forbes obscures his view of the proceedings by manipulating his distance from the events. His point of view fades in and out like that of a camera: "Disgusted beyond the powers of description, we retired to our seats, where also the cha-cha [a slave trader] had retreated; not so his brothers, for I regret to say they remained delighted spectators of the agonies of the death of these innocent victims" (2:51). The agonies of death are a spectacle only for those who remain in the front. The seats are a retreat from the scene. Forbes's very brief rendition of the killings—one that he surmises mostly since he has withdrawn away from the scene— makes no reference to the executioner, a crucial figure for Duncan: "The victim fell at once into the pit beneath. A fall of upwards of twelve feet might have stunned him, and before sense could return the head was cut off, and the body thrown to the mob, who, now armed with clubs and branches, brutally mutilated, and dragged it to a distant pit where it was left as food for the beasts and birds of prey" (2:53).

The "victim fell" and, in the passive voice, "the head was cut off." This deletion of the executioner is analogous to Forbes's own retreat as narrator away from the action. The action happens without an actor, and it is recounted without a witness. Forbes returns to the scene only to describe the aftermath of the killing. The mob violently disperses the body over the landscape. Indeed, it creates the landscape of violence that Forbes has named a few paragraphs earlier, the "place of sacrifice." When he sees the "grizzly bleeding heads" of the victims, which are displayed in a place apart from the bodies, he informs the reader, "We could not have expected any mercy would have been shown, and therefore were prepared for the spectacle" (2:53). "Mercy" is ambiguous here; it could apply to the victims, but it could also apply to Forbes and his companions, who are not spared this scene. Forbes casts himself as a victim when a scene of violence is forced upon him.

Wilmot shared Forbes's defensiveness about being a witness to such violence. A naval officer with experience similar to Forbes's, Wilmot came, however, from a prominent family; he was the fourth son of Sir John Eardley-Wilmot, a renowned legal scholar. In 1851 Wilmot participated in a naval attack against King Cocioco of Lagos, who had refused to stop trading in slaves and had forbidden the British fleet to go upriver toward Lagos. The confrontation that followed the British defiance of King Cocioco's interdiction was described by Clowes as "costly and ineffective but most bravely conducted" (6:368). Seeking success in neighboring territory, Wilmot went on a mission to Dahomey (1862–1863), where, as his account shows, British demands to stop the sacrifices and the slave trade were again rebuffed. Burton, who followed him to Dahomey late in 1863, used Wilmot's report on his visit as his source on the details of human sacrifices.

Unlike Forbes, Wilmot interprets the native's willingness to display himself as a recognition of the westerner's authority:

I found all remonstrances in vain, and that it would be useless to get up and walk away without seeing everything that was interesting in the

country. My object was to witness the manners and customs of the King
and his people, and as the King appeared so friendly disposed, and had
got up so many things solely for my sake, I was determined to bear with
patience and see what the end would be. . . . I have reason to believe that
my line of conduct was rewarded by the whole country being laid open
before us.   *(in Burton 2:236)*

Wilmot's acquiescence to the spectacle facilitates a conquest: "the whole
country being laid open before us." Here the reference is no longer to a specific site, the place of sacrifice, but to the "whole country." In a manner
reminiscent of the explorers analyzed by Pratt, Wilmot represses his anxiety over his own self-mastery by reordering the scene.

Burton judged Wilmot's account as objective and Forbes's as unreliable
because of what he characterized as Forbes's emotionalism. In reference
to Forbes's description of the Dahomean "Amazon" army, Burton tells us,
"Commander Forbes, who drew, as artists say, 'from feeling,' was the first
to colour the melodramatic picture with a 'sensation' and picturesqueness,
a sentiment and a wild romance, in which the real object is wholly wanting" (Burton 2:42). By drawing and coloring, Forbes undermines his own
authority as an observer. Indeed, Forbes is at fault because he makes explicit his interference in the reordering of the scene, while Wilmot pretends that he reports passively, however unwilling a witness he might be.
Moreover, Burton overlooks the way in which Forbes deploys his senti-
mentality to demarcate his Englishness in an environment where that
identity is threatened.

These narratives as a group repeat a specific iconography, a landscape
littered with bodies and skeletons. The iconography becomes especially
vivid when the authors obsess over numbers. How many skeletons did they
see? How many skulls? Duncan succumbed to this obsession. The linear
parataxis of his text creates a logic of accumulation, indeed an aesthetic of
excess, which he sustains throughout his description of Dahomean culture.
The number of bodies and human skulls he sees on display multiplies uncontrollably during the course of his narrative. When he first arrives in Dahomey, he sees three bodies suspended in public view. After he delivers his
antislavery message to King Guezo (a message the king rejected), Duncan
sees two, then three thousand skulls. Although these skulls do not represent

recent killings, Duncan exploits the numbers rhetorically to create the impression of an accelerated rate of killing gone out of control.

In addition to Wilmot's report, Burton included as an appendix to his text another independent account of the sacrifices, a letter by a missionary in Whydah, Peter W. Bernasko.[18] The letter, which appeared originally in the *Wesleyan Missionary Notices* on February 25, 1861, is Bernasko's account of the sacrifices that took place in July 1860. Although Bernasko traveled to Abomey especially to report on the sacrifices and is cited by Burton because he was a witness, he provides little detail about the killings. Instead, the preoccupation with numbers dominates his narrative. Bernasko stresses the serial accumulation of killings: first one man, then another, then four more before the actual ritual has begun (in Burton 2:223). When the ritual begins, he is still asleep. One hundred men are killed before he wakes up. The heads on display also accumulate. At a particular gate in the palace, he sees first "ninety human heads, cut off that morning, and the poor creatures' blood flowed on the ground like a flood. The heads lay up on swish beds at each side of the gate, for public view" (in Burton 2:225–6). Then he adds the following: "I saw at the same gate, sixty heads laid upon the same place; and, on three days again, thirty-six heads laid up. [The king] made four platforms in their large market-place, and on which he threw cowries and cloths to his people, and sacrificed there about sixty souls. I dare say he killed more than two thousand" (in Burton 2:226). Bernasko's final assessment (two thousand killings) seems arbitrary. At a certain point the accuracy to which these numbers pretend is no longer convincing.

In *A Mission to Gelele, King of Dahome* (1864), Burton gives us the most extreme and paradoxical example of the absent witness. Africa repeatedly presented Burton with frustration. His expedition to Lake Taganyika with Speke and his failure to reach Lake Victoria from there (in 1857–1858) was the beginning of a series of missed opportunities in Africa. Speke was lionized in London and Burton ignored. When he returned to Africa, he regarded his appointment as consul in Fernando Po in 1861 (he served until 1864) as a "governmental crumb" that he accepted only in the hope of acquiring a "governmental loaf" down the road (quoted in Brodie 194). Before his expedition to Dahomey from Fernando Po, Burton went to Gabon in an attempt to authenticate Chaillu's claims to have discovered the gorilla. The trip (which is recounted in *Two Trips to Gorilla Land* [1876]) was also a failure. Burton saw only one gorilla, and he did not kill it. His ambition had been to send an unmutilated gorilla carcass to the British Museum. The best he could do was to send parts of a chimpanzee: "The skin has been sent home and I have also transmitted the head and penis in a keg of rum for Professor Burke. Will you kindly let him know this. I promised him a gorilla's brain and will do my best to keep my word, but it may be some time before that can be done" (Burton cited in Brodie 210). Next, he went to Dahomey from Fernando Po on an antislavery mission.

In Dahomey Burton asserts his authority by refusing the king's insistent request that he be present at the ceremony. Although he removes himself from the scene and dissociates himself from the sacrifices, he renders the sacrifices diffuse; they are implied everywhere in his representation of Dahomey. For Burton, the sacrifices are an integral part of the ambience of Dahomey: "During the night, at times, the deep sound of the death-drum and the loud report of a musket informed us that some mortal spirit had fled" (2:18). The absolute identity between Dahomey—the place and people—and human sacrifice is unambiguous. "It is evident that to abolish human sacrifice," Burton tells his reader, "is to abolish Dahomey" (2:17). Dahomey is human sacrifice; human sacrifice has been rendered into a place, but a place that is felt, not seen. Although he discredits Forbes, Burton colludes with Forbes's assessment that Dahomey is an "effluvium."

Dancing and drums add to the violent ambience of the place. During the customs the dancing is a figurative decapitation, a surrogate to the action of the sacrifices that Burton will not describe:

> The dancers stamped, wriggled, kicked the dust with one foot, sang, shuffled, and wrung their hands—there is ever a suspicion of beheading in these performances—bending almost double, ducking heads, moving side-ways to right and left, fronting and facing everywhere, especially presenting the back, converting forefingers into strigils, working the arms as in Mediterranean swimming, and ending in a prestissimo and very violent movement of the shoulders, hips, and loins.   *(2:7)*

The repeated references to dancing demonstrate that, though Burton will not represent the killings directly, he deploys their symbols. The account of the sacrifices is deferred and placed in an appended, borrowed text. But the sacrifices as symbols are constantly circulated.

It is possible to register here in the active narration of a surrogate event (dancing as substitute for the sacrifices Burton refuses to see) the same type of textual pleasure gleaned in Duncan's active narration. Duncan claims that he participated in the decapitation dance: "Civility would not allow me to refuse; and although I never was an excellent dancer, I did my best on this occasion, and gained the applause of his Majesty, as well as the deafening applause of all present except the Ashantees and some Portuguese, who were extremely jealous of me, particularly as the King never condescended to notice any of them during their stay at Dahomey" (1:255). Duncan is eager as a child to perform and be praised. He enjoys his status as favored guest. Such complicity can only be indulged in surreptitiously by Burton. His engagement is registered through his description of the swaying bodies and their symbolic, violent undoing.

Duncan's dancing scene was revised yet again. Unlike Burton, J. A. Skertchly danced; he had to as a prisoner of King Gelele. But he gave a more reticent account of the dancing than Duncan: "After ten minutes of very violent exercise under a midday sun, I was permitted to retire, and Gelele drank my health" (296). Skertchly, an entomologist, was captured by Gelele in 1871 and remained in the Dahomean capital for eight months. His stay in Dahomey, therefore, is not the fulfillment of an ambition but its disappointment. In *Dahomey As It Is* (1874), Skertchly described a people instead of insects.

A captive and thus an unwilling presence, he does not need to reinvent himself as an absent witness. Instead, he exploits his status as prisoner to authorize his testimony of the sacrifices. In his preface, he declares:

> [I] was condemned to be the recipient of savage honours and to sit an unwilling spectator of the notorious Annual Customs of the country; my feelings being grievously harassed by the thought that I had discovered one of the richest localities in Western Africa, while the polite imprisonment, as it were, to which I was subjected, entirely precluded my making any collection. *(viii)*

His posture is that of a disaffected, objective observer, yet his prose belies him. Skertchly downplays the executions, which he says are no different from executions anywhere (193). But he emphasizes the ritualistic display of bodies and describes Dahomey as a land littered with exposed corpses.

Once again, the description of corpses on exhibition parallels the "verbal paintings" of landscape under conquest by the imperial gaze. This is where the energy of Skertchly's prose lies:

> A few yards to the north we come upon the first victim, a fine stalwart fellow, suspended by the ankles and knees to the crosspole of one of the gallows. His arms hung limp, and the eyes were staring with a glassy look, while his mouth was pegged open, as were all others. This was done to show that in death they repented of their crimes, and wished to warn the people in the market against falling under the king's just displeasure. All were stark naked, and showed no signs of the knife, save the mutilation before mentioned [genital mutilation], and a slow drip, drip of dark-coloured blood from the mouths and nostrils, and the fractured occiputs, showed that they had been killed by the knobbed club. *(240)*

Three points need to be made here. The victim is first aestheticized; he is a "stalwart fellow." Then the intention of the author is made clear: he will explain how the killing occurred by reconstructing it from the evidence provided by the body. Finally, Skertchly makes us extremely aware of the physicality of the dead body. "Drip, drip" is realistic, sensual detail that re-creates the experience of observing the dead body and not of the killing itself. Moreover, the passage vacillates curiously between the description of one dead body and unspecified references to many dead bodies.

Consistent with the accumulative style that I have been highlighting, Skertchly goes on to describe the rest of the scene as an unfolding landscape of scattered bodies: "Two other gallows beyond have the same ghastly fruit, and opposite the Uhunglo gate of the Coomassie palace two victims depended from the same cross-pole" (240).[19] The paragraph following also begins in a similar fashion: "Five single bodies depended from as many gallows in a circle" (241).

Absent from the actual killings but there to witness and testify to the aftermath, Skertchly creates pictures; a narrative of what happened must be surmised by the pictures. His travelogue pretends that it represents Dahomey "as it is," freezing it in the aftermath of atrocity, with no past and no future. Having repressed all traces of British complicity in these rituals, Skertchly seems freer than any of the other Victorian travelers to Dahomey to demonize Dahomey. The cumulative effect of these texts is to erase the subjectivity of Africans. Burton's authoritative explanation of Dahomean culture as exclusively sacrificial facilitated the consumption of Dahomey: as an economic resource directly or a cultural symbol for the depravity of the African in general that could be deployed to justify imperialist interventions in other areas of Africa. Hountondji's argument about later ethnophilosophies applies as well to Burton's description of Dahomey: "The black man continues to be the very opposite of an interlocutor; he remains a topic, a voiceless face under private investigation, an object to be defined and not the subject of a possible discourse" (Hountondji 34). The sacrificial landscape, moreover, implies an economy of expending bodies in which the British observers are implicated; through the traces of this economy we can reconstruct their historical complicity in the atrocities they seek to distance from themselves.

The Economy of Expending Bodies

In the introduction to *Six Months' Service in the African Blockade*, Forbes acknowledged that however heroic his efforts on the *Bonetta*, the blockades were an ineffective method for curtailing the slave trade. Articulating the more active attitude toward intervention and the ambition for more direct control that became current in the 1840s, Forbes suggested the following approach: "the introduction of a cheap and useful system of trade under Government superintendence, assisted by a reduction of prices at first, but no presents. Returns for a length of time would be necessarily small, but large quantities of palm and ground nut oil, camwood and ivory, might soon be brought into the market" (vii). An alternative system of exchange is being set up here governed by two conditions: first, that it be a genuine exchange to be distinguished from any aid or interference in the form of a gift; second, that the prices will be low at first but are sure to rise in "time." Thus the passage of time is posited as bringing about an inevitable rise in values, and thus an accumulation of capital.

Since all the missions to Dahomey that I have been examining were motivated in some part by economic concerns, it should not be surprising that the human sacrifices informed the Victorians' understanding of their economic goals and fantasies of riches. The obsession with numbers not only contributed to the creation of phantasmagoric landscapes of death; it was also tied directly into anxieties about money and control over money. I do not mean to suggest here that recording numbers of victims of sacrifice is a meaningless gesture. The problem lies in the method of counting and the use of these numbers to represent Africa.

The sacrifices were preceded and followed by two rituals that rendered money into spectacle: the distribution of cowries to the spectators of the sacrifices, and the display of the king's wealth. Indeed, the sacrifices themselves are seen by Forbes as the dispersal of the king's wealth. They are the king's gifts to his people. As the bodies of the victims fall from the platforms to the crowd below, "the naked ruffians acknowledged the munifescence of their prince" (Forbes 2:52).

In this ritual, the king throws large numbers of cowries (three thousand heaps of cowries, according to Forbes) to the crowd below from his raised position on the platform. This is the same platform from which the victims are thrown to their executioner. Thus money and men are placed as interchangeable symbols of expenditure. In addition to the equivalence of men and money, this ritual sets up a contrast between a primitive behavior (expenditure) and a civilized behavior (accumulation). In a slave trade economy, the interchangeability of men and money is quite literal. The ritual begins to appear perfectly logical. Men are capital, so their expenditure for public consumption is not dissimilar to the uses of cash. The European observers of both these rituals, however, become obsessed with saving: their texts accumulate a record of the numbers (how many bodies and how much money) in an effort to control and inhibit the expenditure, which is wasteful. This temperamental difference becomes a crucial demarcation between the two cultures.

In *Given Time* Derrida provides an alternative way of reading the obsession with saving as an obsession with time. In his analysis of Marcel Mauss's *The Gift*, Derrida shows that through exchange, time accumulates. It is saved up (or suspended, its passage deferred) in the time that elapses from the first act of giving until the exchange is fulfilled with a return act. The gift is in essence a gift of time, according to Derrida. The human sacrifices are disturbing because the expenditure they symbolize works against the notion of exchange. They stress the passage of time, a present without a future. In the slave trade economy where slaves are capital, the sacrifices are a waste, a wishful denial of time and an intransigent refusal to exchange. They are acts of what Derrida calls "economic madness," consumption and destruction without limits. Thus the travelogues record numbers in an obsessive and ineffective effort to thwart waste. Ultimately these texts are also attempts to resist succumbing to a consuming present that will undermine imperialist ambitions that are inherently future-oriented and desire the accumulation of capital.

Wilmot, in particular, stresses the king's ritual distribution of cowries to the mob as part of his account. Wilmot shows that money and human beings are interchangeable signs of wealth that are wasted in an act of communal transgression. In his account the human sacrifices immediately follow the distribution of cowries and other goods: "When all that the king intends throwing away for the day is expended, a short pause ensues, and, by-and-by, is seen inside the platform, the poles mentioned before with live fowls. . . . After the fowls come the goats, then the bull, and lastly the men, who were tumbled down in the same way" (in Burton 2:245–6).

Clearly, for Wilmot this is wasteful, the "throwing away" of money. Everything he sees is part of one action: the serial description of a single action of expenditure. The men "tumbled down in the same way" as the cowries did. To the European observer, this ritual severely tests the efficacy of the logic of accumulation by revealing the attractions of expenditure. The shared complicity of native and European can be located in the slave trade and thus in the history of capitalism. The rituals of the Dahomeans, moreover, suggest in this new light the expressions of a culture grown out of, but in resistance to, the machinations of capital.

In "The Notion of Expenditure," Georges Bataille links the attractions of expenditure as a transgression of capitalist strictures to the European's invention of the "native." From the perspective of a capitalist culture (which is motivated by the accumulation of capital), expenditure is a transgressive act. Bataille's notion of expenditure posits a description of primitive society that is organized around the dialectical opposite of the capitalist ethic of accumulation. Society must expend to maintain its sense of community, and sacrifice is a means of such expenditure. Writing in the 1930s, Bataille laments that the "great and free forms of unproductive social expenditure have disappeared" (124). If Dahomey's rituals are the enactment of such expenditure, they represent the activities of a healthy society by Bataille's standards: "More or less narrowly, social rank is linked to the possession of a fortune, but only on the condition that the fortune be partially sacrificed in unproductive social expenditures such as festivals, spectacles, and games" (123). This expenditure is symbolic of the fact that the king's wealth is the wealth of all, and thus its expenditure reinforces community. Expenditure depicts the stresses of a culture shaped under capitalism by negating this culture. Consistent with Bataille's analysis, Wilmot also invents the primitive as the wasteful.

Counting bodies counteracts the temptation to succumb to uncontrollable spending. The civilized voice of the narrator quantifies the events and thus places them within the framework of an economy. The numbers, the obsessive reference to quantity, demonstrate how a principle of accumulation, more familiar to the narrator and his audience, is reimposed to implement control even as the numbers begin to function simply as numbers, not as representations of individualized human victims. What does seeing two or three thousand skulls mean? The picture of "The Golgotha, Benin" from *The Illustrated London News* (see figure 2.4) shows a phantasmagoric scene, a field covered with thousands of skulls rendered impressionistically. The dehumanization of the victims is twofold: in the kind of death they have suffered, and in the representation of their death as a generalized panorama.[20] In the narratives, the numbers are misleading signs of a precise economy. Despite their intention to exercise control, the authors have rendered the scene unquantifiable in the same way as it is impossible to count the bodies in "The Golgotha, Benin."

For Burton, counting time becomes a huge anxiety. Wilmot had warned travelers to Dahomey, "The custom of this country is delay, delay. No one knows the value of time, nor do they much care about keeping their word" (in Burton 2:235). There are two instances in which the loss of time determines Burton's experience. First, during the enactment of the annual human sacrifices, Burton loses track of a whole day. Native (ritual) time superimposes itself on Burton's sense of "real" time. Then, he had to wait two months before he was given the opportunity to deliver his official message to the king. Moreover, the message, which concerned the important "ticklish subjects of slave export and human sacrifice" (Burton 2:180), could only be delivered after the sacrifices were carried out. Burton waited and then was rebuffed. Therefore, he was a failure as an ambassador, unless he could

FIGURE 2.4   From *The Illustrated London News*, March 27, 1897, "The Golgotha, Benin"

convince his audience back home of the futility of his trip—which is what he attempted. In 1865 Burton argued in front of a Parliamentary committee that Britain should minimize its ties with West Africa. The slave trade had so demoralized the people that they were beyond help (Brodie 209).

His text tries to provide evidence of this demoralization. He devotes most of his narrative to the fifth day of the rituals, which is the day following the sacrifices. During this day, the king makes a public display of his wealth—a long procession that Burton presents as interminable and entirely senseless. He catalogs meticulously the items on display, accumulating over the course of several pages a parataxis of objects, absurdly decontextualized and emptied of their proper significance by the function of their ritualistic display. Moreover, according to Burton, instead of demonstrating the king's wealth, these objects give evidence of his poverty, especially when compared to the material wealth of Europe: "Almost any pawnbroker's shop could boast a collection more costly and less heterogeneous" (2:31–2).

Burton makes a practical assessment that imitates what David Spurr has called the trope of "debasement." Burton diminishes native culture in order to illustrate the abject condition of the native. For Spurr, however, this desire to debase is the product of a repressed desire to identify with the object of debasement: "the obsessive debasement of the Other in colonial discourse arises not simply from fear and the recognition of difference but also, on another level, from the desire for and identification with the other which must be resisted" (80). Although Burton derides the display of the king's wealth, his text imitates it. Moreover, many of the goods on display are symbols of the extensive, shared history of Britain and Dahomey and thus are symbols of a shared guilt in the slave trade. The diminishment of these signs is in turn a repression of the history they announce.

The gesture of diminishment here is so rigorous it affects the form of the text itself. The narrative degenerates into a meaningless and tedious catalog, which extends over several pages. A short example reads as follows:

> Twelve women, also in red. Seventeen fetish pots, three jars, one silver-plated urn, attended by singing women. Twenty casque-women with red tunics, and plumes, and black horsetails. Eight helmet girls, with red plumes, dark crests, and coats, and white loin cloths. Six pieces of plate, a tree, a crane, a monkey, and other things which I could not distinguish.

Some were four feet high, and all were apparently silver, borne by many women on boards. *(2:32)*

Burton does not stop cataloging even when he fails to understand the nature of some of the objects. He proceeds in the same fashion because the catalog does not have the function of explanation. It is the accumulation of raw data. Part of Burton's disenchantment here is the fact that the raw data he has accumulated at the end of this trip resists interpretation.

Forbes also describes the procession of the king's wealth in *Dahomey and the Dahomans* but relegates the catalog of the items on exhibit to an appendix. There he makes explicit the European origin of the items on display, poking fun at the absurdity of their new ceremonial function. For example, one entry reads as follows:

6 ladies of the chamber dressed most magnificently in scarlet and gold tunics, slashed with green silk and satin, with sashes and hankerchiefs of silk, satin, and velvet of every colour; coral and bead necklaces, silver ornaments and wristbands; one wore a Charles II's hat, covered with gold lace and milk-white plumes; the other five wore gilt helmets, with green and red plumes. . . . The scene was now purely theatrical. *(2:238–9)*

In both Forbes and Burton, the parade is also a parade of women (although in other instances men paraded the king's wealth as well). Forbes registers the rich attire of the women as an aesthetic experience; the traces of European culture make the women consumable to his gaze. Burton, on the other hand, sees ugly women in an absurd parade of discarded items that monotonously goes on and on. Forbes's engagement in the spectacle orders it as a theatrical experience that has its own temporality. For Burton the time spent at the parade is tedium, time robbed from him and wasted.

To the reader's dismay, Burton concludes the account of the So-sin customs only to start over again. His extended catalog of the king's wealth is rendered twice because the ritual apparently was celebrated twice in identical fashion. The king had two separate titles and would celebrate the rituals separately in his capacity as ruler in each title. Burton faithfully duplicates this repetition in his text, but the repetition makes his text senseless and amounts to a loss of time. Through his empty, perfunctory text, Burton empties Dahomey of meaning. He is enacting a cultural conquest through a strong-handed erasure. The rhetorical repetition enables Burton to diminish further the value of the customs. "The whole affair was mean in the extreme," Burton reports (2:69). The reader is subjected to another interminable procession:

> 1. Advance guard representing royalty, 4 umbrellas, 40 men and boys escorting Agugun and Ayohi, custodians of the palace. 2. The three great ministers of the crown: a large chair, a parrot or fetish image and stick, 3 flags, fancy umbrella, (lappets with knives and heads of many-coloured cloth), and 50 men. . . . 3. Seven deviced flags.   *(2:82–3)*

This catalog uses numerals to separate the entry of each exhibit and establish it as a distinct moment in a performance that would otherwise lose its contours without these dividing marks. The function of the catalog is to enumerate. Since it replaces the narrative task of recounting the sacrifices, it is provided as the alternative spectacle to Forbes's landscapes of death and the enticements of Duncan's participatory narrative.

Later, colonialism brought about a whole different tenor to the effort of cataloging and displays of material culture. As Annie Coombes has shown, the display and augmentation of objects of material culture was an important function of the cultural project of imperialist conquest. This display, under the control of Western ethnographers who could reinvent the value of the items, created the evidence for the "knowledge of Africa" that justified the superiority of the westerner (Coombes 3). Burton suggests, however, that there is nothing worth knowing about Dahomey unless there is a reasonable prospect of gaining political control over the territory. So long as Dahomey remained strong and independent and able to remind the British of their complicity in the culture of slavery, it was paramount to diminish Dahomey.

Although Burton does not recount how the sacrifices are enacted, he interprets them and explains their significance. His explanation is that human sacrifices are a religious practice.[21] But by alluding to a universalized, culturally unspecific notion of the religious, Burton suppresses the particular history that led to the emergence of this custom. The suppression of native history becomes very apparent in his account of his interview with King Gelele. Gelele's response to Burton's antislavery message draws attention to the history shared between England and the slave-raiding state of Dahomey.

When Burton recounts his exchange with the king, he adapts the paratactic trope of his catalog of the king's wealth to render native speech. Burton anxiously rearranges the king's defiant response so that it appears rhetorically awkward, its effect diminished:

> When the reply was given I perceived that the King and his visitors could not, like many Africans, "pick up the words," that is to say, answer sentence by sentence. Gelele replied in a rambling style, which requires ordering: That the slave trade was the ancestral custom, established by white men, to whom he would sell all they wanted: to the English who, after greatly encouraging the export, had lately turned against it, palm oil and "tree wool:" to the Portuguese, slaves. That a single article would not defray such expenses as those which I had witnessed. Moreover, that the customs of his kingdom compelled him to make war, and that unless he sold he must slay his captives, which England perhaps, would like even less. *(2:183–4)*

The main rhetorical characteristic of this passage is its accumulative style. Fragments are added to the original statement in a paratactic sequence. There is no attempt to revise the statement to reflect the new logic that emerges from the accumulation of discreet fragments. If Burton was reordering native speech, why did he not reorder it further and make it idiomatic? Building on the metaphor of text for culture, Vincent Crapanzano has argued that "the ethnographer does not . . . translate texts the way the translator does. He must first invent them. . . . No text survives him other than his own" (51). Burton invents his text here but also casts it as unassimilable because its content is resistant to his authority.

Yet, despite its rhetorical awkwardness, the king's answer is logical. Its logic rests on a notion of responsibility in which the Europeans are implicated in the savage practices of the Africans. The "ancestral custom" of slave trading was "established by white men." The Europeans shaped the economy that they now want to see reformed, but the bargain being offered to the African kingdom is not economically equitable. Burton perceives his ambassadorship as a cultural mission. Gelele unmasks the true intention of

Burton's mission: it is motivated by economic self-interest. The Dahomean king stresses instead a history of economic interdependence. The practices of slave trading and human sacrifices, moreover, are for him primarily material and not religious practices.

If translation is never just that, but is the invention and constitution of the object being described (as Crapanzano argues), then we also need to remember that the ethnographer's text is not only a product of his own intentions but is conditioned by his historical moment. As James Clifford has said, "structures of meaning are historically bounded and coercive" ("Allegory" 110). One has the distinct sense that Burton's account of Gelele's speech is shaped by such historical pressures. The historical narrative of mutual responsibility articulated by the king is censored by the ideological boundaries within which Burton is writing. Yet the king's message is preserved despite Burton's desire to remold it. Paul Hazoumé is the Dahomean interlocutor who develops fully the implications of the king's historical argument. As we turn to Dahomey's colonial period, the implications of the Victorians' representation of Dahomey for political control become manifest, as we also gain insight into the emergence of a resistant discourse that seeks to explain the ahistoricism of Dahomey as sacrificial landscape.

■■

CHAPTER THREE

Contesting Authenticity: Paul Hazoumé, Ethnography, and Negritude

Evidence of the lasting impression made by the literature on Dahomey and human sacrifice can be found in Michel Leiris's *L'Afrique fantôme*, the diary of his journey with the Dakar-Djibouti expedition (1931–3). In Dahomey, Leiris claimed, "the atmosphere of human sacrifices betrays itself more and more. No more doubt now. Apart from material proofs, fugitive expressions on one or another's face build cumulative evidence. But they only admit the existence of these practices in other villages or in the 'old world'" (123). According to all historical accounts, the sacrifices had ended with colonial rule and the demise of the Dahomean monarchy. All the same, Leiris is compelled to experience Dahomey through Burton's reductionist identification of Dahomey as human sacrifice.

When in 1938 the American anthropologist Melville Herskovits published his classic study on Dahomey (based on field research conducted in 1931), he used Burton, Skertchly, and Forbes as his sources on the human sacrifices. Ambiguously located in history, Herskovits's "ancient West African kingdom" belonged to both past and present. Although the result of fieldwork and thus a report on what Herskovits was able to observe while living near the market square of the capital of Abomey for a few months, the book's subject was a kingdom that did not exist politically any more. Human sacrifices had been part of the precolonial political culture; they are described by Herskovits in the section on "political organization" (2:24). Though Herskovits acknowledged the realities of French colonial rule, his project advances the notion that culture and politics manifest themselves in separate historical spheres. Despite their obsolescence as a practice, Herskovits's presentation of the human sacrifices implicitly argues that they remain part of the culture. Cultural continuity was pivotal to Herskovits's project, since the intent of the study was to "provide materials for those students of New World Negro culture who wish to know more fully the mode of life of the peoples from whom were drawn the ancestors of the Negroes who today inhabit the Americas" (1:iii). An important figure in the establishment of African and African-American studies as academic disciplines in the United States, Herskovits saw the two fields as continuous.[1]

Facing the dilemma of what to restitute historically for his ethnographic account and how much to restrict himself to a description of present-day practices alone, Herskovits argued for the essential similarity of current and past practices despite the fact that no actual sacrifices took place anymore. Thus, instead of describing the grand customs (not the daily, or annual sacrifices that the monarchy exacted but the bigger ceremony that occurred at the death of a king), Herskovits found the closest equivalent, a memorial service held by the last king's, Behanzin's, son in April 1931. A witness to this ceremony, Herskovits contends that the dancing and ritual followed closely the pattern described by the Victorian travelers. Herskovits stressed continuity, albeit in the midst of a cultural diminishment due to the loss of native sovereignty. Thus he tells the reader, "the essential rites, described by all those who visited Dahomey during the days of the monarchy, have persisted despite the overthrow of the kingdom" (2:56).

By the end of the chapter, Herskovits assigns a new function to the monarchy, a function based not on political power but on its role as the preserver of culture and tradition: "It strikingly demonstrates that the royal family deprived of its aboriginal political prerogatives, still keeps alive the traditional ceremonies demanded by worship of its kingly ancestors" (2:69). Since the royal family of Dahomey was complicit in the French conquest, its role as preserver of tradition reveals the interest of colonial authority in fostering notions of tradition. Moreover, in *Le Devoir de violence*, Yambo Ouologuem attacked this complicity between European and native political authorities in inventing notions of tradition that extended the political hegemony of both agencies (see chapter 5 of this study).

The ritual that was performed to honor Behanzin on April 14, 1931, in place of the grand custom that could no longer be performed, is an invented ritual, a collage of practices staged to fulfill the expectations for an appropriate surrogate ceremony. Although I cannot ascertain whether these were staged entirely for Herskovits's benefit, the invented nature of the ritual—performed because its original form had been disallowed—is amply evident from Herskovits's account.[2] Herskovits describes the performance of an improvised imitation of a lost practice. The continuity with the past that Herskovits stresses is more a narrative concern for him—how to shape his ethnographic account of "an ancient West African kingdom"—than a historical reality. Continuity emerges as a powerful principle of emplotment and establishes the logic for the other important principle of emplotment in Herskovits's description—that of a history of diminishment. The Dahomeans are the same peoples, although now diminished in fierceness because of the successful imposition of colonial power.

Arguing for a history that marked change and not continuity, Paul Hazoumé, a native of Dahomey educated by the French missionaries and active in the politics of a nascent nationalist movement in Dahomey in the 1930s, used ethnography to set the record straight.[3] In his two works, the historical novel *Doguicimi* (1938) and the ethnographic monogram *Le Pacte de sang au Dahomey* (1937), Hazoumé brings to light the historical and political function of ritual practices, embedding them firmly in particulars. The meaning and practice of rituals are a response to historical circumstances, and they change accordingly. As regards the human sacrifices specifically (these are the subject of his historical novel), Hazoumé argued that Europeans were complicitous in this practice through their involvement in the slave trade. He saw it as France's moral responsibility to help eradicate the practice. For Hazoumé it is inevitable (and good) that the Dahomeans modernize. Ironically, the attitudes of observers such as Herskovits elicit the reinvention of rituals, emptied now of their historical function, which can serve to maintain the artificial distance between self and other, colonial master and native subject.

Although Hazoumé uses the methods of historical explanation and contextualization to enhance the authority of his ethnographic descriptions, history has meant nothing but trouble for his reputation as a writer. For one it has caused him to be excluded from a literary canon of African fiction. In her pioneer literary history *Black Writers in French* (1963), Lilyan Kesteloot mentions Hazoumé only in passing, dismissing him as "not sufficiently literary" (10). Hazoumé's interest in history disqualified him as a novelist. When Kesteloot refers to Hazoumé again, it is in the context of *Présence africaine*, of which he was one of the founders; in this instance she treats him as a learned ethnologist (281). The historical frame of his ethnographic work was either invisible as history to his European readers, who read allochronically and flattened out the temporal scheme of his presentation, or became a source of grievance for his Dahomean audience, who saw his critical description of Dahomean culture as a justification for colonial rule.[4] Hazoumé continued his efforts to redress the image of Dahomey constructed by Western travelers. But, most important, both his works argue for a political reading of culture that draws a connection between Dahomey's official state culture (of which the human sacrifices were a part) and the history of the slave trade. His historical argument, therefore, calls for a change in political culture; writing within the realities of colonial rule, he holds the French and their civilizing mission responsible for bringing about this change in political culture.

The emphasis on history in Hazoumé's ethnographic work gains its proper resonance when read against the allochronic discourses of those scientists supported by the French colonial government, including Herskovits. Two other French works stand out as instances where the erasure of the Dahomeans as historical subjects takes on particularly contradictory form: Henri Hubert's *Mission scientifique au Dahomey* (1908) and E. G. Waterlot's *Les Bas-Reliefs des bâtiments royaux d'Abomey* (1926), the catalog of the murals on the palace walls of Dahomey.

In *Mission scientifique*, Henri Hubert sets out to collect methodically the available knowledge on France's recently acquired colony in order to assess its value and economic potential.[5] The perusal of conquered territory is a self-aggrandizing gesture: "After the tremendous effort of the conquest, after remarkable results in the pacifying and administration of our African colonies . . . it was imperative to put to use as quickly as possible the productivity of our possessions" (555). Hubert's text is an exemplary scientific text at the service of colonial exploitation and control. It will result in an "*inventaire méthodique*," a catalog of resources (555). Deploying a colonial discourse of what Nicholas Thomas has characterized as "census-like knowledge" (38), Hubert produced a document that quantifies the subject nation. Since the people of Dahomey had proven a particularly difficult case of "pacification," their complete erasure as historical subjects in Hubert's text resonates with violence. The method of quantification objectifies the people of Dahomey so radically that it extends a logic of commodification that pertained to slavery, although historically the Dahomeans were the slave raiders and not the captured.

Perhaps instead of wondering about the brevity of the ethnographic description in Hubert's text, it is more to the point to ask why there is any ethnographic detail at all in the doctoral thesis of a student of meteorology at the Ecole Coloniale. Divided into three sections (geography, the natural sciences—such as meteorology, geology, minerology—and biogeography, a study of the living species in relation to geography), Hubert's book comprises 560 pages of text, several drawings and photographs illustrating geological and minerological formations, one large fold-out map, and a fold-out chart listing the racial characteristics of the people of Dahomey. The scientific description of Dahomey's material resources undertaken in *Mission scientifique* intends to inventory the gains of conquest. The rhetorical containment of the description of a people (they figure only in his chart and sixteen pages of explanatory text) and their integration as one more item in a compilation of resources figures as the most mastering gesture of the text. The description of a people becomes part of a thesis on biogeography, a science that examines the distribution of plants and animals, forms of life wholly susceptible to their environment. The Dahomeans are indistinguishable from plants and animals, treated in like manner as determined by their environment. As in the case of Burton, for Hubert the retrenchment from narrative and the reliance on a text as inventory announce the author's scientific demeanor. These gestures also function as a repression of history, the erasure of the causal links among the items ordered arbitrarily in a list or a chart.

Hubert's text is of particular interest because in it Hubert inadvertently provides evidence of how the possibility of a native history troubled him. Geology proposes a narrative of development in which man has no role. Hubert gets himself in trouble at the point of conjunction between people and land, the point at which he must incorporate this other resource (the people) into his inventory. He invokes and then represses the possibility of a historical account. His chart of the Dahomean people comprises practically the whole of his ethnography (see figure 3.1, which illustrates a small portion of the chart). Hubert explains his thesis on biogeography—that the various peoples of Dahomey settled in the areas most suitable to their characteristics—and then refers the reader to the chart for the evidence on racial diversity.

The chart classifies the Dahomeans by race and geographical location (i.e., the races of the coast, the north, and the south, which are then further subdivided into specific groups such as Fon, Mahi, etc.). This division is then followed by a comparative list of the physical characteristics of each racial group. Under the entries *barbe* (beard) and *moustache* (mustache), we learn that the Fon and the Mahis (both *races du sud* and the people on whom Hazoumé focuses) are *très peu fournie* (sparsely endowed), while under *teint* (skin tone) we learn that the Fon can be distinguished as *rouge-brique* (brick-red) and the Mahis as *rouge-brun* (reddish brown). The chart is the type of document that would result from the careful application of guidelines such as those presented in *Notes and Queries on Anthropology* discussed by Coombes in *Reinventing Africa* (133–5). *Notes and Queries on Anthropology* illustrates different hues of skin, hair, and eye color, for example, and assigns names so as to regularize the description of peoples. This method of classification functions within a colonial ideology that sees "the body as a source of all knowledge regarding the colonized subject" (Coombes 145).

For Hubert, classification not only helps create the illusion of greater control over the colonial subject, it also makes the colony appear richer. The assumption seems to be, the more types, the richer the resources. By extension also, the more types one defines, the greater the reach of the science. It is difficult to mark these distinctions in practice since the difference between

NOM DES RACES	RACES DE LA COTE		
TYPE	Minas (1)	Aïzonnous	Gens du delta de l'Ouémé
Forme du crâne vue d'en haut	ronde		
Visage — Hauteur du diamètre transversal le plus étendu	joues		
Visage — Forme	ovale court		
Nez — Forme	un peu écrasé	écrasé	
Nez — Echancrure à la racine	marquée		
Front	bombé, découvert	large, fuyant	
Ouverture palpébrale	grande, ronde	allongée	
Cils	assez abondants	longs et recourbés	
Bouche	plutôt grande	grande	
Lèvres	épaisses		
Dents	légèrement écartées	avançant	
Incisives	normales	limées en pointe	
Menton — Face	carré	rond	
Menton — Profil	droit	fuyant	
Oreilles	grandes, collées	moyennes, écartées	
Prognatisme	marqué	bien marqué	
Taille	grande		
Membres	grêles	musclés	
Cheveux — Nature	crépus		
Cheveux — Disposition		touffes isolées	
Barbe	assez abondante	néant	
Moustache	rare		
Teint	noir-brun	rouge-brun	

FIGURE 3.1   From Hubert. A portion of the chart of the races of Dahomey. The original measures 31" wide by 18" tall. This reproduction shows the upper-left-hand corner, approximately 6" wide and 12" tall.

rouge-brique and *rouge-brun*, for example, is rather vague, and differences in
skin color do not occur with any predictable consistency. Hubert betrays no
anxiety over the apparent uselessness of the categories since it is the performance of applying these rigid distinctions that establishes his authority. It is
a matter of form, not content. These distinctions seem to create a body of
"methodical" knowledge about France's new colony. Because this is not real
knowledge, Hubert's chart of the races of Dahomey is an excessive gesture,
the transgression of a confident scientist who arrogantly applies his expertise
in one field (biogeography) to the material from other sciences.

Because his classifications are bogus, there is an added burden on Hubert
to make them seem as rigid as possible. The divisions in columns and boxes
on the chart create the distinctions that would otherwise be hardly perceptible; they supply an alternative visual representation, a chart instead of a pho-
tograph, for example. The chart is, therefore, a particularly vicious manner of
representing native peoples, one that erases their humanity completely.

The text that accompanies the chart explains symptomatically the troubles with the catalog. Presented as an extension of the book's assessment of
resources in Dahomey, the *esquisse ethnographique* applies the thesis of biogeography, first used to explain the geographical distribution of animals in
the territory, to natives: "After indicating that the distribution of animal
species was produced by meteorological or geological factors, I showed that
the distribution of human settlements was itself often closely connected to
certain geographical factors, notably the accidental features of the terrain"
(560). Neglecting the Africans completely as historical subjects and assign-
ing them strictly to the realm of nature, Hubert treats them as analogous to
animals. Geography is determining; it enables Hubert to achieve a masterful understanding of the development of these different races because geography ensures that change over time has taken place according to fixed,
unchanging laws: "[the natives] gather . . . according to more or less constant rules" (536).

The desire to control and classify in order to visualize the territory and
its peoples is frustrated, however, by the knowledge that migrations "have
contributed powerfully to the confusion in the racial characteristics of indigenous tribes" (537). This is Hubert's admission that his model of development, which holds that change tends toward ever more rigid differentiation and thus stasis, must confront the evidence of a tendency toward the

opposite: constant movement and a mixture of peoples, a hybridization that renders the colonial subjects unknowable to Hubert. Without reference to history (and, most important, to the slave trade), Hubert will not be able to understand the movement of peoples. The chart, accompanied by the briefly stated thesis of biogeography and verified by the weight of 544 pages on geography, geology, meteorology, and minerology, is thrust against Hubert's admission that there was a history of migration, "Africa being the perfect country for migrations to occur." (537). The chart creates order by fixing peoples in places and giving them unchanging characteristics. It redresses the disordered realities of an actual history that Hubert seems to have no method for learning.

In the attempt to devise a global descriptive strategy, Hubert incorporates the ethnographic within his strategy as an element of the scientific discourse of geography and relicenses the ethnographic in its new affiliation with geography. The mastery of native languages that had been the cornerstone of an earlier scientificity (as in Delafosse's *Manuel dahoméen* [1894]) is no longer important. The possibility of accessing oral history becomes more unlikely as the ahistorical view of native peoples is entrenched. But migrations dangerously hint at histories, and defining people by place can be subverted into a nationalist discourse by the natives themselves. Perhaps no work makes the connection among autoethnography, nationalism, and resistance to colonialism more explicit than Jomo Kenyatta's *Facing Mount Kenya*. Written as a doctoral dissertation under the direction of Malinowski at the London School of Economics and published in 1938 (the same year as Hazoumé's historical novel), *Facing Mount Kenya* became the blueprint for the struggle for land rights that turned into the Mau Mau rebellion and eventually brought about Kenya's independence.

Hazoumé's work, a nationalist ethnography, appeared when ethnography had reached the height of its authority. *Le Pacte de sang* was critically acclaimed in Paris, and in 1938 Hazoumé was invited to join the Institut d'Ethnologie, which had been incorporated by that point into the newly founded Musée de l'Homme. Hazoumé had remained an outsider to the main current of the emergent francophone literature in Paris. Except for a brief visit to Paris to attend the Colonial Exhibition at Vincennes in 1931, Hazoumé resided in Africa until 1938. He was educated exclusively in missionary schools in Africa and was trained as a schoolteacher. Although he collaborated with the negritude writers after World War II (he was one of the founding members of *Présence africaine*), his work was largely ignored by them. For example, there is no entry on Hazoumé in Mongo Beti's *Diction-naire de la Négritude*, although there is an entry on Melville Herskovits. Ha-zoumé was closer in age to René Maran (Hazoumé was born in 1890 and Maran in 1887) than to either Senghor (born 1906), or Césaire (born 1913), although *Doguicimi* (1938) is almost exactly contemporary with Césaire's *Cahier d'un retour au pays natal* (1939).

Hazoumé's ethnographic project has to be understood in the context of his critique of negritude. In a paper delivered at the First Congress of Black Writers at the Sorbonne in 1956, where he was one of the presiders, Ha-zoumé examined retrospectively his own work and the legacy of negritude. The congress, organized under the auspices of *Présence africaine*, was to be a celebration of African culture as well as an occasion to take stock of the de-velopments of recent years.

Twenty years after the completion of his historical novel *Doguicimi*, the Africanist public had not yet committed to a historical discourse on Africa, and Hazoumé's historicist approach remained the exception.[6] Western dis-courses on Africa had offered a "pseudohistory" derived from dualisms that opposed tradition and modernity, primitive and civilized culture. This pseudohistory also "spatialized" the relationship between the West and Africa, placing a "chasm" in between (Comaroff and Comaroff 4–5). Ha-zoumé proposed historicism as a response to Senghorian *humanism*, an idea that was central to Senghor's syncretic goals for an Afro-European cultur-al collaboration of the future but that had been discredited by the more radical factions of negritude (Mudimbe in *Surreptitious* 33).[7] Senghor ad-dressed the future and not the past in his humanistic ideal, seeking to assert what Fabian calls the "coevalness" of African and European experience from the present moment onward. Hazoumé instead prioritized the neces-sity to reexamine the past, to contest and win over the territory of African history and restore the particularity of a multiplicity of points of view with-in Africa.[8]

Senghor's advocacy of Africa's difference (essential and ahistorical) on the one hand, and the assertion that negritude is a new attitude, a response to the experience of the twentieth century, created a paradox of which Ha-zoumé was keenly aware. Where did this Africanness come from if not from a sense of the past? Moreover, isn't the sense of the past itself shaped by the present historical moment and thus under constant transformation? Retrospectively it is easy to see that Hazoumé's paper, "L'Humanisme occidental et l'humanisme africain," presented a departure from the Senghorian position. Hazoumé uses humanism not to achieve synthesis but to demarcate further the differences between the European and the African. European humanism silenced the African past through its various misrepresentations.

Hazoumé's critique of Senghor echoes Sartre's position in "Black Orpheus," his preface to Senghor's landmark anthology of francophone African poetry published in 1948. Mudimbe has argued persuasively that Sartre be considered as a philosopher of negritude, the thinker who sympathetically galvanized the political consciousness of the negritude writers by articulating a more explicit politics for the movement. According to Mudimbe, for Sartre, "negritude signifies, fundamentally tension between the black man's past and future" (*Invention* 87). Yet Sartre's essay was also a critique of negritude that called for a historically changing African identity as opposed to an unchanging essence. According to Mudimbe, "Senghor might have been satisfied" with a "game of opposites" pitting Africa and the West (*Invention* 84). Sartre's critique "established a cardinal synthesis. By rejecting both the colonial rationale and the set of culturally eternal values as bases for society, his brief treatise posited philosophically a relativist perspective for African social studies" (Mudimbe in *Invention* 86). Hazoumé's position in 1956 echoes Sartre's influential essay; yet it is important to remember that Hazoumé's creative work (the ethnography, *Le Pacte de sang*, and the historical novel, *Doguicimi*) predates Sartre by ten years.

In his essay for *Présence africaine*, Hazoumé first distinguishes between two humanisms and then recasts African humanism as African *traditionalism*. He reappropriates the term *traditionalism* and applies it to the systems of knowledge of oral cultures. Knowledge about Africa is possessed by Africans themselves; furthermore, it is particular and local. The opposition between European humanism and African traditionalism stems from the differences between a literate and an oral culture; Africans must learn to present traditionalism as knowledge. Hazoumé urgently calls on Africans to direct their scholarly efforts to the study of their own cultures before the traces of those cultures disappear and along with them the potential for a true understanding of history. He recognizes that a Western education offers advantages for the study of African history so long as it is used in the service of African interests. Africans now have better tools with which to study their own cultures because of the spread of literacy. Moreover, to educate is the obligation of the imperial powers to their subjects, an opportunity earned by Africans through their service to the empire.

Hazoumé sees in the establishment of institutions of higher learning in Africa after World War II a recognition by the imperial powers of the contribution of their colonial subjects to the European war efforts ("L'Humanisme occidental" 31). The opportunity for a Western education is a right of the colonial subjects. Before the establishment of these schools, Africans in French colonies had to go to Paris to attend university; the transferral of institutions of higher learning onto African soil affects Hazoumé's view of the nature of Western education. It is easy to see that Hazoumé thought that Africans needed a Western education in order to defend their own cultures. Moreover, the study of history was key to maintaining an African identity, and recourse to a Western education would help promote African history by Africans. The assimilated, or Western-educated, French colonial subject did not have to—and indeed should not—shed his own history.

Hazoumé's effort to distinguish between a European and an African tradition of knowledge was not an essentializing gesture like Senghor's but a gesture to recognize different histories and points of view. The Europeans' denial of African history could only be redressed by a seizure of consciousness by Africans. Ethnography, the Western humanistic discourse of the other, had represented oral cultures inadequately. Hazoumé explains the process of transcribing oral tradition as a process of translation, and he emphasizes the complexities of the cultural translation over and above those of the linguistic translation. It has been a standard assumption that ethnography aims at "literal translation" until recently, when revisionist proposals for the field have emerged (Comaroff and Comaroff 9). Native Africans, Hazoumé contends, would at least make better translators.

To illustrate his point, Hazoumé draws our attention to a mistake made in a publication by the Institut d'Ethnologie. In an effort to create a record of the artifacts of Dahomey, E. G. Waterlot (the official French printer in Dahomey) undertook to copy and catalog the reliefs on the palace walls of the Dahomey kings. Because of his unawareness of oral tradition, Waterlot, according to Hazoumé, misidentified some of the objects depicted in the reliefs. This is not surprising considering the attitudes of the contributors to Waterlot's volume.

Waterlot's printed catalog was introduced by Lucien Lévy-Bruhl, who, in his assessment of the value of the catalog, stressed the significance of the reliefs as "historical documents of indisputable authenticity, made by the natives themselves" (v). Lévy-Bruhl compared the reliefs explicitly to unreliable oral traditions; the murals were unadulterated and could speak directly of the past. But these assertions of authenticity are highly dubious. Waterlot points out that the images on the reliefs were repeatedly revised and updated by the Dahomeans themselves, and some were extensively restored by the French in 1911. If oral narratives are "adulterated" through their use, then it seems that the reliefs were adulterated in a similar manner and, moreover, the "adulteration" should be considered as an aspect of their history. But instead, Lévy-Bruhl perceives the reliefs erroneously as a stable text and the oral narratives as insufficiently fixed in form; they do not repeat without variation. Lévy-Bruhl's pejorative attitude toward oral traditions ("we are reduced to oral traditions, which are generally not reliable, and which we have no means to control" [v]) robs the natives of their own narratives and guarantees that the historical text is produced by the European.

The reliefs, therefore, are valued because they are available to the Europeans' reception without intermediaries. Since they are images and are not dependent on language, they can be reproduced and circulated in an untranslated form, as reproductions in plaster or photos in a book. Waterlot's catalog ironically illustrates the plaster copies of the originals made by him and given to the Musée d'Ethnologie du Trocadéro (figures 3.2 and 3.3). The reliefs on display, therefore, are not originals.

The reproduceability of the images becomes a prerequisite for the dissemination of the idea of their authenticity. The production of the copies assumes the existence of originals. The adulterated state of the "originals" is obscured by fixing those images as the ones from which copies are made. We encounter here in a perverted state Walter Benjamin's thesis on authenticity and the reproducibility of art. In the case of an African other, reproducibility is the only means to invent and disseminate an authenticity that in practice needs no original.

Since many of the reliefs had already been revised by the Dahomeans themselves, the "authentic" object recedes ever further away from the

FIGURE 3.2   From Waterlot (plate 19). Relief from the Palace of Gelele. The top image depicts, according to Waterlot, the conquest of Ishaga in which the Nago warriors were defeated, their heads cut off and attached to the necks of their horses, and then taken thus to Abomey. In the bottom image, a Dahomean fighter is shown killing a Nago warrior.

FIGURE 3.3   From Waterlot (plate 16). Relief from the Palace of Gelele showing, according to Waterlot, the *goli*. Hazoumé disputes Waterlot's interpretation and suggests that this is the image of a colander.

copy. The evidence that the Dahomeans have restored the murals in the past leads Waterlot to conclude that the older reliefs are of better quality than the restored reliefs, even though the older reliefs are barely visible, lack all traces of color, and will have probably disappeared by the time the catalog is published. His own restoration of these older reliefs (as plaster copies) is more "authentic" than the Dahomeans' restoration that is undertaken as part of their own cultural practice of maintaining and updating the murals.

Waterlot implicitly proposes a thesis of decline: the art of making these reliefs over the centuries has deteriorated into vulgarity and diminished artistry (9). Authenticity recedes from his reader's eager grasp even more. If the murals to be found now in Dahomey are not authentic, then the authentic ones are merely a fiction made visible through Waterlot's "copies" but not to be found in the original anywhere. The copies in the catalog thus have an enhanced value for restoring to view what is otherwise lost.

Waterlot was assisted by native informants (*des informateurs indigènes*) who remain anonymous, whereas the text names its authorities, the linguist Maurice Delafosse and the historian Le Herissé. They provided knowledgeable footnotes to Waterlot's explanation of the reliefs, boosting the scientificity of the project. According to Hazoumé, however, it is not possible to obviate the oral traditions, since the practice of visual representation was tied to the oral histories. The scenes represented function as aides to the transmission of oral history and not as substitutes for the narratives. The reliefs presupposed a knowledge of oral history that even Dahomeans did not necessarily have. They were decoded by what Hazoumé calls a "translator" or interpreter. The reliefs reinforced the collective memory of the community. When Waterlot began to record these reliefs by molding cast copies, copying the colors, and photographing the results, he viewed them as freestanding artifacts and repeatedly misinterpreted them.

The sketch of a jar with many holes, for example, was identified as a *goli*, a sacred jar from which the gods drink (figure 3.3). Hazoumé corrects this interpretation: the sketch depicts nothing more than a common domestic utensil, a colander ("L'Humanisme" 39–40). The reasons for its depiction on the palace mural are historical, not religious. According to Hazoumé's explanation, King Guezo (who reigned from 1818 until 1858) had used the colander as a symbol of the disunited kingdom that he had inherited. He ordered his designated successor to fill the colander with water and follow the wish of the ancestors by keeping the water in the colander. When his successor objected that it was impossible to contain the water since the colander had many holes and he only had ten fingers, Guezo told him that he would have to gather all his people together to help him block the holes with their hands. Otherwise the kingdom would fall apart. The colander, therefore, was a symbol of the collective effort needed to keep the kingdom intact at a time when the threat of conquest by outside forces was increasing. The privileged place of such a common household utensil on the palace mural could easily lead one to misinterpret its significance. Hazoumé explains that a native interpreter of the mural would know immediately that the picture does not depict a *goli*, the sacred jar, because the item depicted is too big to be a *goli*. The native translator would seek a causal explanation of why such a common item as a colander gained such importance.

Hazoumé highlights the content of oral narratives instead of the practices of an oral culture. Knowledge of an oral society, therefore, is produced through the acquisition of these narratives. Hazoumé effectively redraws the discursive field of knowledge about Africa in such a way that the Europeans can only be readers, not cultural producers. He also downplays the significance of writing in French. So long as it is an African doing his own history, it is of secondary importance that he writes in a borrowed language ("L'Humanisme" 42).

The most far-reaching implication of Hazoumé's essay is that the change in point of view renders the historical past of Africa, deleted from the discursive field of knowledge established by ethnography, suddenly visible. Critics of imperialism have repeatedly pointed out that the denial of history to the native was a cornerstone of imperialist ideology. According to David Spurr, the denial of history falls under a larger category of discursive practices, those of *negation*, which addressed the other as "absence, emptiness, nothingness, or death" (92). The effect of the rhetoric of negation on negritude can be assessed through the influence of Leo Frobenius on the movement. According to Christopher Miller, negritude gained its focus after the translation of Leo Frobenius's *Histoire de la civilisation africaine* into French in 1936. Senghor retrospectively claimed that Frobenius "revealed Africa to the world and Africans to themselves" (in Miller *Theories* 16). Hazoumé's difference from negritude stems in part from his not having been affected by Frobenius as the negritude poets were. Not only was he absent from Paris but both his works (*Le Pacte de sang* and *Doguicimi*) were completed before the translation of Frobenius's text into French.[9]

Frobenius's totalizing anthropological study had the important word *histoire* in the title. But *histoire* was an invisible term, obscured by the weight of *civilisation*. Frobenius's thought tended always toward establishing correspondences between Africa and Europe. These correspondences were formulated in clearly allochronic discourse and thus could never have yielded a truly historical account. Fabian has joined a number of detractors of Frobenius in recent years (including Yambo Ouologuem, who lampoons Frobenius in his novel) by raising the issue of complicity between power and objective description. Reading Frobenius's *In the Shadow of the Congo State*

(1907), Fabian notes Frobenius's defense of humor as a rhetorical strategy for self-control at an instance when Frobenius is describing "a catalogue of colonial atrocities." This self-control, Frobenius adds, is mandatory if one wishes to have any control over the natives. Fabian concludes, "We can never be sure, until we face that question directly, whether an ethnographer's "authority" deserves credit as a contribution to knowledge, or whether it merely reproduces the political force and violence it often took to put ethnographers in a position to claim authority" ("White Humor" 61).

The extent to which Frobenius's authority emanated from the appeal of his allochronistic constructions emerges clearly from the discussions of his ideas around the time of New York's Museum of Modern Art's (MoMA's) 1937 exhibit of "prehistoric African rock paintings" based on Frobenius's research. In the catalogue of the exhibit, MoMA's curator, Alfred Barr, noted the "paradox" of exhibiting prehistoric art in a museum of "modern" art. "The art of the twentieth century has already come under the influence of the great tradition of prehistoric mural art," Barr explained, thus the relevance of the exhibit was obvious (9). Perhaps, however, the paradox was invented, since all of the items on exhibit were modern copies and sometimes copies of rock pictures that were not prehistoric. The "paintings" were not dated, and some may have even been modern, contemporary with Frobenius himself.

In a volume of transcribed African folktales (collected and translated from Frobenius's work of the 1920s), which appeared to coincide with the exhibit, Douglas C. Fox explains that Frobenius had set out to find African rock paintings following the discoveries by Rivière of prehistoric cave paintings in northern Spain. According to Fox's anecdotal narration of Frobenius's quest, Frobenius set out to prove that the practice of rock paintings could not have discontinued:

> Young Leo Frobenius . . . asked himself . . . whether it might not have been possible for this older Stone Age culture to have been indigenous to Africa as well as to Europe. It did not seem likely to young Frobenius that anything so alive as that culture could disappear. He recalled the fact that North Africa had not always been a desert, and that it might well have nourished a human culture at a time when glaciers still covered the Southern Pyrenees. . . . The South Africans still painted rock

pictures. . . . Was it possible that the culture of old would still be alive today, *declined, of course,* but still a remainder of a culture which once flourished in Spain? *(African Genesis 13–14, emphasis added)*

In Africa, Frobenius thought to have found a record of a prehistoric culture continuously sustained till today. Africa is posited as a "contemporary" example of prehistoric culture, but the prehistoric is only perceptible in a vulgarized, diminished form. Allochronism does not repress all historical plots; it sets in motion a history of decline that follows a long period without change or history.

African history as decline figures also in Hazoumé's monogram on the blood oath in Dahomey. Decline in this case is tied to the advent of colonialism. The blood oath degenerates into a criminal practice under colonial rule. Hazoumé, however, recuperates the positive significance of the blood oath by uncovering its history. As a result, criminality under colonial rule emerges as resistance to colonialism.

Hazoumé sought to redress the rhetoric of negation in *Le Pacte de sang au Dahomey* (1937) by showing that the description of a present practice was incomplete without a history of its evolution. The blood oath that was still practiced in colonial Dahomey was evidence of a residual cultural memory; the ritual is a trace of a wider history. *Le Pacte* illustrates how cultural memory evolves. Rituals act to preserve cultural identity, but they also register change because the context in which rituals are performed evolves continuously. Hazoumé traces the origins of the practice to a culture of distrust in precolonial Dahomey, a culture that evolved from the ongoing warfare of slave raiding. The blood oath was usually transacted among several parties. It forged stable relationships in political circumstances where everyone was a potential enemy. Because the blood oath created ties that superceded one's loyalties to family and clan, it helped sustain political units of social organization. The king was always the central authority, but he maintained his authority by establishing blood connections with his important subjects. Hazoumé's *Le Pacte de sang au Dahomey* is in fact a political history: he examines the evolution of the blood oath as practiced by Dahomey's kings at each crucial turning point of the state's history. Hazoumé describes the ritual itself only after he has established the historical function of the oath, taking his examples from precolonial Dahomey. The description of the ritual, therefore, contributes to our knowledge of pre-colonial society.

Punishment for breaching the oath was severe, and although the oath had various forms, the threat of retribution was always an elaborate part of the ritual. The most important part of the ceremony usually involved making a small cut to yield a few drops of blood that were then placed on a slice of lemon. The other party would lick the blood off the slice of lemon and proceed to offer his blood in the same manner. Hazoumé describes many variants of this ceremony, some of which involved the use of sacrificial animals and a shared libation in which animal blood was mixed in to symbolize human blood. He stresses the fact that these ceremonies were always conducted in the nude because nudity signified the solemnity of the occasion. The king, who never appeared nude, used a substitute to transact the blood oath in his name.

The historical insight elicited by Hazoumé from his study of the blood oath is that the colonization of Dahomey was a consequence of the breach of this custom. Dahomey fell to the French in 1894 when the oath allying its king to his chosen successor was broken. Under constant siege by the French, the Dahomeans had devised a ruse by which to hold off further attacks: the king would pretend to abdicate in favor of a ruler of whom the French approved. But the king had negotiated a secret agreement with his successor, according to which the king would return to power once the French had stopped their military campaigns. The successor, however, was a French collaborator and broke his oath to the king. By 1900 there was no Dahomean monarchy to speak of.

The blood oath continued to be practiced during the colonial period. However, in Hazoumé's contemporary Dahomey of the 1930s, the blood oath was increasingly associated with criminal behavior. In what amounts to a critique of the colonial system, Hazoumé explains that the loss of political sovereignty forced native practices of social organization underground and into paralegal channels. Consequently, the blood oath helped to form and sustain criminal gangs that set out to accumulate wealth through whatever means. The materialistic values of these gangs reflected the adverse influence of Western culture in Africa.

Interpreted ahistorically, the blood oath explains the cohesiveness of criminal gangs, presenting native custom as an obstacle to the progressive program of the French. When the proper historical context is elaborated, however, it becomes clear that the blood oath has a variable meaning, and its particular evolution into criminal behavior illustrates the moral decline that sets in with the loss of sovereignty. Since in the past the blood oath helped create and sustain Dahomey as a political entity, it is obviously threatening to French authorities who need to discredit it. The colonialist perspective, therefore, authorizes the ethnographic description of the blood oath as criminal behavior that Hazoumé undermines by historicizing his description.

Le Pacte de sang concludes with an "Essai d'analyse critique," which is a good example of Hazoumé's rhetorical strategies: while he identifies this chapter as an instance in which the author will step back and take a critical overview of the practice described in the previous chapters, it is in fact nothing of the sort. Rather, Hazoumé continues his historical project and explains how the increased instability in the latter part of the nineteenth century caused a shift in emphasis that eventually led to a distortion of the oath's original principles. Increasingly the oath became an excuse for meting out punishment: it became an agent of retribution when individuals or families were suspected of breaking their oath. Although Hazoumé does not advocate the reinstitution of the blood oath, he reminds his reader of the good principles (loyalty and community [146]) for which it stood.

While setting out to describe a traditional practice in an ethnographic fashion where it would be easily circumscribed and contained within the established division between tradition and modernity, Hazoumé defies this division and imports the blood oath into modernity. He reminds his reader that the blood oath has not died out as a practice in colonial Dahomey, despite the fact that "today the majority of Dahomeans bless the French conquest" (141). Hazoumé elaborates the historical connections between precolonial Dahomey and the colonial situation and renders the good principles behind this practice available once more for cultural use. The misapplications of the blood oath, and, in fact, the ritual itself, with its use of human and animal blood, should be superceded, but the cultural value of loyalty to one's community is rearticulated through the historical journey that traces the evolution of this practice. Hazoumé renders the ethnographic description into a corollary of the larger historical narration of the oath's evolution as a practice and, more important, of its influence in the history of the community that practiced it.

Criminality and decline are tied to the influence of Europeans, yet colonialism is an order welcomed by most Dahomeans, according to *Le Pacte*. In *Doguicimi* Hazoumé reaches the same conclusion. Both works were written during a period of severe repression by the French authorities, when open criticism of the French was not allowed. But there is more to Hazoumé's position than mere political expediency. The values associated with the criminal gangs, their covetousness and materialism, are tied to the values of the rising capitalist class in Dahomey, which was represented by families who had gained prominence earlier through the slave trade and were, in Hazoumé's eyes, native oppressors. In the 1920s and 1930s there was significant resistance to French colonial policies by a rising nationalist faction composed of Dahomean intellectuals, bureaucrats, and the wealthy bourgeoisie. By the mid-1930s the French had succeeded in crushing this nascent nationalist movement by severely persecuting its most outspoken members. Historian Patrick Manning has identified Hazoumé as a member of the nationalist intelligentsia (*Slavery, Colonialism* 264). However, when the French succeeded in crushing the Dahomean national movement in the 1930s, they divided its factions against each other. The main antagonism existed between the rising Dahomean bourgeoisie, whose economic interests were being stifled by the official French policy to keep capitalist development in the hands of the state (or the French), and the intelligentsia who were critical of the values of this native bourgeoisie since it represented the slave owning and slave dealing class of the past.[10] This meant that in the 1930s Hazoumé's opposition to the class in Dahomean society that represented the interests of a continuing history of oppression made him susceptible to an alliance with the French. This alliance was based on a cultural identification whose political ramifications were the support of the ideals of citizenship and democracy promoted by the French Revolution (*Slavery, Colonialism* 275). As a result Hazoumé, a Dahomean nationalist, could ally himself with France in order to help undermine the hegemony of the native oppressors.

At the outbreak of World War II, Hazoumé became a spokesman against Nazism and traveled throughout Africa speaking on behalf of the Allied cause. He broke definitively with the Afrique Occidentale française (AOF) government, with which he had tacitly sided in the mid-1930s (*Slavery, Colonialism* 272), because the AOF allied itself with the Vichy government.

Hazoumé's commitments were to the ideals of freedom and political equality shaped by his French education and to a nationalist pride that sought to recuperate a Dahomean identity from the violent history that implicated Dahomey in the slave trade.

The source of misunderstanding over Hazoumé's affiliations lies in a tendency to equate anticolonialism with an anti-Western and, in this case, anti-French attitude. If we fail to identify an anti-Western attitude, we do not recognize the resistance to colonialism. Edward Said has shown in his extensive discussion of resistance in *Culture and Imperialism* that the cultural terrain, although hotly contested, was a common meeting ground for France and the francophone intelligentsia (200). The colonial terrain displays an overwhelming "disparity in power between the West and non-West," which made all conditions of writing into the "unequal relationship between unequal interlocutors" (191).[11] To focus exclusively on this inequality, however, promotes the intent of various imperialist discourses of knowledge that must demonstrate that they can efficiently incorporate and recast the discourse of the "weaker" party. To show the limits of these incorporative gestures helps uncover the resistance to dominant discourses.

Disparity in real political power should be a constant reference point for any historical understanding of the culture of resistance to imperialism. The European education of the African intellectual reflected in multiple ways the unequal relationship between cultures. But it also presented Africans during colonialism with the means to define themselves against their oppressors in such terms that their resistance is communicated powerfully as antithesis. Francophone expression (to take just one example) is produced through a process of what Said has called *reinscription*, enacted by the colonized who uses the language and discourses of the colonizer. According to Said's spatial metaphor of *overlapping territories*, the culture of resistance "must to a certain degree work to recover forms already established or at least influenced or infiltrated by the culture of empire" (210). Said aptly characterizes this process of *reinscription* as tragic because it implicitly recognizes the impurity of discourse. The tragedy results from the degree of pressure exercised by the form on the content (216).

A figure from what Mary Louise Pratt has called the *contact zone*, Hazoumé is an example of those "instances in which colonized subjects undertake to represent themselves in ways that engage with the colonizer's own terms." Autoethnographic texts are the native's "response to" ethnographic texts about their own culture. The *contact zone* is a space that, according to Pratt, is usually made invisible, "suppressed by diffusionist accounts of conquest and domination"; it demarcates the "spatial and temporal copresence of subjects previously separated by geographic and historic disjunctures." It is therefore not an in-between space but the space of overlap, and what results cannot be referred to as either "authentic or autochtonous forms of self-representation" (7). Although Pratt's model of the autoethnographic accommodates some resistance in the form of "dialogue with those metropolitan representations," it assumes that the autoethnographer is still engaged in the genre of ethnographic description that systematically represses historical causality. Hazoumé, however, goes further by tying the metropolitan representation of Africa's history of decline to the advent of the Europeans on the continent. Complicity makes the argument for coevalness, which, in turn, makes both narratives of progress or decline that depend on the opposition of Europe and its other seem spurious, since decline and progress are another opposition set up by pseudohistory. The debunking of such pseudohistory is the project of *Doguicimi*, Hazoumé's historical novel, written before *Le Pacte de sang* but published only after the ethnographic work gained critical attention (Manning, in *Francophone Sub-Saharan Africa* 108–9).

■■

CHAPTER FOUR

Resistant History in
Paul Hazoumé's *Doguicimi*

Doguicimi, like Flaubert's *Salammbô* (a novel to which it is frequently compared because of its naturalistic detail and spectacular violence), is named after its female protagonist, a woman of exemplary fidelity who kills herself in a ritualistic suicide and emerges ultimately as a martyr.[1] Read as an allegorical figure of the nation, Doguicimi accomplishes a task conventional to the historical novel: she articulates a critique of the nation's most heroic period from the past as a means of inspiring a renewed nationalism in the present. The action takes place from 1822–1828, the early part of the reign of Guezo (1818–1858), a period in which Dahomey, trading in slaves, would reach the peak of its military power and arrogance. A usurper to the throne, Guezo is depicted by Hazoumé as always seeking to prove the legitimacy of his authority. His zealousness in carrying out the human sacrifices stems from this insecurity, and since the sacrifices were always the sole prerogative of royal power, Guezo uses them to assert his authority spectacularly. Doguicimi, the bride of a prominent prince in Guezo's court, challenges the king's politicization of the sacrifices and articulates an alternative identity for Dahomean nationalism. In *Doguicimi*, therefore, the writing of history is associated with a nationalist project, not merely in opposition to colonial rule but in an attempt to define a national identity against the hegemonic notions of tradition.

The Politics of Sacrifice

Hazoumé's treatment of the human sacrifices in *Doguicimi* is extensive. More effectively than the Victorians' assertions of an atmosphere of human sacrifice, Hazoumé overwhelms his novel with details about the sacrifices. They permeate life at the court completely, from the everyday sacrifices to the most elaborate annual rituals. His descriptions of the violence are excessive, beyond anything we have encountered before. Migan, the sacrificial priest, is presented as an efficient killing machine, a human guillotine, whose skill produces a spectacle of mangled bodies. He is rendered sublime and becomes the face of the god of war, as his unflinching action produces an excess of blood, mutilated body parts, and vomit. Principles of order and disorder are held in a tense balance as the key to the spectacle, an excess that the spectators ("the human wave," 114)[2] seek to consume:

> The "horses" [the human victims] fell and continued to fall. Mêwou, whose gaze never left the base of the altar, moved his arm up and then down as a signal that the next victim should be dispatched to the sacrificial priest. Tirelessly, Migan finished them off with an unerring, sweeping motion. Blood flowed, flowed abundantly, and the sated earth wanted no more to drink. The executioner's assistants wallowed in mud compounded of blood, regurgitated yam puree, and dirt as they busily gathered up the heads and the bodies. The moans of the "horses" that had fallen head first to the ground, their efforts to lift heads that broken necks refused to support, the diligence of the servants who were constantly cleaning the site, the dexterity of Migan whose sturdy arm raised his blood-dripping scimitar and cut off heads in regular rhythm, his face and his clothes splattered with the spurting blood, his expression trans-

figured into the mask of Gou (the god of war), the corner of his mouth continually moving as if he were chewing a stimulant, his body sweating with fury—indeed, everything enraptured the crowd, which feasted its eyes on the spectacle (*la foule qui repaissait délicieusement ses yeux du spectacle*). (*English 113–4, French 165–6*)

The bodies of the victims, deformed and fragmented, come in a constant wave that sets the stage for the excessive consumption of blood and gore that the audience feasts (*repaissait*) its eyes on. Hazoumé's choice of language here could not make the audience's literal consumption more evident. The verb *repaître* literally means to feed; Hazoumé transforms viewing into cannibalism. By extension, reading as a form of consumption also becomes implicated in the cannibalistic impulse and is opposed to the lie of hoarding, saving, accumulating in which the Victorian travelers were invested. Hazoumé subverts the hollow objectivity of Western observers by rendering his readers aware of their presence and complicity through the act of reading. His close-up account of the mutilated bodies as they are being removed from the scene of sacrifice makes a confrontation with the facts of these sacrifices unavoidable. Hazoumé describes directly what Forbes and Skertchly refused to look at. If the Victorians created through their narratives opportunities for the readers to imagine spectacles of violence, Hazoumé leaves nothing to the imagination:

> The "horses" which fell on their heads were always picked up dead, their necks broken, their heads dangling, their skulls shattered, their faces, shoulders, chests, and backs scraped and covered with blood. . . .
>
> Here and there mouths opened and closed three or four times before remaining shut forever; tongues dangled or moved about; eyes started terrifyingly out of their sockets; more than one face was grimacing compulsively. As soon as the head was separated from the body, a few stomachs gave back the yams they had just received. *(113)*

The amount of detail is punishing. Bodies are fragmented (tongues, eyes, heads, stomachs) in a mess of gore that either caters to the reader's masochism or inspires a revolt against it. Unlike the Victorians' refusal to witness and narrate the sacrifices, Hazoumé records the ritual in minute detail as an act of witness. He wants not only to shock but to shape this revulsion into action. By contextualizing the sacrifices in terms of the historical moment, he provides a forum for figuring out a politics, a course of action to redress the legacy of sacrifices.

Hazoumé, alone among the narrators of human sacrifices, goes out of his way to record instances of resistance by the victims. Before recounting the execution of an anonymous mass of victims, Hazoumé gives a detailed account of a captive who resists and speaks out against the inhumanity of the Dahomeans. The resisting victim accuses Guezo of hypocrisy, claiming that the Dahomeans' religious justification of the ritual is not convincing; rather, it is a thin disguise of the political nature of the executions (111–2). Historical narratives emanate from resistance, from voices that defy the powers that be. Moreover, by humanizing the victims and giving them a voice, Hazoumé makes it more difficult for the reader to achieve an aesthetic distance from the account of the killings themselves.

The sacrifices are witnessed by a delegation of "whites" in the novel, who function partially as surrogates for the reader, although the excessiveness of Hazoumé's account disturbs this identification as well.[3] The "whites" ask to be dismissed because they are afraid that "they would risk going mad" if they are forced to stay on and witness more atrocities (149). Although the "whites" depart, enacting the role they played historically (they come, refuse to see, and then leave), the reader remains present by continuing to read and increasingly assumes responsibility for reforming these violent practices. To be able to come and go, to engage and disengage with the violence, allows it to continue both as a real practice with innocent victims and as a dehumanizing spectacularization of Dahomey and then synecdochically of Africa as a whole.

Later in the novel a second delegation of "whites" (this time identified as British) attempts to persuade the king to trade in palm oil. Guezo responds most viciously by presenting the British with the decapitated heads of the maidens who served them dinner (275).[4] The British are derided in the novel for their cowardice. They retreat in terror at this scene. Their refusal to carry out the moral duties imperative from their position as witnesses makes them no better than the perpetrators of the sacrifices. Guezo explicitly charges the "whites" (this time he names them by nationality—Portuguese, British, and French) with introducing the slave trade and then not wanting to face the consequences of these practices: "But didn't you—

the Agoudas, the Glincis, and the Zojagués—introduce the idea and develop a taste for it in this country? Weren't you the ones who constantly armed Dahomey against the small neighboring tribes and encouraged the slave trade by the very transactions that you now consider so infamous?" (278).

The human sacrifices are integrated in historical time and constitute a narrative in the course of which the plot of the novel advances. Therefore the sacrifices are not suspended in ritualistic time outside of history. They are attached to real time and historical circumstance. Hazoumé locates the sacrifices in the context of an evolving history, the lived moment, because it is only through this context that their cultural significance can be grasped. Far from glorifying Dahomey, Hazoumé begins the novel with a political crisis and a military defeat in which three princes are captured by the enemy. Despite the objection of several factions in his court and the oracle's warning, Guezo undertakes a military campaign against the neighboring Mahinou people to avenge their murder of three white "friends" of Dahomey. The defeat of the Dahomeans at the hands of the Mahinous informs this particular celebration of the sacrifices: since the designated victims are Mahinous, the sacrifices are intended to recuperate the lost honor of the Dahomeans in battle and to humiliate the enemy. Although Guezo explains the sacrifices in the traditional manner—they are a religious ritual in which the victims are messengers to the ancestors in the afterlife—Hazoumé presents the sacrifices as political and demonstrates that the king knows this. Doguicimi, moreover, reveals that the king stages the sacrifices at a politically opportune moment. If he were following tradition and religious doctrine, he would do what Doguicimi suggests and wait until after the fate of the missing princes is known. But Guezo wants to stall the military campaign for vengeance while his spies gather enough information to guarantee the campaign's success. He stages the sacrifices as a distraction while his spies go to work.

In this particular instance, which follows military defeat, the ritual brings forth a realignment of power in the kingdom. Historical changes, therefore, result from the enactment of the ritual itself. More specifically, the ritual is the narrative of Migan's rise to power. Migan, the sadistic executioner, caters to the bloodthirsty crowds, and his popularity affects the king's decision making by constricting the king even more narrowly, in a regressive adherence to custom. The excesses depicted here are presented as the apogee of Dahomey's violent culture. The reader learns that the sacrifices have not always had this quality of excess. The excessive zeal found in sacrificing the Mahinou prisoners results from the Dahomeans' defeat by the Mahinous in a campaign undertaken to avenge the murder of three "whites." Moreover, the campaign was undertaken without any military aid from the "whites." Thus Hazoumé links the heightening of violence associated with the sacrifices to the function of this year's rituals as redress to military defeat.

The executioner emerges as a prominent figure in the novel, one who is not merely a type but an individual. Migan's new prominence is signaled early in the narrative of the annual festivities when the king's daughter chooses him as her husband. He is distinguished for being exceptionally efficient, and it is through his characterization of Migan that Hazoumé defines the nature of the ritual.[5] By contrast to Migan, Guezo is moderate and does not seek pleasure in the sacrifices; he views them as a necessity. The crowds (an anonymous, undifferentiated sea of people, *la vague humaine*), inspired by Migan, feast on this sadistic spectacle. Hazoumé depicts this as a collective experience of debasement.

The debasement into excessive violence is couched in gestures of glorification in which the people are reminded of Dahomey's glorious past. Hazoumé deliberately thematizes in the novel the importance of historical practice to the self-constitution of a culture. The official culture of Guezo's Dahomey is steeped in practices of history. The novel begins with the crier's recitation of the royal history of Dahomey.[6] This recitation, a daily ritual, reaches widely into the whole culture in remembrance of its origins. History is also recorded in murals on the palace walls and in paintings on the fabrics of the umbrellas and tents erected for the sacrifices. A "translator" (an interpreter of the pictures) explains their significance to the crowd in an act of collective remembrance that eventually fuels the sense of indignation at defeat. Hazoumé points out, however, that the history in the murals is an edited, self-glorifying narrative that is not truly informative. He tells us, for example, that during this year's festivities the painter of the murals will not paint a new picture because the only event to record is defeat. If defeats are edited out of the national narrative, then the national narrative is false.

Doguicimi articulates an alternative nationalism that criticizes and revises the nationalism that grows out of state power and is economically invested in the slave trade. She presents the king with a dilemma because Guezo recognizes that in her defiance of him, Doguicimi demonstrates the courageous spirit of his people and its women in particular (one of its myths of national identity—Dahomey was notorious for its "Amazon" army). He realizes that to suppress her is to devalue this characteristic: "Ordering the execution of Doguicimi would signify that the most cherished virtues of our ancestors are no longer recognized during my reign. Dahomey would have experienced the day we ceased worshipping the power, courage, and audacity that created it." The king sees in Doguicimi the spirit of the people, the highest national ideals: "this woman who dares attack the king, the very image of power, herself incarnates courage and audacity, the highest virtues in the eyes of the people" (131). To suppress Doguicimi is to attack "courage and audacity" and thus to attack the spirit of the people. Guezo is caught in a bind.

The heroine, however, has also presented problems for *Doguicimi*'s readers because in her critique of the king she seems to endorse colonialism. The history presented by Hazoumé complicates the opposition between traditional culture and France's civilizing mission. Whilst in prison for her defiance of the king, Doguicimi delivers an extended speech, which is usually read as Hazoumé's apology for colonialism.[7] Read, however, as a reinscription of colonial ideology, Doguicimi's speech articulates the historical perspective of the colonized and the demands for just treatment. Doguicimi's account of the colonial relation shows how the rest of the novel can be read against French nationalist myths whereby Hazoumé's appropriation of French ideals (and images from France's revolutionary history in the name of liberty, fraternity, and equality) gives shape to an emerging Dahomean nationalism in the 1930s. As David Spurr has pointed out, the French had moved away from purely strategic and economic arguments for imperialism by the 1930s in the face of critique from such prominent intellectuals as André Gide. Instead, the "colonial empire had been rhetorically endowed with the noblest sentiments of the French Revolution, the humanistic ideals of the Third Republic, and the historical grandeur of French civilization itself" (120). Through his heroine, Hazoumé questions whether the French have lived up to this ideal.

The occasion for Doguicimi's speech is the murder of the maidens who served the British delegation. She learns of this atrocity while in prison and

speaks out against Guezo's senseless violence. Doguicimi begins by giving
an exposition of Dahomey's lengthy history of contact with the Europeans.
In this history Hazoumé deploys a standard rhetorical construct in imperialist ideology: the glorification of one's own empire at the expense of another empire.[8] It culminates in her claim that "Only the rule of the Zojagués [the French] could bring about what the Glincis [the British] came
here to demand—peace for the small tribes around Dahomey, freedom for
the humble, and the reform of brutal customs" (290). The focus of the
speech is an analysis of the ways in which the past has shaped the world in
which the heroine is presently living. When Doguicimi turns to the future,
she warns the French that they will be accountable for their behavior. She
resorts to history in her extended account of the relationship between Europeans and Africans as a way of legitimating her account and of attributing responsibility for present conditions. Historical explanation becomes a
way of rendering justice.

Doguicimi is outraged at the brutal manner in which Guezo has dismissed the British delegation. She grieves for the death of these innocent
maidens who were killed by the king only in order to perform a symbolic
gesture. Yet despite her objection to these murders, she does not disapprove
of Guezo's resistance to the British demands. Calling the British "stinking
beasts," she begins by describing their role in initiating Dahomey to the
slave trade (287–8). The British request that the Dahomeans withdraw immediately from the slave trade is neither practical nor desirable since Dahomey has established a history of military conflicts with its neighbors and
cannot withdraw overnight without risking its territorial integrity. Moreover, Doguicimi is suspicious of the motives of the British, whose past behavior belies their present humanitarianism and who are motivated by
greed (wanting to undermine their competitors) and not by their allies' best
interests. So she asks, "These kings favored the slave trade by all possible
means; how could they change their orientation so abruptly and revolt
against the business to which their country owes its wealth?" (289–90).

In her extensive account of the evolving relationship between Africans
and Europeans during the slave trade, Doguicimi significantly addresses
les blancs and not the British in particular, although the reader has been informed that in this instance "the white men who were fleeing Abomey, the
capital of horrors," were British (287). This generalizing gesture assigns

blame to all whites—a demarcation by race—who participated in the slave trade. But Doguicimi does not only blame the whites. She recognizes Dahomey's complicity: "Stinking beasts whose presence in Dahomey was only tolerated out of an inexcusable complaisance [*une coupable complaisance*, better rendered as "guilty complacency"], you want to meddle in the affairs of this kingdom and even impose your will upon it? (287)." Addressing "whites" as the *bêtes puantes*, Doguicimi also charges Dahomey with *coupable complaisance*, guilty complacency. *Complaisance*, in French, carries with it the meanings of good-natured compliance and the more passive complacency. *Complaisance* is the root cause of complicity in a shared history of shame that, however, should not result in Dahomey relinquishing its sovereignty. This fierce independence characterizes the tenor of most of Doguicimi's speech. Though the Dahomeans should not be killing innocent maidens, *les blancs* are just as guilty and just as bloodstained: "It is out of place for a corrupt person to preach virtue. Your hypocrisy is nauseating to widows and orphans, although they loathe the war that brought on their unhappiness. Your own share of responsibility for the Dahomênous' warlike passions is large" (287–8). At the end of her recapitulation of the wars that cemented the guilty relationship between the "whites" and the Dahomeans, Doguicimi makes reference to the legislated efforts to abolish the slave trade and the failure of the whites to enforce their own laws:

> These white men have merely to prohibit the export of these tools of war, while pledging all of them, never again to send their ships to our shores for the purpose of taking slaves.
>
> But even if they made such a resolution, some of them would continue to engage clandestinely in the slave trade [expecting all along that the slave trade would be reestablished].[9] They have developed too much of a taste for it to give it up completely!   *(290)*

"White men" have been disobeying their own prohibitions against the slave trade and continue to make a demand for slaves. Slavery, therefore, continues to be a problem because it is a habit of white culture.

Doguicimi seems to contradict herself, however. While she harangues the "white men," later in her speech she distinguishes the British from the French and declares her preference for the French. After she completes her historical retrospective of the relationship between Dahomey and the whites, Doguicimi goes on to compare the French and the British. Although the historical record illustrates that whites as a whole are open to criticism (the British having simply been the greediest), it is up to the French to differentiate themselves in the future. Doguicimi's thinking here is consonant with French imperialist ideology, which argued that the French were different as an imperial power because of their revolutionary history. The French Empire brought enlightenment and justice, treating the natives with equality.[10] Doguicimi formulates these tenets of French imperialist ideology in advance of French control of Dahomey. In case they gain control over Dahomey, Doguicimi argues, the French would do well to bring about the necessary softening of Dahomean customs (*l'adoucissement des moeurs*, 397). Despite ample evidence of the past cruelty of the French, Doguicimi concedes, there is hope for the future. Hazoumé is reinscribing and not merely parroting French ideology because, embedded in a historical account, these ideological claims to moral superiority can be evaluated against an actual record of imperial rule. He implicitly asks the reader, did the French live up to their stated standards and did they fulfill the expectations of justice-minded colonial peoples?

Moreover, Doguicimi is also suggesting that the French will be held accountable for how they rule because they will face the possibility of revolt. If in the future the Dahomeans become dissatisfied with French rule, they could revolt. Although one of Doguicimi's auditors in the prison quickly intervenes to declare that the Dahomeans are too passive to revolt, Hazoumé has introduced the notion that the French should be accountable for their policies. When Doguicimi softens her stance by answering that "all we need is for the Zojagués to understand their duties of protection toward the Dahomênous to show evidence of their loyalty" (295), she is demarcating the paternalistic contract that holds both sides hostage. But paternalism is not enough. The empire cannot only be a disciplinary force; it must also be nurturing and protective. Doguicimi calls on France to be a mother as well: "be for him the Mother and Father whom he always, and despite appearances to the contrary sees, in his Sovereign; goodness has a more powerful hold over his heart than tyranny, which he never mistakes for moral or physical superiority" (292). It is key to read historically here. Since Doguicimi says these things in the late 1820s about the future, Hazoumé is not affirming

French imperialism but making its ideology sound hollow in light of the repressive colonial rule of the late 1930s. Was France, Hazoumé asks, fulfilling its mission from the Revolution to manifest as a state and nation the spirit of justice? Doguicimi implores, "Let your decisions be inspired by justice, and let a sense of humanity constantly govern any sanctions you might apply" (292). Doguicimi sets up a standard against which Hazoumé invites us to measure the record of French rule.

But the French are also entrusted with the preservation of true Dahomean culture, not the excesses of the sacrifices in which all whites are complicit along with the state power in precolonial Dahomey but a culture based on their values: "family solidarity, courage, personal dignity, fidelity toward friends, scrupulous honesty, sense of justice, and a deep religious feeling" (291). These qualities are still present despite the corruption evident in the human sacrifices; the continuation of tyrannical rule (in which whites are implicated both as slave traders and as potential colonial rulers) would eventually destroy a society based on these ideals. Doguicimi is a character that harks back to an ideal of Dahomey before slave trading. She remembers this past and invokes its moral order before the advent of the greed and materialism introduced by Europeans (291). Having corrupted the Africans and rendered them materialistic and covetous in their image, the Europeans now must help provide the conditions within which Dahomean culture can renew itself from its roots and in the process redeem themselves as well.[11]

Doguicimi represents an alternative constellation of traditional values that challenge the politically exploited notions of authenticity, notions that have implicated violence as a constitutive element of this cultural authenticity. Moreover, as a woman who struggles to uphold her loyalty to her husband (she rejects the advances of the king's son while she is in prison), Doguicimi radically challenges the attribution of cultural authenticity to state power and the monarchic tradition. A Dahomean identity need not have the sanction of official power. Doguicimi points to the possibility of alternative spheres of attribution: not the state (its military exploits and sacrifices) but those of domesticity and individual action. Moreover, her humble origins (she married above her station), connect her to the people. Doguicimi reinterprets loyalty—a quality highly valued in her culture—as loyalty to one's personal commitments. Her husband, Toffa, who at the beginning of the novel is presented as the most nationalistic of the princes because he argues against Guezo's desire to go to war to defend the honor of the "whites," denigrates the values that Doguicimi espouses because he assumes that all women are unfaithful. His traditionalism is a denigration of the domestic and what it stands for. Doguicimi, therefore, opposes both the greedy materialism of the Dahomean monarchy and her husband's "male" nationalism that denigrates the family. For Doguicimi the nation should be modeled after the family and function as an extension of the domestic circle.

La patrie of colonized Africa in the 1930s was France. If Guezo stands for a state structure that was ostensibly independent but was enabled by Europe's presence in Africa, then it is important to recognize that the state apparatus imposed by French colonial rule that succeeded the Dahomean monarchy is in significant ways continuous with the institutions of Guezo's rule. If Hazoumé damns the Dahomean monarchy, he is by extension damning colonial rule. This claim can not be objected to on the basis of what is usually interpreted as Doguicimi's pro-French statement; Doguicimi's speech reinforces my argument here that Hazoumé wants to stress the continuity of Dahomey's historical development in the nineteenth century. Commitment to family and personal ties can be interpreted to mean in this context a commitment to one's people, the brotherhood of Africans, a belief in "fraternity." This interpretation is reinforced by the ideas of Dahomean independence with which Toffa is identified. Toffa, not Guezo, is a purer nationalist, one who thinks of maintaining his people's independence on racial lines. From his perspective in the 1930s, however, Hazoumé rejects this narrow racialism. Doguicimi upstages her husband by being loyal to him in the face of his disloyalty (he rejects her because he assumes, despite her protests, that if he goes to war she will betray him), and thus extends loyalty to mean an embrace of a fraternity of humanity as a whole. Universal humanistic values articulated from the "native's" perspective have an accusatory tone, a function of the process of reinscription that charges the French with the ideals expressed in their own rhetoric.

While authority can be imposed through force, its legitimacy is more difficult to establish. Tradition helps legitimize authority and, since there are at least three competing versions of tradition (represented by Guezo, Toffa, and Doguicimi, respectively), doubt is cast on the human sacrifices as a traditional practice. Guezo finds it necessary to display signs of his authority constantly, and since only kings can order human sacrifices, he feels bound to the ritual. As he explains to his designated heir:

> In the eyes of Foreigners and even Dahomênous who only judge by appearances, the king is the image of power. Yet I do not have all the authority I am reputed to have in this kingdom. *Imprisoned in tradition, obsessed with custom* from which I must not stray by a single step, and petitioned by those in my entourage, I am, most of the time, no more than an instrument in a multitude of hands that are invisible to the people, who attribute many so-called royal acts to me, although in reality they have been conceived and executed by my secret Masters. The king is perhaps the person with the least freedom in this entire kingdom, and yet he is at the same time the most unhappy, because he is obliged to walk in the ruts of tradition and submit to the will of the court at the very moment when he is expected to maintain the dignity of being in command; he must often permit actions to take place in front of his eyes, even when his conscience disapproves of them.   *(153–4, emphasis added)*

Trapped by appearances, Guezo must perform the sacrifices to be king. Feeling ironically like the least free member of the kingdom, Guezo laments the extent to which his society is tradition-bound. In this extraordinary speech, "foreigners" and Dahomeans equally desire the violent spectacle of the human sacrifices. Corroborating Bataille's theory of human sacrifice, Guezo sees the performance of the ritual of sacrifice as an obligation to his people. Human sacrifice, as Bataille tells us, is a way in which to share in the prerogatives of power and the material wealth of the nation. The assumption is that should Guezo fail to make his authority visible in spectacles of violence, he will not be recognized as king. Although adherence to tradition legitimizes his authority in the eyes of both the "foreigners" and the people, the confession of his unease with it delegitimizes it; according to the novel's point of view, tradition leads him to act unjustly. The king's searching meditation about the prerogatives of his power further historicizes Hazoumé's account of Dahomey.

The institution of the monarchy has a history; its authority has always been precarious. From its inception as a state, Dahomey had been the scene of political reform. Having broken from the Aja tradition of government by council, the Dahomeans granted their king complete authority. Whereas in traditional Aja culture one's allegiance to the kingdom followed after the more powerful ties to the extended family (Akinjogbin 16–17), the Dahomeans submitted themselves directly to their king and were therefore united by their identification with Dahomey as a state. In the context of Hazoumé's novel, Dahomey is an evolving entity. Moreover, despite the constant references to the past and to tradition, Dahomey is a fairly new state.

Having attained the throne by forcing the abdication of his predecessor, Guezo established a new royal line. The newness, however, needed to be disguised in Dahomey's own denial of historical process: Guezo's rule emerges out of historical contests that have no place in a traditional explanation of regal authority as divine. Strict adherence to tradition disguises history and extends the trappings of legitimacy to Guezo's rule. The early years of his reign were dominated by the forces of reaction, although historians who examine his entire reign credit Guezo with starting the transition from the slave trade to the palm oil trade. When he came to power, Guezo was expected to correct the failings of his predecessor, who had been unsuccessful in the slave trade and had not managed to prevail over the neighboring Oyo to whom Dahomey owed a crippling annual tax (Akinjogbin 201). Guezo reinvigorated the slave trade, initiating as a consequence a revival and strengthening of Dahomey's war culture. In his reign Dahomey pulled out of its economic depression and broke off its obligations to the Oyo. But, as Hazoumé shows, Guezo also implicated Dahomey further in a history of Afro-European contact.

Reinscribing the French Revolution

Another dimension of Hazoumé's reinscription is that he borrows from a well-known historical myth of French nationalism, Michelet's account of Joan of Arc's martyrdom and Michelet's interpretation of the French Revolution through the meaning of Joan of Arc. Hazoumé casts Doguicimi as a Joan of Arc figure forecasting the emergent nation through her martyrdom.[12] Hazoumé draws from Michelet's argument that the awakening of the people in the march to the Bastille is a reincarnation of the spirit of Joan of Arc. She is the prophetic, first manifestation of the people's will—the spirit of justice rising in indignation—which then becomes more fully realized in the glorious moment of July 14, 1789. Cast in the terms of this reinscription, Doguicimi becomes a symbol of Dahomean national becoming.

In his review of *Doguicimi* Maran recognized the echoes of French epic in the novel and drew a parallel between Doguicimi and Aude, Roland's bride, who dies when she learns of Roland's demise in battle. Hazoumé's rendition of Doguicimi's suicide surpasses the medieval epic in beauty according to Maran (quoted in Fabre, "De *Batouala* à *Doguicimi*" 247).[13] The comparison to Joan of Arc (and especially to Michelet's account of her martyrdom) is even more evocative. It is in the manner of their deaths that Joan of Arc and Doguicimi are similar. Although Joan of Arc led the French in victory against the English invaders, she was abandoned by her king and sentenced to die by the Inquisition as a witch. Her martyrdom took place during a particularly violent period of European history, and it recalls this history by explicitly setting the emergence of a new nation (France) against the regressive influence of religious orthodoxy gone amok—a situation not unlike the practice of human sacrifice (once religious but increasingly political) whose excesses are associated with politics. Moreover, the terms with which Michelet praises Joan of Arc are echoed in *Doguicimi.* Joan of Arc undertakes her martyrdom, according to Michelet, as a conscious choice. She could have escaped it but does not. So her choice is excessive, unnecessary, done from the heart, and there are no miracles involved. Michelet naturalizes Joan of Arc; the sublimity of her sacrifice is that she suffered consciously: "Sacrifice is hardly just accepted and submitted to; death is hardly passive" (*Jeanne d'Arque* iv).

Doguicimi presents an alternative narrative of sacrifice, that of self-sacrifice. Spurned by her king (she has been imprisoned and threatened with death despite the fact that her military strategy to defend the nation proves to be correct), she buries herself alive at her husband's funeral. Although custom does require that a wife kill herself at her husband's funeral, Toffa's disloyalty and the favor of the king's son would have exempted Doguicimi from this fate (375–6). Hazoumé also presents Doguicimi's act as excessive. Not only does she choose death, but the way she dies is extreme. She takes the injunction of custom literally and buries herself alive with her husband's remains. In the past, the reader is told, no one has taken the custom literally. When women have carried out the custom, they have first poisoned

themselves and then thrown themselves in their husbands' graves. Doguicimi's extreme adherence to custom appears tragic and wasteful. Yet it also
makes her loyalty very visible and indicts her society for not recognizing it.
Doguicimi's self-sacrifice revises the narrative of sacrifice presented by the
novel. It changes the historical import of sacrifice by widening its resonance. Michelet credited Joan of Arc for unifying (and inventing) the
French nation: "Let's remember always, Frenchmen, that for us the nation
was born of the heart of a woman" (*Jeanne d'Arque* ix). Doguicimi's example
could do the same for an independent Dahomey.

Joan of Arc, who was beatified in 1909 and canonized in 1920, has consistently been used as a symbol of French resistance to foreign threats. Although the most pressing foreign threat to French national borders in the
late nineteenth and early twentieth centuries was Germany, the fact that
Joan of Arc fought against the English echoes in the context of imperialism
and France's competitive relationship with Britain. Moreover, her death implicated her own king who, out of political expediency, did not defend her.
Joan of Arc's story identifies a split between the monarchy and the true nation (the people) that Michelet exploited by identifying in her heroism the
first manifestation of the spontaneous spirit of justice in the people.[14] The
French Revolution was a collective rather than individual manifestation of
this unity, but it did not fulfill this potential. Justice in the revolution mani-
fested itself only in flashes and was not sustained. Political divisions inter-
fered with the fulfillment of justice (the mission of the nation), and Michelet
expected history to complete the manifestation of the nation as justice in
the future. These expectations reinforce Doguicimi's own expectations of
just colonial rule, projected as a transitional phase for Dahomey's history.

An extension of Hazoumé's project in his ethnographic work, his reinscription of Michelet appropriates and revises the colonizer's discourse to
constitute a practice of borrowed speech that articulates resistance. Another figure emerges as particularly important to Hazoumé's work: Georges
Hardy, the historian and honorary director of the Ecole Coloniale. A theo-
rist of colonial education, Hardy advocated the instruction of French history in the colonies because he believed that the "natives" were eager to
adopt a history more glorious than their own. In *Une Conquête morale* (1917),
Hardy argued that it was a mistake to believe that native Africans did not
understand history or were not susceptible to the seductions of great his-

torical narratives. Their oral traditions indicated otherwise to Hardy, who did not want the French to abdicate the opportunity to tell history, ceding it to the traditional griots and other opportunists (in Hardy's assessment) who so far had had a greater influence than a historian such as Michelet (Hardy's example) could have ever dreamed of (238):

> The only way to destroy this treacherous nonsense [*ces calembredaines per-fides*] is to confront the [griots's tales] methodically with true history, which would be perhaps less seductive but finding in its certainty and or-derliness its power of persuasion, would end up triumphing over the gri-ots. We have come to a poor country, ravaged by tyrants, depopulated by slave traders; we have established peace for everyone, we have put an end to raids and the slave trade, we have spread culture and built hospi-tals. What griot's tale could be ingenious enough to diminish such straightforward accomplishments? And isn't it obvious what gains are made for French power by proving and justifying itself in such manner?
>
> *(239–240).*

The history of colonization emerges as the most glorious, "epic" chapter of France's history, one that must be taught in colonial schools. It is also the as-pect of the national history that recuperates the nation born out of the French Revolution.

The affiliation between French imperialist ideology and the uses of the history of the French Revolution become even more apparent in a volume published in 1934 by the Centre de Synthèse Internationale on the problem of mobs in history. Georges Lefebvre contributed an influential essay on the revolutionary mob, in which he argued that mobs are not arbitrary, unor-ganized masses but are structured and rational. Georges Hardy contributed another essay in this volume on *la foule primitive* in which he argued that prim-itive societies are basically mobs because in them a collective identity is stronger than any individual identity (24–25). Although the subject of mobs was inspired in the 1930s by fear of Nazism and collective behavior, it had been sensationalized by notions of the primitive. In this discussion of mobs, a French notion of savagery (that of revolutionary mobs) is transferred onto the primitive outside Europe and then reimported rhetorically to character-ize that of which France wants to purge itself. Lefebvre dates the use of the word "*la foule*" to the 1890s, a whole century after the revolution.

Surely these depictions of the mob were informed by the characterization of natives in imperialist literature and the growing tendency to speak of
the working classes as primitives.[15] Hazoumé, in his act of reinscription,
makes *la foule* similar to the bloodthirsty revolutionary mob that we find in
reactionary accounts of the French Revolution. Indeed, it is possible to see
his account of the human sacrifices in Dahomey in the context of the revolutionary festivals and the constant threat of violence during the French
Revolution. Whereas liberal historians such as Michelet saw the revolutionary festivals as nonviolent (what Mona Ozouf has described as "the spontaneous convergence of different wills" 16), the conservative, antirevolution-
ary historians understood the revolutionary festivals as orgies. Ozouf quotes
Lanfrey, who described them as "a permanent orgy purporting to be the cult
of reason" (in Ozouf 28). The festival creates a permissive circle of excessive acts. What they mask, however, is an extraordinarily disciplined society
in which violence is contained in festivals. The accounts of the human sacrifices by Hazoumé, therefore, had an elaborate context specific to French
history, especially for a reader such as Hardy who wrote about the mob.

Doguicimi appeared with a preface by Hardy in which he introduced Hazoumé to the French public as an example of the achievements of assimilationist policy.[16] Praising the scientificity of Hazoumé's *Le Pacte de sang au Dahomey*, Hardy points out that it took less than forty years of French colonial
rule to produce a native scientist the equal of any Frenchman (9).[17] Hardy's
praise for Hazoumé served to glorify the empire and to silence the political
implications of the novel. He reads *Doguicimi* as an extension of the ethnographic work, overlooking the historicity of both the novel and *Le Pacte*.

By characterizing the novel as ethnography, Hardy also discounts its fictional qualities. "The novel form which [Hazoumé] thought wise to
adopt," he says, "was only a matter of appearances" (10). In Hardy's arguments we revisit the terms of Maran's self-defense, except that now they are
articulated by a figure representing the colonial establishment. Hazoumé's
work, according to Hardy, is "perfectly objective," and "he invents nothing" (10–11). The novelistic qualities of the work are accounted for by characterizing it as a "psychological story" (*une histoire psychologique*), a story not
of individuals, however, but of a whole society: "a series of animated and
colored scenes, a reanimation [*une résurrection*] of facts and actions" (10–
11).[18] Despite the emphasis on facts, Hardy discounts the historical content

of the novel. He refers to facts that pertain to the representation of the character of a people, an ethnographic rather than a historical undertaking. He reduces the novel to "having the value of intelligent 'reporting' " (11), a statement that displays the features of allochronic discourse: how can a history covering a period one hundred years ago be a work of "reportage?" What is the past for Hazoumé is for Hardy only another place in the ethnographic present. The generic recasting of the novel into "reportage" diminishes the literariness of the work as well. Literariness invites interpretation; "facts" do not.

Hardy's emphasis on facts contradict the author's own statements in the epilogue, where Hazoumé goes out of his way to present Doguicimi as his invention. Recapitulating the entire plot by repeating "I imagined that," Hazoumé presents his emplotment of this historical account as his interpretation and ends the novel with a reference to the triumph of French colonial rule in bringing "peace, liberty, and humanity" (382). Written at a time of severe censorship of Dahomean writers, these words are ironic, and Hazoumé's insistent reminder of the fictionality of his work invites us to read with literary devices, such as irony, at hand. Doguicimi is the author's invention not simply as a fictional character but as a historical possibility for a postcolonial nation.

■■

CHAPTER FIVE

History as Transgression in
Le Devoir de violence

If colonialism engendered a discourse of resistant history, how has post-colonialism reshaped this discourse? Yambo Ouologuem's *Le Devoir de violence* and Ben Okri's *The Famished Road* are novels that reexamine the last years of colonial rule, both to deconstruct the expectations about independence that have failed to materialize and to liberate from this process of deconstruction new possibilities for historical becoming. Trenchantly critical of the past and, more specifically, of the way the past has been understood, Ouologuem and Okri are at pains to invent a new historical paradigm that will articulate the continuities between the colonial and postcolonial eras so that the historical becoming of African nations can be driven less by the mythologizing ide-ologies of a moneyed and politically empowered elite. Ouologuem and Okri cry out for the democratization of the historical narratives of nation.

Instead of resistance, therefore, the key term in these projects is trans-gression. In part, this transgression addresses the continued deconstruction of ethnographic paradigms. In *Le Devoir*, Frobenius is lampooned in the context of a parody of realistic fiction. In *The Famished Road*, Madame Koto and her bar symbolize the ethnographic reinvented by Africans themselves and surviving as a contradictory but potent place of tradition. While the recurrence of the ethnographic establishes a continuity with my concerns, the transgressive ambitions of Ouologuem and Okri lead them beyond reaction. The desire here is to purge the negativity of reaction and emerge regenerated. Okri creates an elaborate metaphor to represent transgression; Ouologuem invents a poetics of transgression—what I call a molesting text that is less representational than deconstructing.[1]

Ouologuem refuses to occupy the oppositional "native" point of view, and his novel generates a historical perspective that dismantles the persistent Manichaean polarizations of Africanist discourse. Instead of resistance, therefore, Ouologuem's novel suggests transgression. As a poetics, transgression subverts the suspension of narrative enacted through the spectacularization of violence. Furthermore, it engenders a new space of narration with particular resonance for historical understanding, as Foucault's discussion of transgression implies.

Foucault argued that transgression does not function simply as the surpassing of limits but as a way of making the limits conscious. Transgression does not guarantee liberation. It punctuates the limits in such a way that the implicit boundaries of the world we act in are made explicit:

> Transgression is neither violence in a divided world (in an ethical world) nor a victory over limits (in a dialectical or revolutionary world); and exactly for this reason, its role is to measure the excessive distance that it opens at the heart of the limit and to trace the flashing line that causes the limit to arise. Transgression contains nothing negative, but affirms limited being—affirms the limitlessness into which it leaps as it opens this zone to existence for the first time.   *("Preface to Transgression" 35)*

Paradoxically, transgression delimits a "space" that we cannot visualize since transgression is about a crossing, about motion, not about place. Through transgression we confront the void beyond the limit and gain a heightened awareness of what the limit is. Foucault excludes transgression from two dominant emplotting mechanisms: the divided world or Manichaean good and evil that, for our reference here, can be applied to Fanon's analysis of colonialism, and the dialectical plot of history or Hegelianism that has defined the West's progressive historiography and that, again for our reference, has been a consistent sore point for African historians.

In Ouologuem's case, the practice of history by the novelist is a constant effort to cross the limits in which Africa has been circumscribed through its encounter with Europe. Postcoloniality, which lies beyond the end of the novel (the novel recounts events just up to the eve of independence), is the void into which Africa must be born. In discussing Ouologuem's novel, Wole Soyinka casts it precisely in terms of a historical void. *Le Devoir* is, according to Soyinka, a "fiercely partisan book on behalf of an immense historical vacuum" (104).[2] Despite independence (which is a reality at the time of the novel's composition), Africa has not yet emerged into the postcolonial space. If we follow Foucault's formulation of the transgressive, one never enters the void but constantly revises the limit through a heightened awareness of it. "The excessive distance that [transgression] opens at the heart of the limit" is a vantage point from which to do history. Excess is offered as opposed to the impossibility of an outsider's position because although excess affords a vantage point, it is also clearly a position *of* and belonging to the limit.

In independence, the spectacularization of Africa as a place of violence remains seductive so that it urgently needs to be deconstructed and historicized. To do so, Ouologuem undertook an attack on nativism whose implications continue to be debated in postcolonial theory.[3] Read against Ayi Kwei Armah's *Two Thousand Seasons*, Ouologuem's project has been repeatedly described as negative.[4] For example, Soyinka praises Armah for maintaining his revolutionary idealism despite his realistic ("rationalize[d]") depiction of violence: "Most remarkable of all in a book which is hardly squeamish in its depiction of violence, is Armah's insistence on a revolutionary integrity, a refusal to be trapped into promoting the increasingly fashionable rhetoric of violence for its own sake" (114). Addressed to the "particular audience of Armah's own race," according to Soyinka, *Two Thousand Seasons* attempts to galvanize a regeneration (112). These positive attributes highlight the novel's significant differences with Ouologuem's "negative" project.[5]

Ouologuem addresses himself to an audience with which he does not sympathize, an audience whose habits of reading he wants to subvert by making it subject to the same violence that it perpetrates on its objects of reading. Both these realms of violence (the reader's and the writer's) are symbolic, but they shape the ideology that perpetrates actual violence: against Africans, women, and the proletariat and, alternatively, by the revolutionary author, against all forms of usurped privilege. Moreover, Ouologuem's enterprise has special relevance for my concerns in this book. He undertakes to parody systematically the established discourses of representation of Africa, targeting most extensively the conjunction between the novel and an ethnographic ethos.[6] In the chapter "The Night of the Giants," Ouologuem subverts the realistic aesthetic of most African fiction and makes the subject of his representation the lampooning of the ethnographer who had the greatest influence on African writing, Leo Frobenius. "The Night of the Giants" is putatively realistic (certainly more so than the other chapters of the novel). But Ouologuem attacks the pretense of objectivity, the distance of the third-person narrator from his subject and implied reader, a reader who supposedly receives the text passively. While Armah, as Neil Lazarus has argued, attempts a "remythologization of African history" (216), Ouologuem distrusts any mythologization.[7] Ouologuem writes from the perspective of the dispossessed, those he refers to with the demeaning name the *négraille* (translated by Ralph Manheim in the Heinemann edition as "the niggertrash"). *Négraille* renders the African populace visible and invisible at once: it is a shocking reference that draws attention to the dehumanization of Black Africa. At the same time, however, the appellation obscures the identity of these people—they appear as what they have been made into; they are viewed (even when sympathetically) from the outside. Ouologuem, like Frantz Fanon who referred to the dispossessed of Africa as *les damnés de la terre*, tries to take an interior point of view by enabling a history from the perspective of those he calls the serfs, the illiterate servant class. Many have turned to Fanon's discussion of violence to read *Le Devoir* (see Aizenberg, and Lang, for example). But Ouologuem offers a distinct approach to interiority, not Fanon's psychoanalytic method but a representational strategy that deconstructs accepted identities and power relations.

Ouologuem's history emerges from the lacunae created through his ironic undercutting of accepted historical plots. He attacks with equal venom those who want to reinvent Africa as a lost Eden, glorifying its precolo-

nial past, and those invested in notions of progressive history and the civilizing mission of the Europeans. Moreover, Ouologuem's history is never
articulated explicitly but occupies the space that is left over. After every
available narrative has been mocked, our sympathies are inevitably directed to find an alternative point of view. For example, Ouologuem demonstrates the process through which the dynasty of the Saifs (a fictional invention of the author's) turns into a heroic and glorified party once it is
opposed to the ambitious European invaders, even though the dynasty is
renowned for its cruelty. Ouologuem's narrator explains, "The popular
imagination transformed defeat into genius and dictatorship of a tyrannical dynasty into an eternal glory" (33).[8] Although nominally opposed, European and native authorities require each other. The Europeans aid the rehabilitation of the native authority. In common with the Saifs, they live off
of the *négraille*, first during many years of slave trading and then during the
colonial period when, according to Ouologuem, the Saifs' resistance to
colonialism paradoxically helps the interests of the Europeans by keeping
the people subjugated. The reader can espouse neither point of view since
the popular imagination here is no longer opposed to the repressive authority but has become an instrument of it.

Ouologuem traces the changing perspective of the "popular imagination"; in precolonial times the people popularly lamented the fate of *cent
millions de damnés* sold into slavery (18, French), and later they celebrated the
glory of the Saifs on the basis of an ill-founded racial solidarity that masked
the real dynamics of class conflicts, of the privileged against the dispossessed.[9] The Saifs had known how to exploit the authority of oral legends.
Aided by the influence of the Europeans who legitimated anything that appeared authentic, the oral legends gave the Saifs even greater legitimacy. In
a process similar to the reproduction of the murals on the palace walls of
Dahomey, the Europeans help invent African authenticity. In this instance,
they consequently shore up the repressive native authorities as well. The
dispossession of the *négraille* becomes even more acute. Exiled from both
oral and written discourses of history, they are voiceless.

Ouologuem's historian narrator begins by pushing back the origin of
African history: "To recount the bloody adventure of the niggertrash—
shame to the worthless paupers!—there would be no need to go back beyond the present century; but the true history of the Blacks begins much

earlier, with the Saifs, in the year 1202" (3). This revisionist gesture also turns out to be bogus.[10] If the narrator's intent is to begin a "true history" in 1202, the narrative that begins in 1202, ironically subverts this intent. What we learn between the cracks of the purportedly true history is that the Saifs and the *négraille* are created simultaneously as oppositional identities in the colonial encounter that legitimates the Saifs by authenticating them as ancient. The Saifs in turn delegitimate the *négraille* by identifying them as modern and diminished. It is in opposition to the poverty and deprivation of the populace that the Saifs were glorious: "rising far above the common lot, it endowed the legend of the Saifs with the splendor in which the dreamers of African unity sun themselves to this day" (5). Ouologuem shows how the "niggertrash" are severed from history. According to this revisionist history, they are purportedly new, a product of colonialism, whereas the Saifs date from ancient times.

According to the terms of this history, Ouologuem himself is an alienated member of the *négraille*. As a Western-educated African, he has his origins in those people who were sent to the missionaries to be educated because they were perceived by the Saif as dispensable. In order to write from the point of view of the *négraille*, Ouologuem performs a return to his people—although he must overcome the alienation that is the result of his education. Other writers and many politicians have solved this problem by appealing to the unifying identity of race, but for Ouologuem's classist analysis racial solidarity is not relevant.

My readings of Ouologuem and Okri consider illiteracy and the dispossession of voice as problems of historical practice.[11] I address these problems initially through narratology, by looking at constructions of the reader and raising the issue of his/her complicity in the erotic violence of the text. I then demonstrate how Ouologuem exploits the distinction made by Genette in his analysis of point of view between mood ("who sees?") and voice ("who speaks?") (*Narrative Discourse* 186). In factual history, mood and voice work together to reinforce the authority of the historian, which rests in part on their reciprocity. In fictional histories, however, mood and voice can contest each other openly. Ouologuem separates into two distinct areas of concern the problem of who sees the action from the problem of who speaks the history. As a result, a crisis arises in the authority of the historian, a crisis Ouologuem does not seek to resolve but to highlight.

The problem for Ouologuem (as for Okri) is one of narrative method: how to write a history from the point of view of the dispossessed without reenacting a further dispossession by taking over their point of view. If the people of Africa have been erased from history because their point of view is repeatedly co-opted, as in the cynical manipulation and reinvention of the popular memory, how does one record this history without duplicating such a dispossession? The problem here is less one of legitimacy than of power. Irony in *Le Devoir de violence* highlights a disjunction between who speaks and who sees, establishing a distance between the narrator and the history being narrated. If the sadistic enjoyment in violence is a narrative of power, for example, Ouologuem's irony undercuts it by reminding us that the perpetrators are powerless in their enjoyment.

Molesting the Reader

Ouologuem adopts a mixture of styles to explore how certain types of narrative have been legitimated by imitating authentic forms—and, in their path, have invented those authentic narrative forms. Each of the four chapters of the novel incorporates a mixture of oral and written styles, but as the narrative advances chronologically into the modern period, the mixture becomes more varied and challenging. The first two chapters (which treat precolonial history and the wars with the Europeans at the end of the nineteenth century) imitate oral accounts and early forms of written history such as chronicles. As we move into the account of the colonial period where the stories of the servant class take center stage and the text's form becomes more novelistic (or at least here the parodies are directed at the novel as form), Ouologuem continues to resort to oral conventions whenever he praises the traditional ruling dynasty of the Saifs. Of course, the praise is ironic, but as it is reiterated it unmasks the rehabilitation of oral narratives—a countermeasure to Europeanization—as bogus.[12] Repeating praises of the Saifs is not enough to erase the reader's memory of the atrocities performed with the Saifs' sanction.

In the third and longest chapter in the novel, "The Night of the Giants," violence is not treated as spectacle. Here we encounter a molesting, invasive text that involves the reader intimately in the violence perpetrated. Ouologuem narrates the story of the serfs from the inside, staging an attack on the reader as literally as it is possible to do.

"The Night of the Giants" reads like a novel within a novel, the discrete history of one period, the period of colonialism. Although thematically Ouologuem connects what happened during colonialism to precolonial violence, the chapter divisions of the novel follow the accepted periodization of African history and the length of each section corresponds to the extent of the written record on these periods.[13] Thus the first two chapters are short. The first chapter, "The Legend of the Saifs," covers six centuries in a mere twenty-four pages; the second chapter, "Ecstasy and Agony," covers the wars against the European conquest, a short period in numbers of years but a time in which the historical record started to thicken. The last chapter deals with the immediate pre-independence period, bringing Ouologuem's narrative to the threshold of independence but not beyond. Independence is posited as a historical void into which Africa must emerge. Writing in the late 1960s after independence, Ouologuem seems to think that African nations have yet to step into that void.

"The Night of the Giants" traces the emergence of the new class of Western-educated Africans from the serfs whose lives had been at the mercy of the ruling dynasty. Although most of this history depicts the continued deprivation and subjugation of the servant class, Ouologuem skillfully shows how the administrators of the future independent nations rise out of the *négraille*. His story is cautionary but hopeful. It poses a question that it refrains from answering: will Raymond Kassoumi be completely corrupted by his double consciousness and his cultural confusion, or does he genuinely represent a new generation and new hope for Africa?

Through a poetics of transgression, Ouologuem sets out to molest his readers, to invade and change their consciousness. Any act of interpretation is the construction of a reader, and any text calls forth multiple readers (Culler 67). The "stories of reading" told by critics about their experiences as readers of particular texts establish the reader's authority by invariably insisting that reading results in knowledge (Culler 79).[14] Jonathan Culler finds the repeated rehearsal of this conclusion in "stories of reading" unsettling. But the kind of reader who experiences reading as a mastery of the text is indeed one of the readers that Ouologuem wishes to discredit: an authoritarian reader who reads to impose his or her power over the text, the reader as voyeur who wants to masterfully (re)shape the text. The difficulty in *Le Devoir* is that the novel's eroticism seems to invite such a reader. It is only when we address the transgressive energies of the text that we get beyond this dynamic of domination.

Indeed, in the argument that I would like to sketch here, Ouologuem's text calls forth at least two types of readers. In addition to the mastering, voyeuristic reader, there is the reader who, in Georges Poulet's terms, falls prey to the text, who at once assimilates the complex sensibility of the book yet remains aware of its otherness:

> From the moment I become a prey to what I read, I begin to share the use of my consciousness with this being whom I have tried to define and who is the conscious subject ensconced at the heart of the work. He and I, we start having a common consciousness. Doubtless, within this community of feeling, the parts played by each of us are not of equal importance. The consciousness inherent in the work is active and potent; it occupies the foreground; it is clearly related to its *own* world, to objects which are *its* objects. In opposition, I myself, although conscious of whatever it may be conscious of, play a much more humble role content to record passively all that is going on in me. A lag takes place, a sort of schizoid distinction between what I feel and what the other feels; a confused awareness of delay, so that the work seems first to think of itself, and then to inform me of what it has thought. Thus I often have the impression, while reading, of simply witnessing an action which at the same time concerns and yet does not concern me. This provokes a certain feeling of surprise within me. I am a consciousness astonished by an existence which is not mine, but which I experience as though it were mine.   *(Poulet in Tompkins 47–8)*

What interests me in this "story of reading" is the movement of Poulet's thought from reading as an invasion of the reader's consciousness by the text to an acknowledgment, at the end of Poulet's description, of the alien otherness of the text that has so suddenly invaded one. Reading is an assimilation of the text's consciousness from which the reader does not seem to be able to safeguard him or herself and, at the same time, a continued heightened awareness of otherness. Reading is a confrontation of the other from an interior point of view which, however, does not revoke the otherness of the text in relation to the reader. Poulet is a *witness* to the text who, unlike the mastering reader, does not feel compelled to authorize the action but who, without losing his own selfhood, realizes the text's consciousness.

Ouologuem sets up an analogy between seeing and reading. Exploiting Poulet's discussion of reading, I find the crucial difference here between an act of witness that yields testimony and an act of voyeurism that yields fantasy. Taking my cue from Poulet, I would like to suggest that witnessing does not require objectivity. Objectivity is an impossible goal in any case. Witnessing, in fact, entails an emotional involvement in what one sees; to use Poulet's terms, the witness "falls prey" to what he reads (or sees, in my analogy). But witnessing also calls up an awareness of distance from what one sees, a heightened notion of one's own selfhood in opposition to what one sees, often in the form of a moral judgment. Voyeurism, on the other hand, colonizes what it sees; it undertakes an othering of what it sees through which it posits a fantasy identity for the self. The Victorian travelers to Dahomey reacted to the dangers of voyeurism in their refusal to see, which in the end amounted also to a refusal to witness because they erased the subjectivity of the Dahomeans. In the absence of their direct testimony of the sacrifices, they produced through suggestion a landscape of generalized violence, something to look away from.

Let me turn to some concrete examples regarding *Le Devoir de violence* that revisit the problem of voyeurism and the challenges of testimony. I have referred earlier in this book to the ironies evoked by the reception of *Le Devoir* as the first "genuine" African novel in French. Some of the early reviewers of the novel linked their assessment of the novel's authenticity explicitly to its erotic content. However, their argument for authenticity (in which they cited the eroticism as evidence) undermines the claims for the novel's authenticity because it reveals a conventional tendency to identify an authentic Africa with an excessively sexualized and violent place. Drawing from Culler's description of the authoritarian reader, I suggest that these critics read Ouologuem in a mastering, voyeuristic way and, consequently, do not read him at all.

The reception of *Le Devoir* affords a very good example of this kind of reading. The *Times Literary Supplement* (*TLS*) published an unsigned review of the novel when it received the Prix Renaudot in 1968 (three years before the novel's publication in English and before the plagiarism controversy) that articulates clearly the readerly pleasures in the erotic. Reiterating the French reviewers' praise of the novel's authenticity, the *TLS* reviewer states: "despite [Ouologuem's] three French university degrees and now, the imprimatur of Paris's Fleet Street, nothing written in a European language could be farther from a European tradition than *Le Devoir de violence*. The journalists who decide the Prix Renaudot have chosen an African who writes as an African and not as some aspirant to the Boulevard Saint Michel" (1425). The review, which is incredibly entitled "Genital Reminders," undermines the novel's historicism by pitting the historical content against the erotic. The "human interest" in the novel lies in Ouologuem's treatment of sex not history. The reviewer dismisses history as "too dry, too national-epical." Ouologuem "spice[s]" his novel with "sorcery and unnatural death, a taste of cannibalism, black magic and eroticism."

Failing to recognize these as conventional elements in the European discourse about Africa, the reviewer goes on to stress his particular pleasure in finding that all these practices are "centred principally on the various treatments of the genitalia: they are tortured, worshipped, gratified, doctored, torn out, eaten, even used for procreation, rarely ignored." Eroticism displaces historicism. And the eroticism is directed at fragmented bodies, objectified for the reader's pleasure. While the terms in his title ("Genital Reminders") demonstrate the derogation of history to the narrative of the violence done to "already" dismembered bodies, the reviewer's list of actions records his own pleasurable reinvention of the spectacle in terms that are totally consonant with the European discourse on Africa, sexualizing the bodies of Africans by dismembering them. As a gloss on Ouologuem's novel, the reviewer's list is wholly inadequate. Considered as an independent text about the *authentically* African, the review perniciously perpetuates stereotypes and draws a "genuine" African author on the side of the dominating European perspective. The reception of Ouologuem's novel among Africans (like the reception of *Doguicimi*) was largely negative because the novel seems to lend itself so easily to such co-optation. But the *TLS* reviewer seriously misreads the novel, taking the consensual sex literally and ignoring the guilt that Ouologuem attributes (to Chevalier and Sankolo, for example) in the scenes of violence.

What makes an analysis of the novel so challenging is that Ouologuem seems to invite the kind of displacement in which the historical is obscured by the erotic, if only in the end to redirect our attention to a different kind of history. Ouologuem explores the dynamics of a rhetorical strategy that enables the displacement of the historical by the erotic in part by re-creating that dynamic. This displacement occurs largely through the aesthetics of spectacle. It is this mechanism of representation that Ouologuem wants us to become aware of and that I call a history.

To make his critical point (his historical argument), Ouologuem disengages the erotic from the spectacular. Chevalier's enucleation (a possible reference to Bataille's transgressive poetics in *L'Histoire de l'oeil*) renders clearly the object of Ouologuem's attack: the controlling gaze of the colonizer, which is easily defeated by the Saif's surreptitious gaze, his spying. Chevalier's corpse lies bathed in blood, "his right eye open, red, hollowed—and on the floor beside him his eyeball, round and purple, a bloody pear, lay spitted on the tip of a table knife" (64). Chevalier, a sexual predator and a political oppressor, lies enucleated and symbolically castrated. The eye stares at its own orb in a complete subversion of the gaze.

In his misreading, the *TLS* reviewer posits the violence as a natural extension of the erotic; he praises Ouologuem for restoring this insight to the European reader without guilt. Putting aside the issue of the reader's pleasures in these scenes and his guilt, I would argue that Ouologuem's narration certainly attributes guilt. To perceive Ouologuem's attribution of guilt, however, the scenes must be read as part of a narrative, as connected to each other, and not as intervals of spectacle that disrupt narrative. One of the reasons for which Chevalier is punished is that he victimizes the women that the Saif offers to him. In fact, he victimizes them twice: by perpetrating sexual violence and by alienating them from their own experience, rendering them into voyeurs of themselves. The women's pleasure is their humiliation. The scene between Chevalier and Awa, for example, is generated through Chevalier's desire for the spectacle of an eroticized African woman; Awa in this scene looks at herself through his point of view. In the novel, narrative, however, ultimately subsumes spectacle. When seen as one narrative, the different pornographic episodes in the novel link the women's alienation to their violent emergence from this alienation.

The episode that ends in Chevalier's enucleation begins when an African woman (Awa) is sent as a spy to Chevalier, the colonial official. Chevalier has been receiving native women from the Saif habitually so he does not suspect

Awa as a spy. Although Awa goes there knowing that she will (by the Saif's order) offer her body, the scene is narrated as a scene of seduction and thus as Chevalier's fantasy. Chevalier's apartment is described through Awa's reactions to it: "Awa was breathless with delight at the pink hangings, the semicircular bed, and the silk counterpane which seemed to be strewn with rose petals" (55).[15] In the account of the sexual encounter, Awa's consent is not won through the action but is established narratologically by co-opting her point of view in the telling of the story. Awa's experience is increasingly absorbed into Chevalier's point of view as his fantasy of her seduction. This violence constitutes a second order of action that is an extension and completion of the physical molestation of Awa.

After Chevalier "excites" Awa by having the dogs assault her sexually, he asks Awa for her impressions of this experience. Her answer is, "Oh! I've never seen anything like it" (*Oh! jamais je n'avais encore vu ça*) (English 57, French 71). This is an odd answer; Awa stands outside her own experience, observing it rather than feeling it. Already objectified, she views herself from outside herself, serving Chevalier's pleasure, which is extended through the recognition that Awa now sees herself as he has invented her.

When the passage continues in indirect discourse and the narrator attributes to Awa great sexual excitement, the excitement reflects Chevalier's understanding of "[his] little black girl" and not Awa's consciousness (57). Awa, turned into an animal through Chevalier's objectification, registers Chevalier's desire:

> A slap from him made her bark, she coiled up with pleasure, panting under his cruel caress, manipulating him like a queen or a skillful whore. Her mouth was still hungry for this man's pink, plump molusk, and the tongue in her mouth itched to suck at the pearl of sumptuous orient that flowed, foaming as though regretfully, from the stem. *(57)*

The assertion that her "bark" is a sign of pleasure is made through the fiction of her consent. The excessive language, the parody of the pornographic, sets in motion a molestation of the reader who (if we follow Poulet) is both drawn complicitly into the action and able through Ouologuem's ironies to recognize that Awa is not herself in these scenes but has turned into what Chevalier wants her to be.[16] The backlash to this violence is Chevalier's enucleation. But Ouologuem carries the consequences of this scene even further to Awa's own violent death, which disrupts the Manichaean opposition between Awa (native victim) and Chevalier (alien victimizer).

The scene between Awa and Chevalier, moreover, lies at the center of the plagiarism controversy surrounding this novel. The controversies over Ouologuem's alleged plagiarism were ignited by Graham Greene's complaint that Ouologuem had lifted a scene from Greene's *It's a Battlefield*.[17] In fact, the sensibility that the *TLS* reviewer appreciates as genuinely African is borrowed from a European novelist and shows up in Ouologuem as a displaced convention. The subtext of Graham Greene's *It's a Battlefield*, a pornographic male fantasy of being suspended between a crippling ennui and constantly renewed sexual opportunities, surfaces as the main narrative action in Ouologuem's text. Ouologuem writes from his own experience as a reader of Greene and represents the fantasies implied by Greene's characters but disallowed by Greene.[18]

Critics have read from Greene to Ouologuem, positing (within the framework of the plagiarism controversy) Ouologuem's text as deviant. Thus Christopher Miller reads the violent action by the novel's characters as an allegory of Ouologuem's textual violence. The African past emerges as "a purloined, kidnapped, and usurped origin, as an originary violence that precludes the autonomy of any given object, leaving only a void" (*Blank* 233). Miller's thesis subordinates the eroticism to something else (textual theft, the subversion of origins). History is treated only as it relates to the theme of origins. But it is possible to do something with history more directly here.

Reading backward from Ouologuem to Greene, the scene in Greene's novel from which Ouologuem "plagiarized" suddenly appears shocking. By making explicit the erotic undercurrent of the scene in Greene's novel, the scene of outrageous sex in *Le Devoir* in the end is consonant, not dissonant, with the mood of Greene's novel. The eroticism is not incidental, and its transposition from one text to the other contains a part of Ouologuem's historical thesis.

Greene's novel has no content that bears directly on Africa. The Assistant Commissioner (a police officer and central character in the novel) has had a career in the British imperial service and has derived his notions about police work in India. However, he plays no part in the scene that Ouologuem "plagiarizes." Because Ouologuem's rewriting of Graham Greene's scene functions as an exposition of the undercurrent energies of that novel, it draws our

attention to the implications of these attitudes for Afro-European contact.
The attitudes that lead to bestiality are not a response to Africa; rather, they
are imported to Africa and made explicit there. The West has built its historical identity through an elaborate process of othering. Ouologuem demonstrates that instances of othering are really self-constructions.

Textual theft as a strategy of representation comments not only on the
invented nature of origins but also on the problem of point of view. Indeed,
Miller cites Ouologuem's claims that he used the passage from Graham
Greene in order to express a position that would be impermissible to him as
an African.[19] Although Ouologuem is not specific about what exactly would
be impermissible for him to say, a reading of *It's a Battlefield* makes this matter fairly clear. The borrowed thematic element from Greene is the male
character's fantasy of the woman's sexual availability. Greene writes: "Her
body was ready for enjoyment; the deep peace of sensuality covered all the
fears and perplexities of the day; she never felt more at home than in a bed
or a man's arms" (58). Reading backward from Ouologuem to Greene, we
are keenly aware that this passage rests heavily on the presumed sexual
availability of the woman. (The characters in Greene's novel, by the way,
do not consummate their relationship in their encounter.) As an extension
of this, the scene in *Le Devoir* stresses Awa's consent and pleasure in her extreme objectification. The rendition of female sexuality is a far more significant borrowing from *It's a Battlefield* than, for example, the details of the
setting of the scene in Mr. Surrogate's or Chevalier's apartment.

Like the other women in the novel, Awa suffers the most extreme objectification and, in the end, dies violently at the hands of her fiancé, Sankolo.
Ouologuem's rejection of the oppositional native point of view as an adequate position from which to write African history is particularly evident in
his treatment of the violence of Africans against Africans. Early on in the
novel he provides a historical explanation for violence against women in
Africa. The sexual abuse of women in Africa begins, according to the narrator, at a specific moment in the history of colonization (48). According to
Ouologuem's fictional history, the Saif passed regressive laws during the
early years of colonization that tightened the prohibitions against women's
sexuality. The loss of political sovereignty to the French led the Saif to seek
other areas in which he could impose his authority and compensate for his
political irrelevance. As he sought to regulate private lives more thorough-

ly, women became the objects of such control (48). Thus, not only were women circumcized, but the Saif enforced ritual infibulation (the sewing up of the vagina), a practice that had never before been enforced. Like Hazoumé, Ouologuem links the presence of the French to a hardening of native "traditions."[20]

In the scene that results in Awa's death, she becomes the scapegoat for her fiancé's impotence and humiliation. Her death is another instance in which the novel's excessive violence parodies Africanist discourse. This is how Awa dies after an extensive beating:

> Sankolo seized Awa by the throat. His knife whirled, twice he planted it in her left breast, slitted her belly from top to bottom. Suddenly expelled, her pink viscera crackled. He didn't even know whether the woman had screamed. He licked the blade, put the knife away in his belt. Covered the corpse with a wall of mud. *(93)*

Where is the "natural" connection between eroticism and violence that the *TLS* reviewer claims? Such a view makes him complicitous in Sankolo's pleasure while the molested reader shirks away from Sankolo.

Sankolo's barbarism here is induced by a profound sense of powerlessness and self-hate that stems from his subjugation to both African and European oppressors. His violent rage is triggered by what he interprets as the look of hatred on Awa's face as she watches him masturbate. However, the narrative contradicts Sankolo's assumption about Awa's feelings because, throughout his violent attack on her, we are told that she loves him (92). Ouologuem develops this scene by elaborating two different plots for the same action: one plot is constructed through Sankolo's point of view, the other through Awa's. The incompatibility of the two is absolute.

Sankolo's rage is an extension of the same acting out that leads him to masturbate violently as he watches the Saif's son make love to Shrobenius's blond daughter, Sonia. The pleasure he derives in the killing of Awa (cutting her with a knife, licking the blade) is displaced from the frustrations of the earlier scene of masturbation. Sankolo is humiliated by Awa's gaze, which catches him unawares. Reading the erotics of spectacle in continuum with the previous scene between Chevalier and Awa, we understand that Awa's gaze emasculates Sankolo. It objectifies him and fixes him in the passive (female) position, while allowing Awa to subversively occupy the male position. I do not mean to imply that Awa does this intentionally, but simply to stress that as a man who finds himself the object of someone's gaze, Sankolo becomes conscious of his emasculation.

His reaction to Awa's gaze also reveals the intent of his own gaze on Madoubo and Sonia. The aim of his masturbatory fantasy is to humiliate the son of his master and the white woman (who is, in fact, being doubly controlled by both men). Awa's death is a surrogate for Sankolo's orgasm, "his death agony" (91). She interrupts him before his orgasm, and for this he kills her. The killing of Awa is presented by Ouologuem as the completion of the sexual act that began with Sankolo's arousal. He kills because he is prevented from having an orgasm. By killing Awa, Sankolo incorporates her into the action of his fantasy and defeats her independent point of view.

Alternatively (reading from Awa's point of view), Awa's position in the scene is analogous to the reader's: she has watched and listened to Sankolo as he coaxes the two lovers and himself into a frenzy of excitement. Unprepared to assume the authority of her position as a spectator to objectify and control, she is instead a reader who falls prey to the scene Sankolo presents her with. Her sympathetic engagement leads to her consummation:

> He struck Awa a light blow on the cheek. She raised her hands in defense. He struck her full in the mouth, looking away with one eye, at the couple disporting in the truck [Madoubo and Sonia]. That gave him a terrible air of detachment, as though to destroy Awa he needed only half his will.
>
> He went on striking her haphazardly, absently—less interested in punishing her than in making blood flow and inflicting pain. Awa's hands were of no use to her; she made no attempt to return the blows, she loved him, she was tortured by the horror and degradation of this physical struggle. *(92)*

Sankolo is erasing Awa's subjectivity here by venting on her the pain he wants to inflict on Madoubo and Sonia. The simultaneity of the two actions (he watches the lovemaking and beats Awa) suggests that she exists for him only as an instrument for his anger. Awa's subjectivity is preserved, however, by the narrator's indirect discourse: "She was tortured by the horror and degradation of this physical struggle." Sankolo is oblivious to her suffering.

It is clear that Ouologuem perceives Awa as an innocent victim, thus attributing guilt to Sankolo, condemning his pleasure in killing Awa. To summarize this scene as illustrating the natural connection between eroticism and violence is not only to participate in Awa's erasure but to deny Ouologuem's own voice, the inflection of his own subjectivity in the scene. The sentence "That gave him a terrible air of detachment, as though to destroy Awa he needed only half his will" is perceived through the narrator and not through either character. It indicates Sankolo's repression of his conscience, his own dehumanization in the violence that, when narrated from his own point of view (for example, the description of Sankolo licking the blade), he enjoys. While Sankolo watches Madoubo and Sonia, much of his hatred is actually directed at Madoubo. Gender and racial hatred, which motivate Sankolo's feelings toward Sonia, take a secondary place here to his class hatred. It is Madoubo's privilege that he desires; Sankolo, too, wants to master and conquer. He transgresses into Madoubo's space and takes on Madoubo's position. Sankolo is cast as what I have called the voyeuristic reader, who violently misreads through his desires. Indeed, he produces an extensive pornographic text of his own as he talks himself through Madoubo and Sonia's lovemaking. Pointing his penis toward the couple, Sankolo masturbates as he urges them (and himself) on (90-91). Sankolo's soliloquy is parodic. He is laughable here, talking to his penis: "Tell me, my member, have you seen the two white pigeons in the dovecote?" (90). His humiliation, however, soon turns to violent rage. As he watches Madoubo and Sonia, Sankolo gives the impression of willing the action he desires. The confrontation between Awa and Sankolo then turns into a confrontation between two types of reading, two postures, one wanting to master, the other susceptible to penetration. This is what happens in the most novelized section of Ouologuem's fictional history. By turning to issues of narration and how Ouologuem handles irony, we can see perhaps where we, as readers of Ouologuem, might stand.

Focalization and the Writing of History

When Ouologuem posits contradictory plots for the same series of events, the effect in his narration is to pit mood and voice against each other.[21] As Genette has shown, determining point of view involves at least two distinct narrative operations: mood and voice. Genette discusses mood in terms of focalization and voice in terms of the "identity of the narrator" (186). The constant shifts in perspective in the novel are due to Ouologuem's reliance on internal focalization, but since the history is focalized through eyes that belong to other parties openly inimical to the *négraille*, the instances of internal focalization in the novel constantly reenact the dispossession of the people.

Early in the novel we are told that "tradition loses itself in legend, for there are few written accounts and the versions of the elders diverge from those of the griots, which differ in turn from those of the chroniclers" (6). Ouologuem's historian-narrator then gives us some of the different versions, histories with distinct plots, some glorifying the Saifs, some reviling them, all relying on many unexplainable events. For example, the recurring presence of the vengeful asps is either accounted for as an act of providence or given as evidence of the Saifs' mystical powers to train the snakes so they can punish their enemies secretly, without leaving evidence. The breakdown of tradition into multiple legends marks the passage of time and suggests that history traces the emergence of multiple competing stories; it records the dissonance of multiple points of view. The uncertainty created by these multiple plots is not an indication of the narrator's reticence to tell us what he knows but an indication that factual knowledge is hard to come by. By providing us with many competing explanations, Ouologuem undercuts the authority of both historical explanation and the "objective," nonnarrative explanations of anthropology.

Ouologuem presents what appears to be explanation only to reveal that he is casting doubt on the legitimacy of large constructs (such as the "popular imagination") because they get continually renewed without representing what they claim to represent. Speaking from a moment in the postcolonial present, the narrator assesses the importance of Saif al-Heit in such a manner as to draw attention to the fact that any act of remembrance—whether it be through the "popular imagination," "Black romanticism," or the work of the "chroniclers" or the oral historians who preceded them—testifies to the dynasty's enduring dominance. All acts of remembrance can be exploited to perpetuate their influence:

> Whether truth or invention, the legend of Saif Isaac al-Heit still haunts
> Black romanticism and the political thinking of the notables in a good
> many republics. For his memory strikes the popular imagination. Chron-

iclers draw on the oral tradition to enrich his cult and through him celebrate the glorious era of the first States with their wise philosopher-king,
whose history has called not only archaeology, history, and numismatics
but also the natural sciences and ethnology to their highest tasks.   *(8)*

A genealogy of stories is mapped here, which starts with the oral traditions,
moves on to the chroniclers, then to black romanticism, and finally to the
"popular imagination," a timeless entity that refers interchangeably to the
people in the 1960s and the 1500s.

Ouologuem proceeds to give an account that contradicts this glorious
characterization and shows no evidence of how those responsible for shaping the "popular imagination" could possibly remember the Saif al-Heit
fondly. A narrative of excessive violence ensues, which deals primarily with
the history of the slave trade. Citing another oral authority, the narrator recounts how "a hundred million of the damned—so moan the troubadours
of Nakem when the evening vomits forth its starry diamonds—were carried
away." The problem here, however, is that the tone of disapproval eventually emerges from language that mimics the European officials' accounts of
"primitive" behavior and thus cannot be trusted by the reader as an opinion (and explanation) endorsed by the narrator. Although accounted for in
indirect discourse, voice and mood work in opposite directions here. For example, Ouologuem is describing the types of tribes that raided other tribes:

> Cruel peoples, whose speech is kind of croaking, fierce killers, men of
> the jungle, living in a state of bestiality, mating with the first woman they
> find, tall in stature and horrible to look upon, hairy men with abnor-
> mally long nails, the Zulus, Jaga, and Masai feed on human flesh and go
> naked, armed with shields, darts, and daggers. Savage in their customs
> and daily lives, they know no faith nor law nor king. In the early dawn
> they crawl out of their wretched forest huts and destroy everything be-
> fore them with fire and sword.   *(13)*

The absurd list of physical characteristics is reminiscent of Hubert's catalog: tall, hairy men, with long nails who are really beasts. The narrative of
violence escalates to extensive descriptions of the cannibalistic consumption of prisoners, the making literal of the consumption of capital I have
discussed in terms of the human sacrifices. Although Ouologuem wants us

to understand the full extent of the violence of the slave trade on the people of Africa, accounts of their sufferings are only available second-hand, mediated through a discourse of horror that dehumanizes the victims as much as the perpetrators. We must read against the grain once again to retrieve any sense of the people's history, but mostly we become aware of how inaccessible this history really is.

Ouologuem also satirizes the liberal European sympathetic to the African's plight under colonialism. An interesting elision occurs in this version of history as a result of the liberal's tendency to blame all on empire and capital and obscure the complicity of the African ruling class in creating the Europeans' impressions. In the novel the anthropologist Shrobenius (a lampooning of Leo Frobenius) relies on Saif to collect information about native life, but Ouologuem shows Saif inventing "facts" on Africa to cater to Shrobenius's whims (87, 94). Through Shrobenius, Ouologuem indicts negritude's naïveté in building its notions of an African past on Frobenius's ideas of an authentically artistic Africanness (see Miller in *Theories*). Ouologuem's attack on anthropology implicates the Africans themselves.[22]

The narrative that accounts for African history as the fall from grace, a process of degradation and corruption after the arrival of the Europeans in Africa, is authored by Shrobenius in the novel. The critique of empire, therefore, is assigned to the European perspective. "It was only when white imperialism," Shrobenius explains, "infiltrated the country with its colonial violence and materialism that this highly civilized people fell abruptly into a state of savagery" (94). This point of view mirrors Saif's own rationale for the source of his authority: the Saif aims disingenuously to restore African civilization. Shrobenius becomes the mouthpiece for a historical narrative that shores up the authority and legitimacy of an African ruling class that is then relegitimated, reempowered. While Shrobenius tries to rid himself of Europe's guilt, he helps perpetuate the legitimacy of Africa's tyrants.

In "The Night of the Giants," Ouologuem locates historical memory as the repressed cultural awareness and identity of individual characters. Raymond-Spartacus Kassoumi, Tambira and Kassoumi's son, represents the new generation of Western-educated Africans whose origins are in the *négraille*. He has a vision whilst he is dislocated and homesick in Paris that awakens him to a sense of history beyond his own victimization. First he sees in a vision of remembrance (similar to those that Azaro is susceptible in

Okri's *The Famished Road*) life in Africa in the heyday of the slave trade: "he saw ships, he saw through holes in the sky, slaves going to work, women being sold, children being flung into the water, priests, soldiers in armor, men in chains, oarsmen; he saw slave traders and their niggertrash." Then the vision is interrupted by an awareness from the "depths of forgetfulness," a feeling of "delirium," followed by "cries rising to the surface of that muddy water in which his memory of famous names and places he knew, recognized, and understood itself" (156). Raymond finds the "profound meaning of his own destruction"—by which he is referring to his homosexuality. The historical here informs the personal; a reconciliation occurs between Raymond's acquired culture and his African identity marked, in his memory's recognition of those things he had learned, famous places and people.

Yet there is a troubling way in which Raymond, despite the internal focalization of this passage, remains outside himself and his own insight. His memory thinks and feels, not the whole of him. Rendered visually as a scene of recognition, Raymond's experience remains unassimilated, external. He relates to the vision as a witness, moved by what he sees but in the end separate from it. Through this process he understands "the profound meaning of his own destruction," thus complicating the act of witness that is here an act against the self. The full implications of Raymond's self-destruction are revealed after his return to Africa, when his participation in the transition to independence incorporates him as part of the political machinery of the Saif.

As an example of a Fanonian "native intellectual," Raymond is caught in a double bind. He is also the character whose biography brings him closest to Ouologuem himself, but Ouologuem wants to position himself a step beyond Raymond. Tragically, Raymond's memory does not belong to himself; determined through historical processes beyond his control, he gives expression to their destructive impact on his self. Yet Ouologuem aspires to break out of this determinism; he wants to occupy the line of that consciousness of history (to deploy Foucault's terminology) in his transgressive direction to break out of the native intellectual's double bind. Indeed, Raymond's experience in Paris echoes a subgenre of African fiction, the narrative of education in the European metropolis (the student usually has a romantic entanglement with a white woman) of which Maran's *Un Homme pareil aux autres* is a paradigmatic text. This is the novel that Fanon discusses at length in *Black Skin, White Masks* to explain the native intellectual's psychology as an abandoned child. Ouologuem rejects the vantage point of this psychological drama as a place from which to do history.

As an African novelist proposing to write a true history of an invented African kingdom, Ouologuem draws attention to the difficulty of disengaging from existing plots. By parodying the existing plots as pornographic excess, Ouologuem sets up a transgressive poetics that highlights anew the limits of the existing discourses about Africa. His irony attacks both sides of a historically constituted opposition, establishing transgression as a means to transcend the interdependence of the opposing sides in the Manichaean conflict of colonialism.

Fanon described the colonial situation as unequivocally Manichaean and predicted that its resolution had to be violent. The native, according to Fanon, emerges as a subject only at the moment of his resistance, making his history possible through resistance:

> The settler makes history and is conscious of making it. And because he constantly refers to the history of his mother country, he clearly indicates that he himself is the extension of that mother country. Thus the history which he writes is not the history of the country which he plunders but the history of his own nation. . . .
>
> The immobility to which the native is condemned can only be called into question if the native decides to put an end to the history of colonization—the history of pillage—and to bring into existence the history of the nation—the history of decolonization. *(The Wretched of the Earth 51)*

Decolonization is the point of departure for history from the native's point of view. More recently Edward Said has posited the "native point of view" as a position in continuing resistance to the "discipline and praxis of anthropology" ("Representing the Colonized" 219). But the unifying point of resistance that Said appeals for is resisted by some postcolonial writers. The problem for Ouologuem is that the space of opposition, the rhetorical position of the "native point of view," has been usurped, and the usurpers' stories are indeed unreliable because they are generated to safeguard the usurpers' own interests.

It has been an assumption of my reading so far that Ouologuem's political engagement is identifiable, that he writes from the point of view of the dispossessed and that there is thus a closer affinity between what he does and Said's contention, despite the rejection of the oppositional stance. Ouologuem's destabilizing transgressive poetics and his molestation of the reader (a reader who, as the *TLS* review demonstrated, stands in a similar way in relation to the text as Shrobenius does to Africa) aim at an active engagement with other points of view instead of occupying a space of unilateral opposition. For Ouologuem, history does not move through dialectical oppositions but through a process of assimilations and adoptions that implicate and sully those who claim it.

Transgression destabilizes by producing multiple engagements. As I have noted earlier, it does not demarcate a space as such, nor does it define a new subject position for the author. Instead, it destabilizes the boundaries that are in place.

In the last chapter ("Dawn"), the narrator disappears until the final two paragraphs, where he returns to address the issue of historical memory:

> Often, it is true, the soul desires to dream the echo of happiness, an echo that has no past. [*Souvent il est vrai, l'âme veut rêver l'écho sans passé du bonheur.*] But projected into the world, one cannot help recalling that Saif, mourned three million times, is forever born to history beneath the hot ashes of more than thirty African republics. *(181–2)*

This is an injunction to the reader to remember because forgetfulness leads to the repetition of past violence. The Saif's legacy is constantly present, and it is implied, therefore, that resistance to it must be constantly renewed. In the absence of a narrator for most of the last chapter, we are confronted with a decentered text that approximates in its form the decentering of history that Ouologuem has been enacting all along. The narrator's reemergence at the very end identifies history with a constant effort to remember against the desire to forget.

Paul Veyne has argued that forgetfulness comes to us more naturally than a conscious historical engagement. In a passage from *Writing History* that introduces the metaphor of the road for history, Veyne distinguishes between man's historicity and the practice of history:

> For man is so naturally historical that he cannot distinguish the beginning of what comes to him from the past. With that, he is not naturally

historiographical; this body of knowledge is less a treasure of memories than a stage reached. He treats a piece of land or a custom without any more thought than if it were a bit of nature. *Historicity means only that man is always at some stage of his road, that he can only go from the point he has reached, and that he finds it very natural to be at the stage of his cultural way.* Action has no need to know the genesis of the recipes, tools, and customs that it uses. Certainly, if we are geometers, we belong, said Husserl, to the community of geometers past and future; but Husserl also said that the sense of cultural works "formed a sediment"; that, far from the present referring to the past, it was the past that had to be "reactivated" in order to be alive and present.   *(73, emphasis added)*

So historicity is to be distinguished from the historiographical, and the historiographical (the writing and narrating of history) is the process bound up with conscious remembrance. Historiography is for Veyne a critical enterprise that meets with resistances and impediments, a process that needs constant vigilance to remain vital. This is the struggle that the closing of Ouologuem's novel calls up. Okri's *The Famished Road*, on the other hand, exploits the imagery of the road of man's historicity as what Foucault called the space of the line, the limit that transgression makes conscious in an effort to combat the collective forgetfulness that has shaped postcolonial nationalisms.

⁛

CHAPTER SIX

Temporality and the Geographies of the Nation: "The Future Present" in *The Famished Road*

The violence and political instability of postindependence Africa indicates the failure of nationalisms, but it has also created a history of nationalisms, conflicting and contested narratives of what has happened since independence and of what defines African nations today. Novelists have engaged insightfully with the problem of nation, and Nigeria perhaps more than any other affords us with a sustained novelistic discussion of the nation. Dubbed "the trouble with Nigeria" (the title of Achebe's political diatribe of 1983), the ongoing discussion about Nigerian nationalism has produced, most important, Wole Soyinka's *The Interpreters* (1965) and *Season of Anomy* (1973), Achebe's *Man of the People* (1966) and *Anthills of the Savannah* (1987), Buchi Emecheta's *Destination Biafra* (1982), Ken Saro-Wiwa's *Sozaboy: A Novel in Rotten English* (1985), and Ben Okri's *The Famished Road* (1991). A pattern emerges from this brief list of the most influential works: a flourish of novels exploring national questions in the mid-sixties before the Nigerian civil war and then a renewed focus on nationalism in the 1980s.[1]

It is the most recent group of novels that interests me. Much like the "condition of England" novels of the 1840s, which helped shape public debate but also established important historiographical and narrative paradigms for England, these Nigerian novels that treat the "trouble with Nigeria" are dissenting from official narratives of nationalism while also recommitting to the nation, a nation reshaping in postindependence.

Out of this group of novels, Okri's fantastic narrative paradoxically fits most closely the rubric of the classical, nineteenth-century historical novel. Although Okri's fantastic is a reinvigorated realism, it is the historical setting that distinguishes this novel. Set in 1950s Nigeria (forty-plus years before the time of its composition), *The Famished Road* revisits the recent past much like Walter Scott's *Waverley, Or 'Tis Sixty Years Since*, in a conventional gesture that invites an analysis of the author's present in view of the decade of the 1950s that gave birth to independence. With the same gesture Okri also revisits the first prolific period of Nigerian literature in English, resuscitating, with a difference—a sharp political consciousness—the fantastic, wandering tales of Amos Tutuola, while also rewriting the social consciousness novels of Cyprian Ekwensi by focusing not on metropolitan Lagos but on an unnamed provincial town. Furthermore, Okri renews Achebe's historical project from *Things Fall Apart* and *Arrow of God*, which are also set fifty years or so before the author's time. But the differences in execution, of course, are many: Okri's first-person narration, the absence of place-names, the surreal settings and magical actions. The world of the characters is also different in a concrete way: the basic material security enjoyed by Achebe's characters is completely gone in Okri's novel. All these differences mark the new perspective of a postindependence author.

Geography is a recurrent preoccupation in the novels on the trouble with Nigeria. Achebe's *Anthills of the Savannah* posits this problem paradigmatically. In a key scene in the novel, Chris escapes from the city to his native province in order to save his life. In this journey in the midst of political crisis, he becomes newly aware of the nation, not as a problem of the state and of governance but as a geographical entity first and foremost whose logic then needs to find expression in a system of governance:

A few kilometers north of Agbata there was a fairly long bridge over a completely dry river-bed and beyond it a huge sign-board saying: WEL-COME TO SOUTH ABAZON. It was amazing, thought Chris, how provincial boundaries drawn by all accounts quite arbitrarily by the British fifty years ago and more sometimes coincided so completely with reality. Be-yond the dried up river there was hardly a yard of transition; you drove straight into scrubland which two years without rain had virtually turned to desert.   *(193)*

What is real here is geography; the landscape delineates the border with all its implications for governance and history. As Chris contemplates the arbitrari-ness of the British division of the land, an arbitrariness that ignored the Africans' presence on their own land, he also recognizes that these divisions make the land newly readable. It is impossible at this point to remove the boundary from Chris's consciousness of the place. If one of colonialism's legacies was to demarcate land, then Chris is recognizing that what was in one context an arbitrary act was in another an act of reading whose logic emerges when Chris revisits the familiar landscape as land denuded of history.

Chris not only discovers the British reading of the land. He discovers the realism of Ikem's prose poem "Pillar of Fire: A Hymn to the Sun," in which the anthills of Abazon are described as the kernels of history. Achebe's nar-rator describes Chris's discovery: "Perhaps it was seeing the anthills in the scorched landscape that set him off revealing in details he had not before experienced how the searing accuracy of the poet's eye was primed not on fancy but fact" (194). The landscape mediates Chris and Ikem's divergent understandings and creates a consensual imaginary from which a national consciousness could emerge. Ikem writes the poem out of his remembrance of a place; Chris understands the poem fully only after seeing the place again. Furthermore, as a result of his reading, Chris also understands the place in new way. In this neat manner Achebe makes a powerful argument for the political relevance of art, which, even when highly imaginative, is al-ways grounded in reality ("not on fancy but fact").

The central question regarding geography's role in a historiographical project asks, where does history fit between geography—a set of boundaries that delimits a varied terrain and forces a coherence over it—and state pol-itics, the pressing necessity of governance? Is history, as Neil ten Kortenaar argues for *Anthills of the Savannah,* invented anew to make sense of geographical boundaries and forge a nation?[2] Or must it be accountable for the incoherences of real circumstances? Isn't a responsible and enlightening history one that unmasks myths, that strives to elaborate the most complex and inclusive plots? In such a project, geography is not simply a set of confining boundaries but increasingly a storytelling paradigm for laying out contiguous narratives that suggest rather than force coherence from a multiplicity of places and their points of contact.

The naive narrator of Saro-Wiwa's *Sozaboy* discovers something similar to this paradigm. In his unheroic and ultimately unsuccessful Odyssean return home from war, he reverses the sequential travel from village to village that marked his departure for war. On his way to war each new place was genuinely new to him since he had never traveled. Each place was also marked by its potential enemy status, an artificial difference generated out of the competing nationalisms of the Biafran conflict. On his return the places are all the same, not the same as before the war but the same in their devastation. The ruinous effects of war have made the demarcations of village and region meaningless, re-creating an uncannily homogeneous landscape out of violence. "I will not allow anybody to tell me that this is enemy and the other one is not enemy," he decides (139). Sozaboy thus articulates a nonsectarian consciousness, and there is a glimpse in Sozaboy's understanding of the potential for a real nation to be born out of this war.

But Saro-Wiwa is not an optimist. Sozaboy's deconstruction of the term *enemy* follows the failed recognition scene in which Sozaboy, having returned to his devastated home village of Dukana that now looks like all the other devastated villages (129), announces himself to his friends in hiding, " 'Duzia, I am Sozaboy,' I said." Duzia's disappointing reply is "If you want to kill me, do it quick quick, no wasting time" (130). Duzia not only fails to recognize his friend, he fails to recognize a soldier from his side of the conflict. All soldiers are enemies of the people. When he is eventually recognized, Sozaboy is believed to be a ghost returned from the dead. The problem of recognition here is accentuated by the fact that Sozaboy has no name; he announces himself as "soldierboy," and his anonymity destabilizes his identity so that he is what others see him as. Sozaboy joined the war out of ignorance, and the understanding he gained was the consciousness of his complete powerlessness, marked most emphatically by his homelessness at the end of the novel: "[the war] have made me like person wey get leprosy because I have no town again. . . . I will just run and run and run and run and run" (181). Sozaboy is homeless for two reasons: he is shunned because he is an ex-soldier, and his home village was completely destroyed and deserted, so he has no place to return to. Thoroughly uprooted, Sozaboy belongs nowhere until the history of the Biafran conflict is claimed. Saro-Wiwa's novel contributes to this project of claiming history. By producing the narrative of Sozaboy's discovery of his powerlessness, Saro-Wiwa reclaims the experience of many that is denied in the postwar national consciousness. The eloquence and moving emotional immediacy of Sozaboy's storytelling lays claim to the ideals of nationalism betrayed.

Anthills of the Savannah and *Sozaboy* are very different novels aesthetically and politically. Yet their authors both turn to the landscape of Nigeria to create new narrative space for a reexamination of the nation. *The Famished Road* pushes this possibility to an extreme, using descriptions of landscape as a cinematic screen on which to project unfolding images that hanker for emplotment. Deploying a narrator who belongs somewhere in between Achebe's elites and Saro-Wiwa's illiterate soldier (Azaro belongs to the downtrodden but is educated and highly literate), Okri attempts to find a creative solution to the divisions that have threatened the implosion of postcolonial Nigerian society and thus to create a national narrative through the mediating figure of Azaro.

When *The Famished Road* was awarded the Booker Prize in 1991, it was immediately characterized by reviewers as an allegory for the emergence of a nation.[3] Although Okri's fantastic tale invites an allegorical interpretation, the identification of its protagonist's childhood narrative with Nigeria's national emergence opens up as many interpretive problems as it solves. But the problems are not Okri's alone. As Basil Davidson puts it, colonialism systematically eradicated indigenous political systems in Africa and set the stage for the emergence of "modern" states in a violently created historical vacuum (48–49). Okri sets *The Famished Road* in the years immediately before independence to describe the creation of this vacuum, the consequences of which are examined directly in Achebe's and Saro-Wiwa's novels.

From her independence in 1960, Nigeria has been in continuous danger of dissolution. Emerging from what Crawford Young has explained as the

British belief in the "higher viability of larger sovereign units" at independence (240), Nigeria is in the most literal sense an invented nation, a federated, multiethnic state bound by territorial borders that make geographical but not cultural or historical sense—except in terms of the record of British imperialism. Her boundaries at independence had been established by the British in 1914, when they consolidated the protectorates of Northern and Southern Nigeria into one colony under the governorship of Frederick Lugard. The name *Nigeria* was invented by a London *Times* journalist on January 8, 1897, as a less cumbersome and more convenient name for the "Royal Niger Company Territories" (Coleman 41–44). Thus Obafemi Awolowo noted in *Path to Nigerian Freedom* (1947): "Nigeria is not a nation. It is a mere geographical expression. There are no 'Nigerians' in the same sense as there are 'English,' 'Welsh,' or 'French.' The word 'Nigerian' is merely the distinctive appellation to distinguish those who live within the boundaries of Nigeria from those who do not" (47–48). Territory, not nationality, demarcated Nigeria. The colonial and postcolonial state were both lacking one of the primary elements of legitimation, a coherent nationalist ideology (Young 32).

In the late 1930s, when demands for self-government became current, Nigerians were struggling not so much as nationalists but as Africans resisting humiliating, colonialist rule. For example, Nnamdi Azikiwe (who became the first president of the Federal Republic of Nigeria) presented his influential *Renascent Africa* as an anticolonialist tract that defined the conflict in racial terms and was shaped by ideas of Black Nationalism that Azikiwe had been exposed to during his stay in the United States from 1925–1934. A meaningful concept of the nation has been struggling to emerge in the constant negotiation of the conflicting ideals of Nigerian unity and federalism since independence. Internal boundaries, therefore, have been the enduring bone of contention. Nigeria was divided into three governing regions by the British in preparation for self-government in 1954 (the Lyttleton Constitution). Then, in 1967, under General Gowon's regime and on the eve of civil war, Nigeria was divided into twelve regions. In 1976 it was further divided into nineteen regions. The defeat of Biafra's bid for independence in the civil war of 1967–1970 was largely perceived as a victory for national unity, yet Nigerians are still wondering in the 1990s, "Will Nigeria survive?" (Olukushi and Agbu 74–75).

Theories of nationalism have been mostly diachronic, explaining the emergence of nations as histories or fictions but in either case as narratives of time and development against which is contrasted an essential, unchanging, and ahistorical notion of a people, an ethnicity. Benedict Anderson explains eloquently the pervasiveness and power of nationalist ideologies as a result of the concept's transportability: a sense of nation, in Anderson's theory, can be carried over, shared pervasively by an *imagined community* in either a diasporic or settled situation because it is essentially a powerful fiction of belief and depends less on real historical circumstances than it does on a convincing imaginative narrative that creates and then fosters "a deep horizontal comradeship" (16).

While Anderson, writing in 1983, galvanized our thinking about nationalism precisely because he freed the discourse of nation from fixed geographical borders and stressed the narrative elements of its ideology, he was still thinking of nationalism primarily as a liberationalist tool, believing in its potential to set people free in a variety of flexibly defined national entities. Yet in the case of the African postcolonial states, we are presented with the repeated and widespread failure of national narratives that do not hold, even if they have been created in large part by the dynamics of language and print culture that Anderson so clearly elucidates (see especially 122). Partha Chatterjee, writing from the perspective of the third world and responding sympathetically to Anderson's insistence on the inventedness of nation, sees these failures as a result of the "derivativeness" of nationalist discourse. For Chatterjee, it is a borrowed, ill-fitting story that does not explain the past of postcolonial nations but recasts them as versions of European nations (19–22).

Indeed, we need once again to focus on the relation between territory and nation, to reanchor our examination of nationalism in terms of geographical boundaries and, consequently, the relation between state power and nation. Young has explored this conjunction of issues fruitfully in his study of the colonial state, and he sketched the implications of this history for the postcolonial state. He usefully refocuses the problem of nationalism on the artificially created borders of postcolonial states. But between Anderson and Young there is room to think some more about the narrative problem of nation, not only diachronically as emergence, progress, and development but synchronically as place. Okri's contribution is to address the nation as a problem of place and to try to invent a way of narrating place that addresses the synchronicity through which we experience place historically. He does so by focusing on the synchronic space of memory as the revelation of contiguous and competing spaces that resist narratives of nation. Indeed, Okri speaks of nation indirectly through the problem of forgetfulness. He reconfigures a resistant sense of nation by confronting the repression of history in nationalist discourse. If forgetfulness "constitutes the *beginning* of the nation's narrative" according to Homi Bhabha ("DissemiNation" 310), then Okri's novel, by attacking forgetfulness, is about the lived, historical resistance to nationhood. The nation being forged by Nigerians since independence is a history to which Nigerians must lay claim.

Bhabha, who has a particularly important place in the discussion of nation as Bakhtinian chronotope, attempts to rehabilitate the nation as a liberationist tool by uncovering its liminality and what he names its duplicity, a "double time" and "spatial disjunction" (297). He stresses the "temporality of representation" (292) as an added, disruptive temporality that ultimately provides discursive space for subaltern voices in opposition to historicism. But this temporality is enabled through the forgetfulness of nationalist discourse ("the beginning of the nation's narrative"), precisely Okri's target. Bhabha analyzes the nation as a chronotope, a narrative intersection of time and space determinants. Using Bakhtin as a bridge between Bhabha and Okri, I argue that Okri, by rejecting liminality in favor of transgression, stages a fictional refutation of Bhabha's theoretical elaborations and restates with passion the need for a commitment to historicism.

There has been a tendency in the critique of Africanist discourses, and in postcolonial theory in general, to be suspicious and ultimately dismissive of historicism as a method of knowing the subaltern.[4] Okri cautions his reader against such a position by showing relentlessly the real material and spiritual impoverishment of the Nigerian people as their passage into postmodernity is transacted tragically as a passage out of historical consciousness.

Okri addresses Nigeria's birth in *The Famished Road* through the metaphor of the abiku child—a spirit child, according to Yoruba belief, who returns repeatedly to the same parents only to die over and over in infancy.[5] Azaro, the protagonist, is an abiku child who determines to stay among the living after his second birth; hence he is named after Lazarus who returned from the dead. Azaro's choice of life is contrasted to that of another abiku child in the novel, Ade, who chooses to return to the spirits. Ade explains the analogy between the abiku and the nation: "Our country," he tells Azaro, "is an abiku country. Like the spirit-child, it keeps coming and going. One day it will decide to remain" (478).

The opening sequence of the novel, a birth scene or creation myth in which Azaro breaks into life from the spirit world, articulates a rejection of liminality, of the in-betweenness that is the abiku child's privilege, in favor of the limitations and concreteness of life. "But this time," Azaro explains, "somewhere in the interspace between the spirit world and the Living, I chose to stay. . . . It is terrible to forever remain in-between" (5). The rejection of liminality renders Azaro's emergence into the materiality and concreteness of life as a transgression, a crossing of boundaries: "I was a spirit-child rebelling against the spirits, wanting to live the earth's life and contradictions. . . . I wanted the liberty of limitations, to have to find or create new roads from this one which is so hungry, this road of our refusal to be" (487).

The collective "refusal to be" is the nation's resistance to emergence and refusal of history, against which Azaro's story provides an oppositional—descriptive and visionary—perspective. Once among the living, he compulsively wanders off into what first appear as imaginary landscapes, landscapes he renders increasingly historical.[6] It is Azaro's explorations of the limit dividing the conscious and unconscious, the real and the repressed, that generate the historical perspective in the novel. Nigeria's imminent emergence into independence and nationhood looms as the void beyond the limit.

The simultaneous and contiguous presence of the material and fantastic that is revealed through Azaro's wanderings yields paradoxically a recognizable political reality. Yet Azaro's transgressions must overcome the added problem of historical forgetfulness that distorts the contours of this political reality. Forgetfulness engulfs the political consciousness of the people even as the relics of their political history remain visible around them.

Azaro's ability to see what his countrymen don't see renders the forgetfulness into a historical phenomenon. For example, a riot that breaks out after the distribution of spoiled milk by the "Party of the Rich" is soon forgotten despite the remaining visible traces of its actuality. Although the burnt campaign van of the politicians—the evidence of the riot—is never removed, it soon disappears from sight. Azaro tells us that the memory of the riot receded as the van's visibility, its presence as a relic, was diminished: "nothing was left to identify the vehicle, or to rescue it from forgetfulness. It wasn't long before it vanished from the street, not because it was no longer there, diminishing with each day's sunglare, but because we had stopped noticing it altogether" (155).

The subject of Azaro's account, therefore, is the people's loss of memory of the riot. The passage of time, the surrender to linear temporality, threatens historical memory. Out of fear of this erasure, Okri subverts diachrony and depicts experiences as synchronicity. In the absence of a collective consciousness, the nation's "refusal to be" diachronically through history and as a process over time, synchronicity forges a record of a history of negation, refusal, and repression.

Instead of retrieving history from the past, Azaro "saw a future history in advance" (314). "In the future present" of his wanderings, he sees the construction of modern Nigeria: "All around, in the future present, a mirage of houses was being built, paths and roads crossed and surrounded the forests in tightening circles, unpainted churches and whitewashed walls of mosques sprang up where the forest was thickest" (242). The outlines of this future history collapse back into the narrative present. In this invented synchronicity, the present in Okri's novel is overburdened. His characters live in a present that has no thrust in time: with the future collapsed back onto the present, the present seems to lead (or to have led) nowhere.

The ambiguities of narrative time in *The Famished Road* take a visual form in the fantastic landscapes that Azaro describes. The past is rendered as the postcolonial period that has not yet unfolded at the time of the novel's action. Through this transposition, Okri challenges the reader to remember the history of the postcolonial period and project it as the dialogic background necessary for understanding the "future history" of Azaro's visions. It is here that Okri imaginatively addresses Bhabha's theory of national narrative.

In "DissemiNation: Time, Narrative, and the Margins of the Modern Nation," Bhabha (nodding to Derrida) reads the nation as a "disjunctive temporality," occurring over a "double-time" that renders it heterogeneous.[7] For Bhabha as for Anderson (whom Bhabha cites), the paradox of nationalism lies in the incommensurability of the nation's historical modernity and its claims of antiquity: nations are in actuality new but fashion themselves by inventing ancient pasts. In this rift between new and old, Bhabha finds a heterogeneous space: "the space of modern nation-people is never simply horizontal." "Disjunctive temporality" turns into a "spatial disjunction" (309) as people carry over their identification of home in their migration or dislocation in order to preserve a sense of belonging. Nationalism is always compensatory, and the nation is never immanent but always transposed. In the temporality of the narration, moreover, the immanence of the nation is posited as a fiction. A narrative of wholeness carries within it a consciousness of fragmentation and is necessarily divided against its own intent. As a result, "The [people's] metaphoric movement requires a kind of doubleness in writing; a *temporality of representation* that moves between cultural formations and social processes without a 'centred' causal logic" (293, emphasis added). Bhabha contrasts this temporality as "non-synchronicity" to Anderson's assertion that the nation is invented in a temporal space analogous to the "meanwhile" of novelistic time. For Bhabha the nation is posited in a "break, not simultaneity but a spatial disjunction" (309). To play on Bhabha's own terms, however, it should be said that the narration ("the temporality of representation") also seeks to separate from and obscure the "meanwhile" of the historical in materialist terms.

The "temporality of representation" posited by Bhabha fractures the horizontal space of the modern nation in which time (history) is metaphorized as landscape. Reading Bakhtin against the grain, Bhabha posits the nation as chronotope in order to disjoin considerations of time and place from each other and to suggest that historicism is not the only way in which we express our consciousness of time. The temporality of representation is a distinct moment, a *performative* moment in which the objects of national becoming in the historicist narrative are the " 'subjects' of a process of signification" (297).

Bhabha contrasts the *performative* to the *pedagogic*. The two make up the double time of the nation's narration that need each other but also work at cross-purposes, making the nation into the essentially disjuncted space that Bhabha describes. The pedagogic narrative is historicist; it explains the present as the result of a process of becoming in a "continuist, accumulative temporality" (297). Performance, by contrast, enacts a constant repetition. It is a static assertion of the uniqueness and sameness of the nation, repressing the memory of the nation's violent, disjunctive beginning and creating a space within which the pedagogical invented narrative can be sustained. In the performative, Bhabha locates political agency, "the exercise of power" (296).

Thus for Bhabha, forgetting, not remembering, emerges as the crucial gesture of nationhood:

> It is through this syntax of forgetting—of being obliged to forget—that the problematic identification of a national people becomes visible. . . . To be obliged to forget—in the construction of the nation's present—is not a question of historical memory; it is the construction of a discourse on society that *performs* the problematic totalization of the national will. . . . Being obliged to forget becomes the basis of remembering the nation, peopling it anew, imagining the possibility of other contending and liberating forms of cultural identification.   *(310)*

Bhabha borrows the phrase to "be obliged to forget" from Ernest Renan, whose definition of the nation as "a daily plebiscite" stresses, according to Bhabha, the performative aspect of a constantly renewed will to nationhood that belongs to the present moment and not the past. Thus, "Renan's will is itself the site of a strange forgetting of the history of the nation's past: the violence involved in establishing the nation's writ" (310). The performative enacts the forgetting. But the performative is also potentially subversive. By inventing an alternative (narrative) temporality, the performative always suggests an incommensurate story that disturbs the cohesiveness of the pedagogic, historical narrative.[8]

Okri, however, posits incommensurate spaces rather than temporalities. The dissonance of the modern nation is for Okri a problem of place. The historical as landscape, a metaphor repressed by Bhabha, resurges in *The Famished Road*, although the landscape is now rendered strange, difficult to read.

The liminal etymologically indicates both a temporal and a spatial designation. While its primary meaning in the *Oxford English Dictionary* is a stage in time (for example, adolescence as a time between childhood and adulthood), its secondary meaning designates space, the space on either side of a boundary or the boundary itself. Both these spatial designations associate the liminal with the margin. Bhabha celebrates the "subaltern voice of the people, a minority discourse that speaks betwixt and between times and places," rendering the nation hybrid, decentered, and disjunctive; the margins' irruption at the center causes the phenomenon of dissemiNation (309). The slippage in Bhabha's use of liminality to apply to the "other time of writing" as both time and space shows that the performative is a supplemental space that operates in the absence of an actual authority over a real space. In the history of national emergence, however, it is the incommensurability of spaces that needs to be confronted. The real agon is always over place, home, belonging, as power and authority over an actual space. Okri's juxtaposition of incommensurate spaces in *The Famished Road* dramatizes the Nigerians' loss of authority over their place as a result of the ravages of colonialism and independence in the terms of a prefigured nationalism that has betrayed them in predictable ways.

The notion of prefiguration also plays a role in Bhabha's discussion. The historical narrative of the pedagogic must posit the nation first as an a priori and distinguish it from its others before it can construct the history of its emergence. The agonistic relationship between the pedagogic and performative arises from the imperative to erase the traces of this prefiguration: "In place of the polarity of a prefigurative self-generating nation itself and extrinsic other nations [a polarity set up by the a priori assumed by the pedagogic], the performative introduces a temporality of the 'in-between' through the 'gap' or 'emptiness' of the signifier that punctuates linguistic difference" (299). The liminal here is introduced as the "temporality of the 'in-between.' " This temporality of the in-between, however, creates a new space, a discursive, enunciatory, performative space. Bhabha says, "The barred Nation It/Self, alienated from its eternal self-generation, becomes a liminal form of social representation, a space that is *internally* marked by cultural difference and the heterogeneous histories of contending peoples, antagonistic authorities, and tense cultural localities" (299). In Bhabha's rhetoric the temporality of actual history is rendered secondary (outside the margins of the liminal and in-between) to the events in a discursive, performative space. The constant contest between the pedagogic and the performative renders the national space liminal.

But liminality can also be construed, as Okri sees it, as the suspension of contest. The traces of prefiguration that this contest seeks to erase (explained earlier as the forgetfulness at the birth of the nation) are historical evidence of the borders of a nation that must be reconfigured. Okri's flattened time—synchronicity mapped out as contiguous, incommensurate spaces—gives way to visions that beg for a new organization of the boundaries of the whole.

The fact that Nigeria is never named in *The Famished Road* merits some attention. In this historical novel there are no place-names at all, not even fictional ones. Place is fragmented into distinct spaces—Madame Koto's bar, Azaro's family compound, the forest, the road, the market that do not have place-names. Although the characters belong to a community, as is evident from the cohesiveness of practices and customs that regulate their lives, the community seems to have no memory of its origins, no awareness of its environment or its connection to this environment. The absence of a sense of place and the forgetfulness to which the characters of Okri's novel seem increasingly doomed go hand in hand. Thus the question becomes, what kind of history is possible in the absence of a sense of place?

This is the problem Okri tries to resolve by disturbing the usual correspondence between time and place that is the cornerstone of realist, historical fiction. The combination of spatial and temporal determinants in narrative, Bakhtin's concept of the chronotope or "time-space," acquires a new configuration in Okri's novel. Bakhtin argued that in all literary chronotopes time takes precedence over place.[9] Place metaphorically describes the effects of time, the impact of historical change: "Time, as it were, thickens, takes on flesh, becomes artistically visible; likewise, space becomes charged and responsive to the movements of time, plot and history" (84). Thus Bakhtin praises Balzac for his ability to "see time in space" (247). Houses in the Balzacian text appear as "materialized history"; they are invented as archaelogical sites to be excavated by the narrator, who renders visible in their simultaneity the traces of the past and the newness of the present.

In Okri's novel there is no such compactness, no thickness of time. There is instead a constantly unfolding surface that is contiguous to actual life and remains unfelt except by Azaro. Space is not a metaphor for the passage of time but has overridden the chronotope to become its primary determinant, begging to be recontained through narrative, causality, and historical discourse. To play with Bakhtin's terms, time does not thicken; it flattens into a space whose borders must be renegotiated. Azaro's transgressions are the necessary preamble to the development of a historical consciousness, a synthesis of this accumulative contiguity.

More than any other space, the road expresses Okri's sense of historical contest. Azaro's relation to the road is one of constant struggle. On the road he witnesses an unstable reality under continuous transformation. Objects, both natural and man-made, are imbued with spirit, and their transformative powers keep the narrator's point of view in constant motion. Azaro confesses about one of his wanderings:

> The roads seemed to me to have a cruel and infinite imagination. All the roads multiplied, reproducing themselves, subdividing themselves, turning in on themselves, like snakes, tails in their mouths, twisting themselves into labyrinths. The road was the worst hallucination of them all, leading towards home and then away from it, without end, with too many signs, and no directions. The road became my torment, my aimless pilgrimage, and I found myself merely walking to discover where all the roads lead to, where they end. *(114–15)*

This description is full of paradoxes. The road has none of the characteristics of a road except the name. It leads nowhere, multiplies uncontrollably, has no stable direction or surface.

The road always seems to carry a double meaning. It is both destiny and historical possibility. In Okri's novel, it represents the folkloric, mythic belief in the famished road and its god that needs to be fed.[10] It also represents the historical fact of economic development and the sacrifices made to achieve this. The forest is constantly receding because of the construction of the road. The road increasingly takes on the burden of representing history, a telos, a resolution of paradoxes. In another incident, Azaro hallucinates that he is guided on the road by a three-headed spirit and has the following conversation:

"Are we travelling this road to the end?"

"Yes," the spirit said, walking as if distance meant nothing.

"But you said the road has no end."

"That's true," said the spirit.

"How can it be true?"

"From a certain point of view the universe seems to be composed of paradoxes. But everything resolves. That is the function of contradiction."

"I don't understand."

"When you can see everything from every imaginable point of view you might begin to understand."

"Can you?"

"No." *(327)*

History is contested ground, a constant unfolding of contradictory forces that will end only when all points of view are subsumed into one consciousness. The end of the road is the end of history. Okri's postcolonial perspective is of a world where the paradigms of historicity imposed on Africa by the Western world have been used up. Instead we emerge into a constant presentness, which has no organization and begs for the invention of a new historical paradigm. Azaro's experiences on the road create sequences of endlessly unfolding visualizations that resist totalization and closure. His transgressive wanderings into fantastic landscapes present a constant challenge to the encroaching forgetfulness.

In language that parodies various paradigms of Western historicism (most notably the Hegelian dialectic, or even a Marxist belief in the inevitably progressive course of history), Okri presents the explanations of the road (of history) as fundamentally unsatisfactory. We are left once again with the earlier image of a paradoxical road without contours, without shape. How is it recognizable as a road? Here Okri echoes intertextually an extensive body of neo-African literature that records an alternative history of emergence. Moreover, books, historical consciousness, and political agency become increasingly linked in the novel, a theme that culminates (as I will show later) in Azaro's father's bid to power and his tragic demise.

The road recurs frequently in African fiction as a symbol of the European intrusion, of colonial conquest, and of the imposition of progressive narratives of history in which the nation emerges as a telos.[11] Independence is a beginning and an end. Okri's novel echoes other works in which the building of a road is both literally a representation of actual events (colonialism was experienced as the building of roads) and metaphorically the symbol for colonialism's fragmentation of traditional cultures and communities. The road bifurcates, divides, and destroys. Ousmane Sembène's novella *Vehi Ciosane* tells such a story: the prospect of a road being built to pass through a village, physically dividing it, destroys the community, which is subsequently dispersed. The child born out of this conflict is a child of incest (the chief of the village fathers a child with his daughter). In Sembène's *God's Bits of Wood* the railroad becomes the site of resistance. In Achebe's *Arrow of God* the conflict that leads to the novel's negative resolution occurs at a construction site for a new road. Ezeulu's son is helping the British build a road, and his defiance of their authority eventually leads to his death. Wole Soyinka has repeatedly resorted to the road for its mythical as well as its contemporary significance. Moreover, his autobiographical *Aké* includes an episode strikingly similar to Azaro's wanderings, the episode where the young Wole leaves the compound walls and follows a band to the market town, where he gets lost.[12]

The road becomes quite literally a text that Azaro must interpret: "I walked on the dissolving streets and among the terrestrial gushes. The air was full of riddles. I walked through books and months and forgotten histories" (307). Wandering is an allegory for reading. Bakhtin treats the road as a recognizable chronotope (in relation to the picaresque novel and its antecedents) and emphasizes the road's capacity to make visible the "sociohistorical heterogeneity of one's own country" (245). But the hero who travels on the road, according to Bakhtin, occupies a privileged space for observation since the scene of ordinary life unfolds on the edges of the road as he passes through. By contrast Azaro sees not only what is on the edges of the road but the road itself, and its shape and contours lose definition. Derrida has also turned to the image of the road for its capacity to illustrate how a process of differentiation unfolds. For Derrida the road is a metaphor for writing: the violent inscription of difference that ruptures the homogeneity of a particular space (*Of Grammatology* 107–8). What Azaro sees at times, however, is the reversal of these processes of history for Bakhtin and writing for Derrida. He sees (as posited by Okri's fiction and thus by implication) the repression, obstruction, and inhibition of meaning.

The forest as a primeval scene is the antithesis to the road, yet it contains a memory of the historical that reveals itself to Azaro in various daydreams. In one such daydream, Azaro wanders into the eyes of a duiker (an antelope) to find himself in "a yellow forest" in which primeval images are everywhere. The visibility of history has been attained through the retrieval of a primeval language, before the sign, in which there is no discontinuity between signifiers and signifieds: "I saw the forms of serene ancestors, men and women for whom the stars were both words and gods, for whom the world and the sky and the earth were a vast language of dreams and omens" (456). From here Azaro wanders over historical time, which is laid out spatially. The fantastic landscape unfolds as Azaro runs all the way to the Atlantic coast and sees the "ghost ships of centuries arriv[ing] endlessly on the shores" (457).

When he physically enters the space of the fantastic, Azaro himself experiences the world as "both words and gods," symbols and meaning. The spatial contiguity of the real and the imaginary in the novel (Azaro wanders physically from one into the other) metaphorically enacts the primeval language found in the antelope daydream. Moreover, while these experiences have a distinct place in the narrative time of the novel, they are curiously disengaged from historical time: the reality depicted here is not validated by any other characters in the novel, despite the fact that what Azaro sees often pertains to changes in Nigeria on the eve of independence. At the very beginning of the novel he witnesses the building of the road: "The clearing was the beginning of an expressway. Building companies had levelled the trees. In places the earth was red" (16). This image recurs throughout the novel, but no other character gives witness to this type of economic development. This is especially baffling in view of the fact that Azaro's father is a manual laborer; we never learn what is being done at the site where he works.

Azaro's visions allow him to see change as process. The building of the road unfolds progressively: "Steadily over days and months, the paths had been widening. Bushes were being burnt, tall grasses cleared, tree stumps uprooted. The area was changing" (104). Aside from Azaro, no one seems aware of these changes. The discontinuity between the novel's real and visionary worlds derives from Okri's examination of the notion of forgetfulness. The real, waking life is one of forgetfulness. It unfolds as a progressive alienation from past events, even as the actions in the novel amass a history of their own: several riots, the election campaigns, the persecution of the photographer, events in the market. No one consciously connects these events to each other to form a meaningful sequence. The photographer provides some temporary records of the riots, but the strictly visual nature of the evidence he can provide limits its usefulness. With the pictures destroyed and the photographer gone, the events recede from the collective consciousness. Thus the violence of the night of vengeance by the Party of the Rich is forgotten: "because the photographer hadn't been there to record what had happened that night, nothing of the events appeared in the newspapers. It was as if the events were never real" (182–83). The dubious authority of photography to license the real is a weak surrogate here for literacy. The real cause of forgetfulness increasingly appears to be illiteracy.

There is a sense in the novel that none of the external spaces (the road, the forest, the market) can be fully explained without taking into account the energies that are cooped up in the interior spaces of Madame Koto's bar and Azaro's home. In these spaces (one public and one private) dialectically opposed versions of the nation are being formed. Madame Koto's monstrous pregnancy (which never comes to term) is another allegory for the birth (or rather the botched birth) of a nation. A figure who represents both tradition and Western influences (liquor, technology, capitalistic exploitation), Madame Koto is a satire of the worst influences shaping the emergent Nigeria. As Madame Koto's stature in the novel increases, she becomes more recognizable as a symbol of colonialism, an amalgamation of invented traditions and Western civilization and know-how.

First Madame Koto takes on the shape of a traditional chief, but tradition is clearly not authenticity here. She appears as the type of chief invented and authorized by "indirect rule" and whose power is resented by the indigenous people:

> She painted her fingernails red. Her eyelashes became more defined. She wore lipstick. She wore high-heeled shoes and moved with an increasingly pronounced limp, walking stick always in hand. She began to resemble a great old chief from ancient times, a reincarnation of splendour and power and clannish might. . . . People glared at her hatefully when she went past.   *(374)*

She also becomes associated with the most extreme witchcraft, including human sacrifices. All of this, combined with her business success and ever-expanding wealth, make her a formidable, monstrous figure representing the material wealth and cultural distortions of this emerging nation (374–75). At her bar, men turn into monsters, drinking and fighting.

Azaro's home, on the other hand, becomes symbolic of the impoverishment and exploitation of the people: small, claustrophobic, unhealthy, plagued with a leaking roof and overrun with bugs and rats, it is never an adequate "home." Always out of control and essentially unsettled (the family's belongings have simply been dumped inside, never arranged [32]), the compound becomes a metaphor for the psychological state of its inhabitants, the dispossessed and dislocated who have no energy to examine the dilapidation of the actual structure nor to redress its unhomeliness (10–11).

From this household, however, will spring resistance. Thus, compared to the bar, Azaro's home is invested with a certain hopefulness. From here will emerge a challenge to both traditional and modern authorities that tragically (as represented by Azaro's father) remains largely unheeded. When the father awakens to political consciousness, his message makes sense but has no impact:

> "THINK DIFFERENTLY," he shouted, "AND YOU WILL CHANGE THE WORLD."
> No one heard him.
> "REMEMBER HOW FREE YOU ARE," he bellowed, "AND YOU WILL TRANSFORM YOUR HUNGER INTO POWER!"
>
> *(419–20)*

For most of the novel, the suppression of memory is a result of spatial fragmentation and discontinuity. Okri's narrative problem is how to invent a new logic of causality and contingency in the traumatic absence of memory. Indeed, narrative emerges in the end of the novel when Azaro narrates to his father the repressed memory of his boxing victory against Yellow Jaguar. This victory is the beginning of the father's political defiance: he defeats the past and learns defiance. But, because his defiance is impotent, it is presented as a kind of madness, although Okri clearly treats the father as tragic and dignified.

The father's boxing match with Yellow Jaguar is a uniquely privileged moment in the text because it forges the two realms of the novel: the mixed realm of Azaro's sensibility and his community's reality. In this episode father and son share the same unreality. The father boxes with a fantastic creature who identifies himself as Yellow Jaguar, a champion boxer returned from the dead. He receives real injuries from the fight, and his recovery is presented by Okri as a rebirth. Because of his father's amnesia, Azaro must recount the events of the fight to his father. It is, therefore, Azaro's retelling of the events, the history of the fight, that convinces the father of what he has accomplished. This history gives Azaro's father a new confidence in his own strength, which then brings about his defiance of authority and his political activism. The tale of his "epic battle with Yellow Jaguar" (363) engenders a rebirth into resistance. Azaro serves as his father's memory. Without history there is no reality, only self-erasure and forgetfulness.

The tragedy of Azaro's father lies in his illiteracy; physical force is his only means to gain the political authority he needs to realize his ambitions as leader of the Party of the Beggars (a party he invents as an alternative to the corrupt and exploitative parties of the Rich and Poor). Boxing, in this instance, also represents an impoverishment of tradition. Although a traditional means through which men win authority, boxing here extends the father's identification with brute force and physical labor and ties him to the silenced history of slavery and domination. As Achille Mbembe has explained, this is a history that must be overcome, deconstructed, in order for there to be a lessened reliance on authoritarian means of asserting political will (100, 105–7). Azaro's father is acting out this history of defeat, and without literacy, he is doomed to repeat it. In *The Famished Road* boxing reveals the vulnerability of the people to physical exploitation. Although the father's message is current and relevant, his means of struggle are antiquated and irrelevant, and destined to fail him.

With the money he earns boxing, the father begins to buy books compulsively even though he cannot read. Azaro, therefore, reads to his father, learning along with him from this vast array of texts:

> He bought books on philosophy, politics, anatomy, science, astrology, Chinese medicine. He bought the Greek and Roman classics. He became fascinated by the Bible. Books on the cabbala intrigued him. He fell in love with the *Arabian Nights*. He listened with eyes shut to the strange words of classical Spanish love poetry and retellings of the lives of Shaka the Zulu and Sundiata the Great. He insisted that I read something to him all the time. *(409)*

Tragically, his efforts throw him further out of sync with his community, and eventually he becomes a clown, a politically irrelevant buffoon. There is no correlation between the father's transcendent impulse to a worldly position—a will to political power through literacy—and the particular historical struggle in which he must involve himself and in which he seems already defeated. A symbol of the disenfranchisement of the people in the decolonization process, Azaro's father is also a figure of transition, belonging incompletely to his moment while echoing the past and prefiguring the future.

The reader, guided by Azaro's sympathetic narration, knows to take the father's dreams and hallucinations seriously: they represent a frustrated awakening to history, the consciousness of which is carried by Azaro, the witness of his father's efforts who acquires a surrogate education in the process. If the father is a more apt allegorical figure for the historical Nigerian people, then Azaro is an idealized version of the people's historian: a sympathetic witness whose imagination and sensibilities record a history that recognizes potential and hope in the most dismal of situations.

Earlier, at the scene of the vengeance of the Party of the Rich where the people are violently attacked, Azaro records a history of despair in a such a way as to leave it open for regeneration through historical memory:

> The hosts of the dead descended into the open bleeding mouth of the earth. I saw them from the van. I watched the world dissolving into a delirium of stories. The dead descended into the forgetfulness of our blue memories, with their indigo eyes and their silver glances. . . . We did not celebrate our resistance. We knew that the troubles were incomplete, that the reprisals had been deferred to another night, when we would have forgotten.   *(182)*

Azaro is a witness, and the witness's voice carries the past into the present. The bleeding earth is rendered as a sacrificial landscape. Okri is railing against the repression of the historical that had laid the groundwork for colonialism. A historical consciousness, therefore, would recognize the continuity that links precolonial, colonial, and postindependence history, a continuity that begs to be confronted but is constantly fractured, hidden, made opaque. If Madame Koto had become a symbol of these repressions in her increasing deformity, then her "opacity" to those around her expresses metaphorically the effects of historical forgetfulness.[13]

In the incident of the boxing match against Yellow Jaguar, the father and Azaro become prophetically aware of the postindependence violence and civil strife. The novel presents a construction of postindependence history from the perspective of a moment that preceded it. Because of this narrative prefiguration, history is experienced as repetition. The collective forgetfulness results from a willingness to accept the premise of repetition: everything becomes the same and recognizable in the same way, which prevents the awareness of change, the consciousness of history. Pre- and postindependence history blend together.

But repetition is also a refusal of history, Azaro explains at the end of the novel. Repetition is the fate of the abiku child who is born many times over only to die in infancy each time, never growing up. When Azaro compares his choice to live with that of Ade's to return to the spirits, he makes the choice the equivalent of an espousal of history rather than a refusal of history. Ade has identified the nation with the condition of the abiku: "Our country is an abiku country. Like the spirit-child, it keeps coming and going" (478). It is within the context of this statement that we must read Azaro's evaluation of his rebellion against the spirit world:

> The spirit-child is an unwilling adventurer into chaos and sunlight, into the dreams of the living and the dead. Things that are not ready, not willing to be born or to become, things for which adequate preparations have been made to sustain their momentous births, things that are not resolved, things bound up with failure and with fear of being, they all keep recurring, keep coming back, and in themselves partake of the spirit-child's condition. They keep coming and going till their time is right. History itself fully demonstrates how things of the world partake of the condition of the spirit-child. . . . There are many nations, civilisations, ideas, half-discoveries, revolutions, loves, art forms, experiments, and historical events that are of this condition and do not know it.   *(487)*

Repetition restates the problem of liminality, a protracted in-betweenness that produces more of the same. But repetition is also largely unconscious, a result of forgetfulness. Consciousness alone can transgress the boundaries set by repetition. Azaro's father's resistance exemplifies an impulse to transcend the limitations of time and place—of other (national) narratives received rather than made. Yet without literacy, this resistance can go nowhere.

In his counternarrative, Okri deconstructs a nation prefigured by the ideology of decolonization as an achieved entity. In planning self-government for their colonial territory, the British viewed independent Nigeria as the endpoint, the fulfillment of a successful civilizing campaign. The nation of Nigeria would be the result, the positive product, of a colonial history.

Margery Perham, writing a dissenting (if admiring) preface to Awolowo's *Path to Nigerian Freedom*, made amply clear that unity into a strong central government is the only condition of nationhood. If Nigeria is not a nation yet as Awolowo claims, then Perham replies, "Britain may for long be required to provide the framework which holds these groups together until they are able to fuse into unity or federation" (14). Independence was to signal the completion of this path to maturity, evidence in and of itself of "fusion." Retrospectively, it is amply clear, as Neil Lazarus has argued, that African nationalists, along with the departing European powers, invested too much in the idea that independence was a true break with the past, a real beginning; this was a willed belief that amounted to a repression of historical consciousness (23). A departure from the novels of disillusion of the late 1960s, *The Famished Road* does not reinvest, as Lazarus argues for those novels, in the messianic hope for the emergence of a true nation. Okri posits the historical nation as a construct of state power from which Nigerians must articulate a dissenting history.

Glancing back to *Anthills of the Savannah* and *Sozaboy*, we can see the importance of localism: without roots, or a home in a particular locality, there can be no stable sense of the whole. And while internal boundaries are being contested, nationalism is a repressive ideology. In *Anthills of the Savannah*, Achebe's characters float. It is a novel that provides only a fleeting opportunity for local identity. Complicit in military rule, the characters fail to save the nation or themselves. *Sozaboy* articulates the power of home by accounting for the devastating effects of its loss. In *The Famished Road*, the most optimistic of these novels, home is saved.[14] Although always on the verge of dissolution and marred by recurring episodes of violence, Azaro's home remains recognizable as a home. However unstable their material conditions, Azaro's family is not uprooted. Moreover, Azaro's wanderings repeatedly punctuate the desire to return home.

Afterword

The project of *Claiming History* could be fairly characterized as literary history. But it also looks at the history in literature, and indeed uses that history to develop its arguments about reclamation, resistance, transgression. Reclamation, claiming that which has been taken away, aptly describes what drives the authors studied here. Laying claim to their point of view in history, Maran, Hazoumé, Achebe, Ouologuem, and Okri situate themselves in the midst of an ongoing Africanist discourse, engage with it critically, and then rewrite its narratives. Before independence, resistance usefully defined a point of view that was situated so as to engage the other, the colonizing perspective that invented Africa as authentically primitive and out of history. In the wake of colonialism, resistance was co-opted by oppressive nationalisms, and so a process of reclamation began all over again—this time, I argued, in the form of transgression, a deliberate crossing of the limits of representation to invent new terms beyond the Manichaean opposition of colonial and anticolonial.

If this describes the history in literature that has concerned me, it does not address the nature of history. In other words, I have implied all along a fuzzy distinction between history (human action that then is described and represented in narratives) and history as always already a set of representations embedded in narrative. Paul Veyne makes this distinction more clearly when he speaks of historicism and the historiographical: historicism is man's condition, his constant becoming on the road of history; the historiographical is his conscious effort to remember and narrate (73). The fuzziness in my treatment of this distinction arises from the complex position of Africans writing historical novels. Their historicism as subjects of history has always been to some degree prefigured by the historiographical enterprises of the European colonizers.

In distinguishing between the novel and historiography, Veyne can simply declare "history is a true novel" and hence not a novel at all, except that it is a story (x). Our knowledge of the past is so limited he tells us, that each "historical novel shrieks out its falsity" because of its realism (25). On the other hand, history is not obligated to explain or to represent what is not known, but simply (although not easily) to declare the limits of its knowledge and from there, through a process he calls "retrodiction," fill in the gaps (see *Writing History*, chapter 8). Unlike explanation, retrodiction does not emplot. A process of induction, retrodiction tries to identify the most probable cause by mapping the circumstances out of which events arose as accurately as possible.

Veyne's theory of history nicely complicates many assumptions about the writing of history that have been based on nineteenth-century notions of historicism as man's consciousness. It posits an ideal toward which historical practice should aim but that does not always describe what we find as readers in texts of history and historical novels. The actual texts produced by our practice of history are much more hybrid in their intent. Even if our knowledge of the past is severely limited, we are compelled to justify our actions through stories of the past, not merely through careful retrodiction but through emplotment, a willful creation of coherence and meaning in our stories.

What I have called the invented traditions of Maran and Achebe, for example, cannot be read outside the context of the compulsion of colonialism to invent traditions. Maran and Achebe make us aware of these linkages that then force a recognition of the historical agency of Africans actively repressed in the project of colonialism. So the history in literature pertains both to what Veyne would call our knowledge of events and what I would call fiction as historiography.

Speaking of the "historiographical operation" and responding in part to Paul Veyne, Michel de Certeau insists on a self-reflective awareness of place in producing history: "Connecting history to a place is the condition of possibility for any social analysis" (69). Much of Veyne's theory strains toward a homogeneous practice of history; different circumstances of writing do not affect the nature of historiography produced. Veyne, however, insists on absolute discursive differences; history and fiction are distinct. De Certeau, on the other hand, usefully focuses on the circumstances of production and on the degree of historians' self-reflectiveness about their present circumstances that they carry over into their accounts of the past. "History," he tells us, "is defined entirely by a relation of language to the (social) body, and therefore by its relation to the limits that the body assigns either in respect to the particular place whence one speaks, or in respect to the other object (past, dead) that is spoken about" (68–69). Thus in most respects one writes the history that is *permissible* at that time and place.

We can readily see how this would be at play in the work of Paul Hazoumé. Navigating the terrain of the permissible while still making your difference heard is not easy. A nationalist who misidentifies with the nationalist faction and then finds himself misallied with the colonizer, Hazoumé occupies a place from which his historical narrative must extricate him. He must write himself out of French imperial ideology. The limits constraining him in de Certeau's sense are the narratives of French nationalism (for example, Michelet's *Histoire de la Révolution*, as we have seen); out of these limits he must fashion a different relation between "language" and "social body." Dissent, therefore, takes the form of an argument for a new place to speak from, ultimately a different nationalism.

The history in literature has as much to do with the agons of the writer's present as it has to do with the past recounted. To return once more to de Certeau:

> On the one hand, writing plays the role of a burial site. . . . On the other hand, it possesses a symbolizing function; it allows a society to situate itself by giving itself a past through language, and it thus opens to the

> present a space of its own. "To mark" a past is to make a place for the
> dead, but also to redistribute the space of possibility, to determine neg-
> atively what *must be done*, and consequently to use the narrativity that
> buries the dead as a way of establishing a place for the living. *(100)*

The emphasis on potentiality here is crucial: one reclaims the past to define
a direction in the present. To abdicate doing so by succumbing to historical
forgetfulness amounts to burying oneself along with the dead. *The Famished
Road* resists this negative possibility, constantly opening the space of the
present against the forces that inhibit remembrance.

By turning to Veyne and de Certeau, I would like to suggest ways of
teasing out the philosophical implications of my discussion of historiography, of the history in literature. But more must be said of *Claiming History's*
method of literary history. I have deliberately avoided in this book a strictly chronological account—hence the treatment of Achebe out of chronological sequence in chapter 1 (and again in the final chapter), as well as the
return to the nineteenth century in chapter 2. More perplexing to some,
however, might be the jump from Hazoumé's 1938 novel to *Le Devoir de violence* at the end of the 1960s. This intervening period, which is not the single focus of any chapter here, is, of course, pivotal both for the emergence
of African nations from colonial rule and the cultural flourishing that accompanied these historical changes. It is also the period most studied by
scholars of the African novel and from which most of our paradigms about
African literature stem.

Claiming History does take this period into account but disperses its attention to it throughout the book. It is the backdrop against which this study
develops. If we are to see the continuities between colonialism and post-
colonialism, we need to expand the historical frame. Agitating against colonialism, Maran and Hazoumé look forward to the same historical period on
which Ouologuem and Okri cast a deliberate retrospective glance. At the
same time the persistent need of Western readers to inaugurate the African
novel shows that insofar as receptionality goes, there is a far greater degree
of continuity than the usual periodization of African literary history—before and after independence—indicates.[1] This problem, in fact, leads us to
the trickiest aspect of "African" literary history, even if we accommodate a
plural possibility of literary histories: separating reception from some kind

of implicitly organic or natural development of an African genre. I would argue strongly against this kind of segregation that leads us to read African literature(s) as a literature apart, when it has from its very inception in the languages of the colonial powers been a literature of response: importing and subverting conventions, mixing styles and expressions, and, after all, narrating and enacting a history of transcultural contact. This makes it like, rather than unlike, other literature, since what I call here "responsiveness" is part of what Jonathan Arac has called the "historicality" of literature, "literature and the literary" as "historical transformations, rather than either fulfillments or invariants" (25).

Nor should the comparative context of African literature be only Europe. Novelists throughout the world read and respond to each other. An awareness of African novels and their reception in Europe, for example, is one important context for understanding the African imaginary of Kenzaburo Oe's *A Personal Matter*. The Japanese writer's own complex relation to the novel is not simply one of margin to center. As de Certeau has shown us, the site from which you speak determines the limits of what you say. We don't have to understand limits as constraints but as boundaries that accommodate overlapping discourses, creating a site of considerable density and richness. To build context in literary history, the first step is to go inside the novel and map its overlapping languages.[2]

We have looked at the history in literature both in the sense of literature's content and as the literary's agency as historically transformative. We have also examined some of the implications of a practice of literary history and the kind of reading that it elicits. All of these approaches explore from different angles a fundamental function of the overlap of literature and history: that is, the need to memorialize. In "Public Memory and Its Discontents," Geoffrey Hartman explains:

> One reason literature remains important is that it counteracts, on the one hand, the impersonality and instability of public memory and, on the other, the determinism and fundamentalism of a collective memory based on identity politics. Literature creates an institution of its own, more personal and focused than public memory yet less monologic than the memorializing fables common to ethnic or nationalist affirmation.
>
> *(85)*

We can see what Hartman is driving at by delineating a distinct space for literature, a public space, where the specificity and urgency of personal experience can maintain its integrity while also being claimed as a part of a communal experience. Hartman goes on from here to posit the problem of "absent memory":

> At the same time, because today the tie between generations—the "living deposit" or "passé vécu," as Halbwachs calls it—is jeopardized, creative activity is often carried on under the negative sign of an "absent memory" (Ellen Fine) or *mémoire trouée* (Henri Raczymow). A missed encounter is evoked through a strenuous, even cerebral exercise of the imagination, as if the link between memory and imagination has been lost. *(85)*

Hartman turns to Toni Morrison's *Beloved* to illustrate his point; the "absent memory," of course, is the experience of slavery. But how well these sentences describe *The Famished Road*, not only because the linkages among the slave trade, colonialism, and postcolonial violence are all "absent memories" but because of the method of retrieval through literature, the "strenuous, even cerebral exercise of the imagination" that Hartman describes. So much of what Okri does is try to reconnect two generations divided by a colossal gap of language and sensibility that renders what Hartman calls collective memory potent and mute at the same time.

But there are also difficulties here for extending Hartman's discussion to African literature. If "literature creates an institution of its own," then Hartman assumes an overlapping space of writers and readers. Although he edges away from national literatures and seems to imply a transnational institution of literature, literature remains discreet, inclusive of a multicultural range of expression but also exclusive in the large numbers of people who remain out of its reach. The same problem resurfaces that we have when we speak of a national literature. In the case of Nigeria and a literature that treats the "trouble with Nigeria," we have to ask: Where are the readers reading and who are they? This is not a new question. It is asked often in the study of African literature.

The fact that much of African literature is read outside of Africa presents special challenges for understanding the dynamics of testimony. Writing from disjuncted communities and in-between places, the authors studied here address not discreet communities from which they are separated because of socioeconomic differences but the points of conjunction of the different worlds on which their hybrid experiences touch. I argued earlier for the strengths of such displacement, such in-betweenness, and I would like to reemphasize this point. Perhaps "an institution of its own" argues not for a real place as such but for geographical crossings. Redefining literature as testimony, Hartman wants to combat "unreal memory" (91), a falsifying, unifying memory. His exemplary poet here is Derek Walcott, who sees his testimonial function as resurrecting fragments. Much of what Walcott speaks of is fragmented precisely because it occupies the unstable place of a conjunction among different cultures and communities with competing aspirations. History happens at these meeting points, these unstable places, and literature's historiographical function is in part to re-create the dynamics of that conjunction and allow narratives buried at the site of these contests to resurface.

NOTES

■■

Introduction

1. An important exception is Amos Tutuola's *The Palm-Wine Drinkard* (1952). This novel's reception in Britain as surrealistic tended to universalize its themes. The surreal avoided the incompatibility of historical specificity and timeless authenticity by suppressing background and context. When African reality was treated as mythical (as in *The Palm-Wine Drinkard*, for example), it was not the work's authenticity that mattered but its articulation of universal values. Ironically, African readers were annoyed by Tutuola's inauthenticity. To English readers Tutuola's unidiomatic language was modernist and the "universal" themes of his tale made the novel easily assimilable to their literary traditions, contributing to its huge success. Tutuola's narrative account of a search among the dead was on a par with those of Orpheus, Heracles, or Aeneas (Moore in Beier 179). In effect, Tutuola was perceived as reinvigorating existent and culturally powerful plots. However, the novel appeared derivative to Nigerians who read it within the context of D. O. Fagunwa's immensely popular Yoruba novels. (For more on Fagunwa's reception see Moore in Beier, and Irele). They questioned why Tutuola reworked the indigenous Yoruba tales in a language he had not mastered when he could follow the earlier example of Fagunwa and write in Yoruba. Moreover, the qualities of the novel that seemed the most appealing to the Europeans (Tutuola's "naïveté" and "freshness" of style) were to the Nigerians the most problematic. The celebration of Tutuola as "a literary noble savage" (Owomoyela 74), or the recognition of his "quaintness" (Irele in *African Experience* 182), seemed offensive.

2. For a reappraisal of the novel and an analysis of its ideological complexity see Christopher Miller, "Literary Studies and African Literature" in Bates and Mudimbe,

eds., *Africa and the Disciplines*, 222–23. According to Miller, the novel's didactic argument for French literacy actively devalues the long tradition of literacy in Arabic.

3. Miller focuses early in his book on Senghor's affirmation of Frobenius's claims for an aestheticized Africa (16–17). I am troubled by the passive reflexiveness of Miller's manner of articulating the relationship between African writers and the founders of an authoritative, Western discourse. Miller argues for Senghor that "My point is of course not that Frobenius was inaccurate in his physical description of African civilization, rather that his writing *rewards* Africa for conforming to a European image of civilization, for acting as a mirror in which a European can contemplate his own idea of beauty" (17). Rewards given for conformity form the basis of Miller's charge that these writers are essentially collaborationists. Here, however, I find Mary Louise Pratt's theorization of the dynamics of representation in *Imperial Eyes* much more useful for uncovering resistance in what may seem as conformity. According to Pratt, when the representation of Africa conforms to European requirements, then the representation is essentially an invention and a masking or camouflaging of the real topos. In the native's conformity to this aestheticization is encoded a resistant questioning of its premises.

4. Maran also tampered with the original version of his text. The second edition, which appeared in 1937 (sixteen years after the first), has an additional chapter inserted between the original chapters 2 and 3. In this new chapter Maran explains in more detail Yassiguindja's motivation for betraying Batouala. The novel had been repeatedly criticized for not having enough plot, and this was Maran's concession to his critics. My analysis of the text is based on the original 1921 edition.

5. The author of *Mission scientifique* (Henri Hubert, born in 1879 and trained as a metereologist and geologist) is not to be confused with Henri Hubert (born in 1872), the sociologist and collaborator of Marcel Mauss.

6. See Roger Caillois's account of Bataille's intent to carry out a human sacrifice in "The Collège de Sociologie," 61–4. Marianna Torgovnik also discusses this incident in *Gone Primitive*, 108.

7. Henri Hubert and Marcel Mauss published their influential study, "Essai sur la nature et la fonction du sacrifice" (1898).

8. See Eric Wolf, *Europe and the People Without History*, where he attempts to redress this erasure. See also Talal Asad's review of Wolf ("Are There Histories of Peoples without Europe?"), where Asad addresses the problem of narrativity in writing the history of a people "without history."

1. The Traditional Cultures of René Maran and Chinua Achebe

1. *Batouala* is dedicated to Gahisto, who published parts of his correspondence with Maran in the volume *Hommage à René Maran*. Their correspondence provides a

valuable record of Maran's anxieties of authorship. In *Hommage*, Maran's letters are cited extensively, and Gahisto narrates his own responses and the history of their correspondence. Before going to Africa, Maran had published a volume of poetry that Gahisto had read and admired (*La Maison du Bonheur* 1909; see *Hommage*, 94–5). Maran was eagerly seeking correspondents in France to keep him connected to the literary scene during his absence. Moreover, he had completed his first novel but had been unable to find a publisher. According to Gahisto, the novel was too slim to be marketed (107). *Djogoni* was eventually published posthumously, but Maran learned from this early rejection to conform more closely to the expectations of potential publishers, expectations that were based on the publishers' construction of a true "black" author. His *roman d'un métis* (novel of a half-cast), *Djogoni*, was not publishable, but *Batouala*, the true African novel, would be.

2. Clifford has discussed the restorative function of certain types of ethnography as "salvage ethnography" (see "On Ethnographic Allegory," 112–3). The Western ethnographer confronts the "other" as already lost and in need of preservation ("salvation") in the ethnographer's text.

3. Delafosse preserves the domain of ethnographic discourse for Western writers to maintain the coherence of the rest of his theory of Africans. Before Leo Frobenius (whose translated writings appeared in France in 1936), Delafosse argued that the sophistication of African cultures was evident in their artistic achievements; Africans were indeed different from Europeans, but they were morally their equals. This dubious division of separate but equal spheres confined the black man's expression to art. The sphere of scientific discourse was preserved for Europeans. For more on Frobenius's influence on Senghor, and negritude more generally, see Christopher Miller's discussion in *Theories of Africans*.

4. Maran implicitly criticized the *broussard* as a type in his 1948 biography of David Livingstone. Deploying a rhetorical method we will see much evidence of later (using an English figure of empire to criticize French imperialist ideology), Maran stresses Livingstone's civilizing influence, his antislavery, the love and devotion he inspired among his native associates—all the signs, in other words, of his civilized status, not the romanticized primitivism of the *broussard*.

5. For an account of Mauss's teaching methods and his relations to his students see Fournier, 502–12.

6. As Ruth Larson has said regarding Leiris, he set out for Africa "with the hope of being relieved of his identity, disarmed and transformed through contact with persons radically different from himself" (237). No such escape was possible, however.

7. In "De *Batouala* à *Doguicimi*," Michel Fabre explains Maran's desire to be objective as a result of his dislocation: "his affiliation with French culture equaled his attraction for the land of his ancestors." Maran's objectivity "seems to come from his alienation as a black educated in European style as much as from aesthetic premises" (239).

8. As a result of his refusal to confront his abandonment, Maran developed a neurosis in which he overintellectualized his experience. According to Fanon, Maran demonstrates "recrimination toward the past, devaluation of self, incapability of being understood as he would like to be" (*Black Skin* 74–5). France betrayed Maran by promising him a cultural home and then by denying him an identity and point of view within that home.

9. In *Hommage* Gahisto reproduces examples of ethnographic details on female and male circumcision cited by Maran in the drafts of *Batouala*, and then comments as follows on Maran's descriptions: "Everything that precedes belongs to the field of ethnography and could very easily support a scholarly study of the Oubanghi-Chari-Tchad black population's mores and habits. I didn't fail to remind my correspondent that the novel as a genre demands action rather than meticulous knowledge, that his work needed a plot" (132). Maran's draft lacked a plot. Gahisto was fully cognizant of Maran's ethnographic ambition and was uneasy with Maran's dismissive attitude toward literature. He tried to steer Maran away from ethnography by reminding him of his earlier intent to write a novel (the failed *Djogoni*). Regarding the problem of knowledge, we may well ask, what about Flaubert or Zola? Did they not aspire to a "meticulous knowledge?"

10. For a full account of the scandal see Iheanacho Egonu, "Le Prix Goncourt de 1921."

11. This is the point missed by those critics of Maran who, like Femi Ojo-Ade, see Maran's negative portrayal of Africanness as denigrating (49–50). The present reality is negative, but it has its causes (colonialism), and we can only imagine what must have been before colonialism through the traces left in the present.

12. See Lukacs's discussion of irony and *created totality* in *The Theory of the Novel*, 75.

13. Ironically one of Maran's conservative critics, René Trautmann, mounted his attack against Maran's anticolonialism by recasting Maran's ethnographic descriptions against him. Batouala's malaise becomes evidence for the natives' *indolence* and *paresse*, subheadings in Trautmann's chapter on "Leurs Qualités intellectuelles" (in *Au Pays de Batouala* 72–9). In the same chapter Trautmann argues that the infantile minds of the natives are a consequence of their practice of genital circumcision, which arrests their development. Infantilism is, therefore (according to Trautmann), cultural (45–7).

14. For example, Graham Huggan has characterized the novel as an ethnographic parody because it shows that cultural restitution is impossible. Huggan finds Achebe's explanations "contrived." They function as warnings against believing in "simplistic or erroneous generalizations about 'primitive cultures'" (114).

15. Achebe has stated explicitly that his novel was a response to Joyce Cary's "superficial picture" of Africa in *Mr. Johnson*. Achebe's goal was to look at the same

reality but "from the inside" (quoted in Innes 698). The insider's point of view, however, becomes more problematic as we advance into the postcolonial period, where the delineation of who is an insider and who an outsider becomes more difficult to determine.

16. For a discussion of *Things Fall Apart* as a resistance novel from a Marxist perspective and against the context of Joyce Cary's *Mister Johnson* see Onyemaechi Udumukwu, "The Antinomy of Anticolonial Discourse."

17. Achebe has admitted to having a tragic sense of the world: "the things that really make the world, the human world, are the serious, the tragic. . . . It is, you know, the man who fails who has a more interesting story than the successful person. . . . Simplicity is part of the success of Hardy and Housman because the tragic situation is very simple; it's not 'convoluted' at all." (Cited in Ezenwa-Ohaeto 46, from interviews with Achebe conducted by Robert M. Wren; see Wren's *Those Magical Years*.)

18. A particularly revealing instance of this is the explanation of the *ikenga* that I discuss in my introduction. By delaying this explanation and then presenting it as Winterbottom's explanation to Clarke, Achebe drives his reader to abandon his trust in ethnographic discourse and respond instead to an African context.

19. The attack on the Abam by the British in 1901 was particularly devastating to the Ibo since the Abam were widely feared as the fiercest warriors of the Ibo. After razing two villages, the British publicly executed an Aro and an Abam leader. The officers responsible for this were later reprimanded by the colonial authorities. The attack against the Abam was part of the Aro expedition. The Aro, also an Ibo group, were the wealthiest of the Ibo. The British acted under the pretense that they were intervening to settle a conflict between tribes. In fact, the Aro, with their warrior allies, the Abam, frequently instigated conflicts with neighboring communities in the struggle to control trade routes. For more information on the history of the Ibo, see Isichei, *A History of the Igbo People*.

20. For Bakhtin literary ("artistic") language is about the representation of other languages. Hybridity is its key feature. As he explains in "Discourse in the Novel": "The artistic image of a language must by its very nature be a linguistic hybrid (an intentional hybrid): it is obligatory for two linguistic consciousnesses to be present, the one being represented and the other doing the representing, with each belonging to a different system of language. Indeed, if there is not a second representing consciousness, if there is no second representing language-intention, then what results is not an *image* [*obraz*] of language but merely a *sample* [*obrazec*] of some other person's language, whether authentic or fabricated" (359). The hybrid makes visible the doubleness of any of the many languages of the heteroglossic. In a novel, the ethnographic comes across not simply as the ethnographic but as the representation of the ethnographic.

2. History, Human Sacrifices, and the Victorian Travelers to Dahomey

1. For a history of the origins of Dahomey as a state and its role in the slave trade see John Iliffe *Africa: The History of a Continent*, chapter 7. In the words of economic historian Karl Polanyi, Dahomey was "an unbreakable society" (9). Formed in the 1600s out of a mixture of disparate ethnic groups that occupied an area without natural borders, Dahomey survived on its military strength, which was consolidated through its participation in the slave trade. By raiding its neighbors and trading slaves for arms, Dahomey maintained its sovereignty. Thus a people who were not united through ethnic or religious bonds developed a war culture and an allegiance to their monarchic dynasty, maintained through extreme discipline and terror. Economic self-interest made Dahomey the enemy of all its neighbors and the natural ally of the European traders in the eighteenth century. Dahomeans and Europeans were "mutual customers" as Polanyi puts it (23).

2. Burton was appointed consul at Fernando Po on the West African coast in 1861. From there he traveled to Dahomey on a mission to persuade the Dahomeans to give up the slave trade and turn to the trade of palm oil. Dahomey's "Amazon" army also held a powerful attraction for Burton, although in the end he declared that the "Amazons" turned out to be disappointing.

3. Dahomey continued to be deeply implicated in the slave trade until the 1870s. Although there is a consensus that captured slaves were slaughtered annually in a ritual custom that had become emblematic of African "savagery," there is no accurate information on the numbers of those killed. For a discussion of how European writers sensationalized accounts of human sacrifice, see Hammond and Jablow, 139.

4. This literature is a spin-off of abolitionist literature, which also "involved the revelation of atrocities" (Brantlinger 175). The booklength accounts by British travelers to Dahomey before the Victorian period are: William Snelgrave, *A New Account of Some Parts of Guinea and the Slave Trade* (1734), William Smith, *A New Voyage to Guinea* (1744), Robert Norris, *Memoirs of the Reign of Bossa Ahadee* (1789), Archibald Dalzel, *History of Dahomy* (1793), and John McLeod, *A Voyage to Africa with Some Account of the Manners and Customs of the Dahoman People* (1820). The Victorians' accounts (six in all) are the subject of this chapter.

5. A good example of the extent to which such accounts of human sacrifice with reference to Dahomey became conventionalized is James Greenwood's *Prince Dick of Dahomey; or, Adventures in the Great Dark Land* (1890). Greenwood, a writer of adventure stories for young boys, sets his novel in Dahomey so that he can make use of a particular body of sensational and predictable material. Human sacrifices, however, have little relevance to his own plot. They are part of the setting as a matter of course.

6. The British withdrew politically as well. Engaged in costly wars with neighboring Ashanti in the 1870s, the British lost interest in Dahomey, and it fell to the French in 1894 after sustained military attack. For the French conquest of Dahomey see David Ross, "Dahomey," in Michael Crowder, ed., *West African Resistance*.

7. Dahomey's dominant role in this relationship had been established from the first visit by an Englishman to the state. Purportedly the first white man to visit Abomey (the capital of Dahomey), Bulfinch Lamb arrived as a prisoner. He was captured by the Dahomeans in their victorious raid against the coastal state of Arda in 1724. He was held in Abomey for two years but treated well and allowed to leave loaded with presents (Forbes I:2–3). From Lamb's own testimony, it is clear that King Trudo brought him to Dahomey in order to persuade him of the Dahomeans' willingness to trade with the British (Lamb in Forbes I:181–95). The campaign of 1724 was an important turning point in the history of Dahomey. Having succeeded against Arda, "the most important slave trading state on the Upper Guinea Coast" at the time, Dahomey had acquired access to the coast and was ready to dominate the slave trade (Polanyi 21).

8. Since Lamb's sojourn in Abomey from 1724 to 1726, the journey to Abomey (located in the interior, past the marshes of the Lama that separated Dahomey from the coast) had presented a geographical challenge. Abomey was experienced as a kind of limit beyond which it was impossible to go. In some instances, other travelers like Skertchly relived Lamb's experience of imprisonment.

9. A point of clarification is in order here. When Duncan describes the killings, he never calls them sacrifices; the killings are explained as punitive executions of enemy tribe members. The events that constituted human sacrifices are not well understood by historians even today. The Dahomeans believed they were sending the victims as messengers to the king's ancestors, but these killings also had a disciplinary function. The victims were either criminals or prisoners of war. Some of the killings reported in the literature as sacrifices were unceremonious. Others were conducted as elaborate rituals. The political nature of the human sacrifices is investigated at length by Paul Hazoumé (a native African from the French colony of Dahomey) in his historical novel *Doguicimi* (1938).

10. Mary Louise Pratt's distinction between scientific and subjective utterance is apt here. Pratt distinguishes the "scientific position of speech" from the position of "subjective experience" thus: "the scientific position of speech is that of an observer fixed on the edge of a space, looking in and/or down upon what is other. Subjective experience, on the other hand, is spoken from a moving position already within or down in the middle of things, looking and being looked at, talking and being talked at" ("Fieldwork" 32). Duncan speaks from subjective experience because, according to him, that is where valuable testimony occurs. Testimony is thus highly personal and to be distinguished from science.

11. Duncan's rendition is in complete contrast to the picture of the scene of execution provided by the illustrations in Forbes's volume. In figure 2.2, for example, the scene foregrounds the mob of naked men, not the executioners or victims.

12. Although there are some similarities between what I am describing here and Christopher Lane's discussion of "colonial *jouissance*" in *The Ruling Passion*, Duncan is ultimately seeking mastery and not the loss of mastery, even in the narrative rendition of the killing. Lane defines "colonial *jouissance*" as a "counterforce" to the imperial ambition to control and master, and thus a drive toward a loss of mastery, a deployment of colonial experience as dissipation (16). He applies it to a description of violence in Kipling that is similar to Duncan's account of this execution, but Lane makes an opposing argument for Kipling: to participate in such violence, even if one is the successful perpetrator and not the victim, is a form of undoing of the self and not of self-preservation (24). Notably, in Lane's example the horror (and pleasure) derives from an exchange of glances between the executioners and the victim, which registers the recognition of the violence as the pleasure. By contrast, Duncan does not personalize the victim.

13. One could push this point further: if all decapitations in Freudian terms are metonymic equivalents for castration, then the violence perpetrated has a particularly sexual (and specifically homophobic) energy. Duncan's intimate scene of execution involves Duncan and the executioner decapitating a third man. The decapitation is shared by Duncan and the native executioner and thus neutralizes or expends the energy of the encounter between Duncan and the executioner.

14. In Barthes's terms the text is "atopic" (29). What for Derrida is expressed in terms of supplement becomes a matter of displacement for Barthes. Thus Barthes argues, "the pleasure of the text is always possible, not as a respite, but as the incongruous—dissociated—passage from another language" (30). Thus displacement, dissociation, disjunction make up the space of the "seam" that is pleasure.

15. See also Forbes's account of his service as commander of the *Bonetta, Six Months' Service in the African Blockade* (1849).

16. According to Forbes the British were optimistic in 1849 that they would prevail on King Guezo to curb the slave trade because his powerful agent and slave dealer, the Brazilian Francisco da Souza, had just died. Sending Duncan as an emissary to correct da Souza's influence seems wrongheaded, however, since Duncan had become good friends with da Souza during his 1845–1846 trip. Duncan rendered his final leave-taking from da Souza very sentimentally: "He was very ill in bed and scarcely able to speak. . . . At parting he shook me by the hand, and in a low whisper bade me a long good-bye, with every wish for my future happiness" (2:297).

17. Forbes's written account, therefore, has the opposite effect of the illustrations in his text (which were not done by him); the illustrations (as in figure 2.2) highlight the mob, although they do not show the actual violence. They anticipate it.

18. Bernasko's relations with the Dahomeans seems to have been strained. Skertchly, who is unsympathetic toward missionaries, cites King Gelele's disapproving comments on Bernasko's personal character: "You say that your people abhor the thoughts of men being sacrificed; that their religion teaches them such things are contrary to the will of the Divine Being. Now we have a "God man" at Whydah, and does he set such an example to my people as I would wish them to follow? Does he not drink till he talks foolishness? Does he not make plenty of mischief by his talebearing, and has he not told lies to the English people about me and my country?" (237–8).

19. The Coomassie palace was the palace built during Guezo's reign. It was named "Coomassie" (which is the name of the Ashanti capital) in order to commemorate Guezo's campaigns against the Ashanti.

20. See also Annie Coombes's discussion of the same image in *Reinventing Africa* 16.

21. Burton characterizes human sacrifice thus: "deplorably mistaken, but perfectly sincere," human sacrifice in Dahomey is "founded upon a purely religious basis" (232). Dahomey is like other cultures in the past. The Druids, Burton reminds his reader, also practiced human sacrifice (232). Through his interpretation, Burton projects the eventual obsolescence of the custom, but he was entirely pessimistic about the chances of Europeans civilizing Africans. For more on Burton's anti-imperialism concerning West Africa see Brodie, 209–10. Moreover, Skertchly repeats Burton's assessment that "the monarch has a bona fide belief, misplaced and fallacious, no doubt, but none the less genuine, that by so doing he is carrying out an act of filial piety" (235). Just like Burton, Skertchly cites the Druids on the one hand, and other African nations on the other, as practitioners of human sacrifice (236). Dahomey, we are to conclude, is not exceptional.

3. Contesting Authenticity: Paul Hazoumé, Ethnography, and Negritude

1. See George Eaton Simpson, *Melville J. Herskovits* (New York: Columbia UP, 1973) for biographical information and for Herskovits's importance in the American academy. Herskovits's work in *Dahomean Narrative* is the source for Henry Louis Gates's "trickster" figure in *The Signifying Monkey*. I have discussed *Dahomean Narrative* at length in "Writing Stories about Tales Told."

2. Herskovits marks these rites as both typical and extraordinary. They are meant to be representative, but they are obviously new: "How the basic outlines of these ceremonies persist was indicated when a rite for the soul of Behanzin, the last King of Dahomey was witnessed, even though this was not a part of the annual customs. It was rather a ceremonial marking the anniversary of the burial of Behanzin, and carried out by his son. . . . Because a description of this ceremony brings the chain of accounts of ceremonials for the royal dead to date, and because it was of a type that has not heretofore been described in the literature, it may be given in de-

tail" (2:57). Herskovits adds a footnote to the above, referring us to a similar scene in Skertchly's text. Herskovits both draws authority from the accounts of the Victorians and needs to distinguish himself as providing something more authentic, or up to date.

3. For details on Dahomey in the 1930s and on Hazoumé's political activities specifically see Patrick Manning, *Slavery, Colonialism.*

4. Jean-Norbert Vignonde sees the two issues (the marginalization of Hazoumé from the literary canon and the absence of an explicit anticolonial statement in his work) as related. The model of the canon, Vignonde argues, was established through Afro-American perceptions of the origins of African literature. Thus negritude (which was closer to the Afro-American position) became the model. Writers not directly linked to negritude were left out, Vignonde writes (34). This argument is largely valid, except that Hazoumé had ties to negritude and the expectation that he articulate an explicit anticolonial statement did not take into account the fact that he was writing in Africa (not Paris), under colonial rule and stringent censorship.

5. This Henri Hubert is a different person from Mauss's collaborator on *Sacrifice.*

6. In *Surreptitious Speech*, Moralis et al. point out that history did not become a major concern in *Présence africaine* until the need to understand neocolonialism became paramount in the late 1960s and 1970s. The evidence given in *Africa and the Disciplines* seems to confirm this assessment. African history as a discipline in university studies was not established until the 1970s. On the same topic see also Philip Curtin's contribution to *The Past Before Us*, 113–30. Curtin maps the emergence of the field of academic African history and describes the different types of scholarship produced.

7. Senghor had been talking about a black humanism since the 1930s, when René Maran had inspired him. In an essay on Maran's *Le Livre de la brousse*, he developed the idea of a new humanism by singling out Maran's synthesis of Western and native knowledges, one based on reason, the other on emotion and the soul (see Steins in Gérard, 1:374–75). The idea of such a synthesis was directed specifically at Césaire, who considered the two identities, the Western and the African, as antithetical (Steins in Gérard 1:375). For Senghor, the African of the twentieth century was irreparably disjointed from the precolonial African. Negritude is not a return to the past but a transposition of Africanness to a new cultural terrain. Summing up negritude's position in 1959, Senghor said: "Negritude even when defined as 'the total of black Africa's cultural values' could only offer us the beginning of a solution to our problem and not the solution itself. We could not go back to our former condition, to a negritude of the sources. . . . To be really ourselves, we had to embody Negro African culture in twentieth-century realities" (quoted in Kesteloot 102–3). Negritude is not a return but a strategy for cultural survival. This was Senghor's assessment of the First Congress of Black Artists.

8. In the preface to *Liberté I*, Senghor reacts to the accusation that negritude is a racist ideology and uses humanism in defense of negritude: "In reality, negritude is a form of humanism" (8). Continuing to argue for the "emotive theory of the African personality" that sets it apart (Irele in Gerard 383–4), Senghor claimed that negritude was the enunciation of the Africans' commitment to live out their experience as difference: "our only concern has been to take on ("assumer") this Negritude by *living* it, and having lived it, to deepen its *meaning*. To present it to the world like a touchstone in the creation of the Universal Civilization, which will be the communal work of all races" (9). Negritude would be a cornerstone in a multicultural synthesis that would give rise to a new knowledge, the knowledge of the *panhumaine* (9). For Senghor, humanism enabled the accommodation of difference (whereby the study of mankind is the study of different cultures) with a commitment to the universal civilization of the future.

9. The manuscript of *Doguicimi* was completed in 1935; see Manning (*Slavery, Colonialism* 328, n. 29). A copy of *Le Pacte* was submitted for publication when Hazoumé traveled to Paris for the Colonial Exhibition in 1931.

10. See Manning *Slavery, Colonialism*, 272–6. As Manning goes on to explain, French policy changed after World War II. As preparations for independence slowly began, the French sought to develop a native capitalist class that would safeguard French economic interests after independence.

11. Said presents the corollary to his argument about resistance when he exposes the dependence of European intellectuals on the enabling presence of the Oriental or the African, a dependence the culture of imperialism has sought to "disguise" (191).

4. Resistant History in Paul Hazoumé's Doguicimi

1. For a comparison of *Doguicimi* and *Salammbô* see Dorothy Blair, *African Literature in French*, 75. With the exception of the volume of essays on *Doguicimi* edited by Robert Mane and Adrien Huannou and published in 1987, most of the critical discussion of Hazoumé has repeatedly tried to introduce him as an important writer, reviewing his career in general terms. See, for example, Adande, Erickson, and Huannou ("Hommage"). Mane and Huannou's *Doguicimi de Paul Hazoumé* includes good discussions of the novel's reception and its critical history.

2. Citations from the novel are from the translation by Richard Bjornson (Washington, D.C.: Three Continents Press, 1990). References to the French text are from the first edition of the novel (Paris: Larose, 1938).

3. Hazoumé mentions "whites," not Europeans, or French or British throughout the scene of the sacrifices, although we learn later of a different delegation of British visitors who ask the king to trade in palm oil, not slaves. "Direct the zeal of your arms

towards the cultivation of your fields" (273), the whites tell the Dahomeans. Hazoumé's identification of the spectators to the sacrifices by race is an indictment of the white race as the consumer of black bodies through both the slave trade and these rituals. "Whites" are in cahoots with the tyrannical Dahomean monarchy.

4. Once again Hazoumé records the victims' perspective. The narrative of the killings of the maidens is focalized through the consciousness of the maidens: "A mouth opens, the tongue emerges, moves about, goes back inside, and reemerges; the child continues to cry. She can no longer be heard, but she is understood; she is proclaiming her innocence, her right to life, and imploring pity for her youth" (275).

5. Although "Migan" is not given a personal name (Migan is a title and not a name), Hazoumé develops him as a character and shows how this particular individual exploits the power given to him by his position.

6. This opening provides a contrast to *Batouala*. Both novels begin by depicting the early morning hours and the routines of waking. In *Batouala* the reader is brought into the hero's bedroom to experience awakening as physical and psychological malaise. This domestic scene contrasts sharply with the public acts that begin the day in *Doguicimi*, where we learn that all beginnings start with an act of remembrance.

7. For a discussion of Doguicimi's speech as transgressive, which links it to her martyrdom at the end of the novel, see Gobina Moukoko, "Les Prises de parole et la mort de Doguicimi."

8. David Spurr identifies the trope of "affirmation" in *The Rhetoric of Empire* whereby the French thought of their own empire as having a unique mission when compared to that of other empires (120). He identifies Georges Hardy as a prominent practitioner of this trope (glorifying the French while denigrating the British). Hardy wrote the preface to *Doguicimi*, and I turn to him later in this chapter when I discuss Hazoumé's practice of reinscription more fully.

9. The bracketed part of the sentence is missing from Bjornson's translation. I am restoring it to the text in my own translation. The French reads, *"en attendant qu'elle fût rétablie officiellement"* (396).

10. For a fuller discussion of this aspect of French ideology see David Spurr's chapter on "Affirmation" in *The Rhetoric of Empire*. Spurr uses Georges Hardy once again as an example. Hardy affirms the uniqueness of French imperialism against the savagery of the British (120).

11. In ways that echo his critique of colonial Dahomey in *Le Pacte de sang au Dahomey*, Hazoumé is addressing in his historical novel the burgeoning capitalist middle class and its culture of greed that emerged during the 1930s and that continues to play a destructive role in postcolonial Africa. The attack on materialism is, therefore, as much a critique of his contemporary, colonial society as it is of precolonial Dahomey. See Patrick Manning (1982) on the economic and political situation in Dahomey in the 1930s.

12. For an alternative reading of Doguicimi in the context of other heroines in African fiction see Arlette Chemain-Degrange's *Emancipation féminine et roman africain*.

13. Maran, who thought that *Doguicimi* was an extremely important book, acknowledged its historical aspect by comparing it to Thomas Mofolo's *Chaka* but stressed the ethnographic elements over the historical. Hazoumé "paints with fidelity, with minutiae, that which he sees, that which he knows, and even to some degree, that which he smells." Hazoumé exhaustively records "beliefs, traditions, rituals, superstitions, fables, legends, proverbs, practices of witchcraft, truth poisons, war dances, funeral dances." The amount of detail, however, makes the novel "indigestible," according to Maran. Despite the integrity of the author, the novel fails to move the reader because it lacks poetry (the quotations from Maran's reviews of *Doguicimi* come from Fabre, "De *Batouala* à *Doguicimi*" 246–8). Considering the different proportions and poetics of *Batouala* and *Doguicimi*, this is not a surprising judgment on Maran's part. Because Hazoumé insists on historical explanation, the model of Maran's realism is not sufficient for him.

14. Michelet accuses Charles VII (whose coronation Joan secured by recapturing Reims from the English) of betraying Joan outright. Michelet stresses this point to glorify Joan's loyalty since she sought by contrast to take all the blame on herself: "I have done ill, my king is not at fault; it is not he who advised me" (*Jeanne d'Arque* 165). Whatever Charles's role, the French, a nation divided between the supporters of the house of Burgundy and those of Charles, are to blame for her death. Captured by the duke of Burgundy, Joan was sold to the English and tried by the Inquisition at the University of Paris by mostly French judges.

15. Particularly relevant here is the discussion of domesticity, capitalism, and imperialism in Comaroff and Comaroff, *Ethnography and the Historical Imagination*, chapter 10, "Homemade Hegemony."

16. Hazoumé was not the only African intellectual to accept Hardy's patronage. Senghor acknowledged the wide influence of Hardy on African writers of the period. In a statement from 1947, Senghor explains: "M. Hardy was a the source of the Néo-Nègre movement. He was important because of his writings but, above all, because of his activities while Director of the Department of Education for French West Africa. He presided at the birth of the William Ponty Teachers' College, giving it an African spirit. In this way he prepared the teachers to undertake respectful and scientific research on African values" (quoted in Hymans 68). This was a particularly costly association for Hazoumé, although without Hardy's help he would not have published *Doguicimi* (Midiohouan 74–7).

17. According to Hardy, *Doguicimi* was proof of the success of French Empire in creating little Frances throughout the world that recognized themselves as the "daughters" of the mother nation and displayed their attachment to their mother ("moving evidence of their attachment" [11]) as *Doguicimi* did.

18. There are some interesting points of contrast here to Maran's *Batouala*, which was recognized as novelistic precisely because it was a psychological story of the protagonist (see *Le Monde* review). Moreover, Maran's own claims of objectitivity echo Hardy's for *Doguicimi*.

5. *History as Transgression in* Le Devoir de violence.

1. Ouologuem's text has been described as transgressive in reference to its textual thefts (see Miller and Randall). The pornographic sequences and his critical portrayal of Africans have also been described as transgressive. My use of the adjective will relate specifically to Ouologuem's conception of the historian's role.

2. Soyinka sees Ouologuem's espousal of the void as a rejection of Hamidou Kane's influential defense of Islamic mysticism in *L'Aventure ambigue*. He compares the endings of the two novels and argues that Ouologuem rejects Islamic mysticism and ambiguity ("Kane's transcendentalist apologia for Islamic spirituality") in favor of history (*Myth, Literature, and the African World* 102). Soyinka links the two novels not only thematically but in form as well. The last chapter of *Le Devoir* reenacts a battle similar to the ending of Kane's novel, mimicking and subverting Kane's novel. Soyinka's reading is persuasive, but Kane is simply one more context here, not the definitive one. For an alternative reading of the existentialist debates in "Dawn" see Nichols.

3. See for example Benita Parry's "Resisting Theory: Theorizing Resistance," whose subtitle is "Two Cheers for Nativism." Parry does a very good job of reviewing the debate on nativism and, although we take opposite stands on the issue, as my reading of Ouologuem will show, there is also considerable affinity in our positions, especially in her casting of nativism as transgressive (177). Parry does not examine Ouologuem.

4. As Robert Fraser points out in his study of Armah's novelistic oeuvre, the comparison stems from the shared influence of Schwartz-Bart's *Le Dernier des justes* and expresses itself on the epic scope of the historical frame of Ouologuem's and Armah's novels and the treatment of sacrifice in relation to the history of a race (65).

5. In his article comparing Ouologuem and Armah, George Lang claims that *Two Thousand Seasons* is intended as a reply to Ouologuem, "a repudiation of the negativity" of *Le Devoir* (387). To do so, Armah returns to the discourse of negritude, according to Lang: "he has . . . reintroduced the principle motifs of Négritude and . . . fused them into a program which is Fanonist in essence, though more the Fanon of *Peau noire, masques blancs,* who was concerned with the psychic effects of cultural alienation, than that of *Les Damnés de la terre,* who affirmed that the only effective catharsis would be violent and political" (394).

6. In his comparative reading of Armah and Ouologuem, Derek Wright stress-

es the orality of both novels as a feature shared in common. Whereas Armah does unambiguously imitate oral forms because he sees them as regenerative, Ouologuem, I would argue, is squarely focused on conventions of writing even when he treats orality. He is interested in the usurped authority of orality that appears in written discourses that claim to be authentic.

7. These two novels are grouped together often because they seem exceptional and, in their exceptionality, similar. I would rather see the emphasis placed on a rare moment where critics consistently feel compelled to read anglophone and francophone traditions comparatively because these authors' works resonate so powerfully than make an argument that insists on the similarities between *Le devoir* and *Two Thousand Seasons* and then segregates them from other novels. These novels sent out ripples throughout the literature of a period of particular significance (from 1965 to 1975, approximately), and they should anchor a comparative and synthetic reading.

In this spirit, I propose a different comparison that seems fruitful but has not been made. Ouologuem's attack on the reader and his deployment of the representation of sexual violence to accomplish this shares some important common ground with Bessie Head's *A Question of Power* (1974). As I have argued elsewhere (see "Authority and Invention in the Fiction of Bessie Head"), Head writes from the perspective of a subject defined by sexual violence that is carried out in large part through language. She is almost totally blocked in this novel by the awareness (similar to Ouologuem's) that her readers are unlikely to read her sympathetically; much that will motivate the reading of a narrative of an African woman's struggles with mental illness and sexual abuse will seek to dominate her. To use this autobiographical novel as a tool of liberation, Head knows she must effect a change in her reader, and she, too, explores the aesthetics of molestation.

The comparison to Head as opposed to Armah highlights Ouologuem's concerns with an ethics of representation in historical narratives that explore the consequences of violent othering. This moves away from a more canonical definition of historical narrative as the unfolding of a span of time, a history of development, which is the model of historicism of *Two Thousand Seasons*, with its epic span and oral qualities. History, moreover, is far from irrelevant to Head, who in the end seeks to constitute her subjectivity historically, forging a symbolic link between her land and her sex ("Authority and Invention" 18, 22–3). Head's career was marked by constant experimentation with genre, and it reverses the progression we find in the development of African fiction away from the ethnographic. Her early novels are unambiguously realistic. *A Question of Power* is a departure from the convention, an experimental novel. It was followed by a collection of short stories that are more ethnographic (*The Collector of Treasures* 1977), and finally *Serowe: Village of the Rain Wind* (1981), a historical ethnography. This return to ethnography yields a transformed genre. An oral history of her adopted home in Botswana, it is a powerful, multivoiced text that does not offer a unitary history but a history of many stories.

8. Citations from the novel are from the translation by Ralph Manheim (Portsmouth, N.H.: Heinemann, 1971; Paris: Seuil, 1968).

9. For a discussion of Ouologuem's debunking of oral sources see Aizenberg, Wright, and Barkan.

10. This bogus revisionism is "borrowed" from *Le Dernier des justes*, André Schwartz-Bart's novel that Ouologuem allegedly plagiarized. In his novel, however, Schwartz-Bart intends the revisionism sincerely.

11. In the extensive critical literature on *Le Devoir*, only Aliko Songolo identifies the problem of literacy as pivotal to the dispossession of the *négraille*. See "Fiction et subversion," 17–21. I also follow Songolo's lead here in stressing a narratological approach to the novel.

12. Songolo pushes this point even further. He argues that oral narrative conventions are used in the novel to announce the narrator's intention to mock ("Fiction et subversion" 25).

13. For a discussion of the novel's linear chronology see Schikora, 74.

14. Here Culler has Stanley Fish's model of the reader (from *Is There a Text in This Class?*) in mind, especially the complete assumption of the reader's authority over the text.

15. Seth I. Wolitz uses the focalization through Awa in his defense of Ouologuem's plagiarism to show how Ouologuem's text made meaningful changes to Greene's. "[The voice] of Greene's narrator takes on an omniscient objectivity. Ouologuem, on the other hand, narrates the scene through Awa's vision, and thus from the perspective of an African spy, curious of European luxury, conscious of her duties. . . . By making us share Awa's perspective, the narrator offers us not only a psychological view of the way in which Awa perceives, thinks, and acts but also the sight of an African woman facing the reality of colonialism" (133, my translation).

16. Robert Philipson argues instead that "the passage that describes the governor's surrender metaphorically deconstructs the colonialist discourse of discovery and conquest" (226). Stressing the governor's *jouissance*, Philipson argues that it renders him powerless. But Philipson also assumes that Awa's pleasure is genuine, a point my reading gives reasons to doubt.

17. I will limit myself here to a reading of Greene, but the plagiarism controversy involved at least two more works of fiction, Maupassant's *Boule de suif* and André Schwartz-Bart's *Le Dernier des justes*. For discussions of the plagiarism controversy see Miller, Randal, Sellin, Wolitz, and Songolo.

18. As Eileen Julien has argued forcefully, Ouologuem's reader is unambiguously male.

19. Miller makes reference to Ouologuem's contention that he had placed the various passages in question in quotation marks, which his publisher deleted. Moreover, Ouologuem contended that it was necessary for him as an African to borrow these passages because the point of view he wished to express was impermissible to an African (cited in Miller 223–4).

20. This explanation is provided as part of Tambira's story of abuse. See Julien for a fuller treatment of this aspect of Ouologuem's portrayal of women.

21. A gloss on Genette's terminology is in order here. In his attempt to devise more concise terms for accounting for point of view in narrative, Genette distinguished among three types of mood, or focalization, in third-person narratives: nonfocalized, internally focalized, and externally focalized narratives. Briefly the distinction among these types stems from the narrator's perspective on the internal thought patterns of the characters. If the narrator has absolute authority over his subject and knows more than the character about the character's experience, then we have an instance of nonfocalized narrative. Perspective is created entirely by the narrator and is not communicated through the character's consciousness. Internal focalization provides us with the character's own self-awareness. The voice is the narrator's but the experience is accounted for through the character's understanding. External focalization gives us neither the narrator's insights nor the character's own awareness of experience. It presents the character's actions as a spectacle to the reader without explanation.

22. Huggan makes an interesting connection between the issue of textual theft and the critique of anthropology: "Ouologuem's refusal to respect the 'sanctity' of textual origins reflects further on the double standards of diffusionist ethnographies where the origins of a culture are inscribed within the wider framework of a redemptive narrative of the West proclaiming its 'salvation' of Africa. Ouologuem's postulation of the origin as a site of duplicity and/or violent contestation thus mines the contradictions inherent in a European anthropological project in which the alleged retrieval of another culture's origins provides a spurious moral justification for the material success of one's own" (117).

6. Temporality and the Geographies of the Nation: "The Future Present" *in* The Famished Road

1. There are complicated literary and historical reasons that contribute to this pattern, and I do not mean to imply that there were no novels of significance in the 1970s. What I am focusing on here are novels that deal with the national problem and try to raise public consciousness about it. Many novels in the 1970s dealt with social issues, as, for example, the feminist work of Buchi Emecheta and Flora Nwapa, and the works of socially conscious writers such as John Munonye and

T. M. Aluko. Much of Soyinka's poetic and dramatic work was also written in the 1970s.

2. In his article on *Anthills in the Savannah*, Kortenaar argues that "The memory that would create a communal identity must be selective. Not memory but invented memory is necessary for the nation" (67). In his concluding paragraph he raises the following doubts about the persuasiveness of such invented histories: "Nations everywhere are artificial, but in Europe the tropes of consent and descent have been naturalized; in Africa, their artificiality cannot be disguised. . . . Achebe's desire in the novel to redeem the nation is inevitably compromised in the postmodern, postnational moment in which he is writing. . . . Is he perhaps admitting that a Nigerian identity cannot be imagined?" (72).

3. Henry Louis Gates, for example, in his review for the *New York Times*, hails *The Famished Road* as a new stylistic departure for the African novel in English, which up until Okri had been consistently realistic. Okri has disclaimed both the labels "fantastic" and "magic realism." He prefers "expanded sense of reality," as he stated at the London International Book Festival on March 16, 1996, insisting therefore on the realism of his endeavor. Moreover, both Gates and Anthony Appiah (reviewing for *The Nation*) stress the novel's allegory for the emergence of Nigeria. Okri was the first black African writer to receive the Booker Prize. Established in 1969, the Booker is open to all citizens of the British Commonwealth whose novels are published in Britain. Others to have won the Booker from Africa are Nadine Gordimer (*The Conservationist* [1974]) and J. M. Coetzee (*The Life and Times of Michael K* [1983]), both white South Africans.

4. See the concluding chapter of V. Y. Mudimbe's *The Invention of Africa*, where he uses a spatial paradigm—a geography—to criticize the treatment of African history in Western historicism. Also see Mudimbe, ed., *Africa and the Disciplines* (especially the chapter on history). For a discussion of nationalism as a problem of knowledge and Western historicism see Partha Chatterjee, *Nationalist Thought and the Colonial World*, 1–35.

5. Gates discusses Okri's use of Yoruba mythology extensively in his review of the novel and stresses the need to understand it intertextually since it functions as a literary influence on Okri. Okri is not himself Yoruba but has absorbed this mythology through the literary influence of Soyinka, as well as earlier writers such as Fagunwa and Tutuola. The argument about literary influence across ethnic lines is persuasive evidence of national identity. In his review Appiah calls the abiku child a belief of "Nigerian tradition," silencing the specifically Yoruba reference. In the novel, no ethnic or national groups are named.

6. The descriptive passages are the heart of the novel, not mere padding as Charles Johnson claimed in his review for *TLS* (April 19, 1991). The landscapes that

Azaro witnesses in his wanderings are not separate from the sociohistorical reality of his family's poverty but a commentary on these conditions.

7. There is some slippage in Bhabha's terms. What he means by disjunctive temporality turns into "spatial disjunction" later in the essay (309).

8. Bhabha leaves himself vulnerable here to a type of reverse allochrony. See Fabian, *Time and the Other*.

9. Bakhtin explains: "in literature the primary category of the chronotope is time." The chronotope is the fusion of "spatial and temporal indicators," but it is the way in which space comes to represent time that establishes generic distinctions in literature (85).

10. In fact, Azaro has the vision of the road quoted above after eating the sacrifices left on the road (114).

11. The forest is a precursor of this image in the works of Fagunwa and Tutuola.

12. In *Aké* Soyinka also includes the portrait of an abiku child, Tinu, who tortures her parents with her whimsicality.

13. Okri writes: "She became, in the collective eyes of the people, a fabulous and monstrous creation. It did not matter that some people insisted that it was her political enemies who put out all these stories. The stories distorted our perception of her reality for ever. Slowly, they took her life over, made themselves real, and made her opaque in our eyes" (374). The opacity, moreover, is the expression of political intent.

14. My discussion here is limited to *The Famished Road* and not its disappointing sequel, *Songs of Enchantment*, in which Okri produces a parody of himself. Pushing his abiku metaphor too far, Okri produces what seems like a series of set episodes on the theme of *The Famished Road*. Lacking are the richness of the earlier novel's images; most disappointing, the courageous optimism of *The Famished Road* is trivialized.

Afterword

1. This periodization has contributed to the largely thematic critical literature of African novels. The periodization that divides absolutely between pre- and postindependence carries with it immense ideological baggage, which is more often than not used to filter the literary works and thus homogenize them.

2. Arac describes the problem with traditional literary history in similar terms, as an omission of reading: "Much of the longstanding discontent—from René Wellek to Paul de Man—with traditional, positivist and philological, literary histories comes from their failure actively to read the materials they name and order, even though the materials, as literature, demand to be read, not only cited" (24).

WORKS CITED

■

Achebe, Chinua. *Anthills of the Savannah*. 1987. New York: Anchor, 1988.

———. *Arrow of God*. 1964. New York: Anchor, 1989.

———. *Things Fall Apart*. 1958. New York: Anchor, 1959.

Adande, Alexandre Senou. "Paul Hazoumé: Ecrivain et chercheur." *Présence africaine* 114 (1980): 197–203.

Afolayan, A. "Language and Sources of Amos Tutuola." In Christopher Haywood, ed., *Perspectives on African Literature*, pp. 49–63. London: Heinemann, 1968.

Aizenberg, Edna. "Historical Subversion and Violence of Representation in García Marquez and Ouologuem." *PMLA* 107.5 (1992): 1235–52.

Ajayi, J. F. Ade. "Nineteenth-Century Origins of Nigerian Nationalism." *Journal of the Historical Society of Nigeria* 2.2 (1961): 196–210.

Ajayi, J. F. Ade and B. O. Oloruntimehin, "West Africa in the Anti-Slave Trade Era." In J. D. Fage and Edmund Oliver, eds., *The Cambridge History of Africa*, Vol. 5 (1790–1870), John E. Flint, ed. Cambridge, England: Cambridge University Press, 1976.

Akinjogbin, J. A. *Dahomey and Its Neighbors: 1708–1818*. Cambridge, England: Cambridge University Press, 1967.

Anderson, Benedict. *Imagined Communities: Reflections on the Origin and Spread of Nationalism*. London: Verso, 1991.

Appiah, K. Anthony. "Is the Post- in Postmodernism the Post- in Postcolonial?" *Critical Inquiry* 17.2 (1991): 336–57.

———. "Out of Africa: Topologies of Nativism." *Yale Journal of Criticism* 2.1 (1988): 153–78.

———. "Spiritual Realism." *The Nation*. August 3/10, 1992. 146–8.

Arac, Jonathan. "What Is the History of Literature?" In Brown, *Uses of Literary History*, pp. 23–33.

Armah, Ayi Kwei. *Two Thousand Seasons*. 1973. London: Heinemann, 1979.

Asad, Talal. "Are There Histories of Peoples without Europe? A Review Article." *Comparative Studies in Society and History* 29.3 (1987): 594–607.

———, ed. *Anthropology and the Colonial Encounter*. New York: Humanities Press, 1973.

Awolowo, Obafemi. *Path to Nigerian Freedom*. 1947. London: Faber and Faber, 1977.

Azikiwe, Nnamdi. *Renascent Africa*. Accra: by the author, 1937.

Bakhtin, M. M. *The Dialogic Imagination*. Trans. Caryl Emerson and Michael Holquist. Austin: University of Texas Press, 1981.

Barkan, Sandra. "*Le Devoir de violence*: A Non-History." In Anyidoho, Kofi, et al., eds., *Interdisciplinary Dimensions of African Literature*, pp. 101–12. Washington, D.C.: Three Continents, 1985.

Barker, Francis, Peter Hulme, and Margeret Iversen. *Colonial Discourse/Postconial Theory*. Manchester: Manchester University Press, 1994.

Barthes, Roland. *The Pleasure of the Text*. Trans. Richard Miller. Oxford: Basil Blackwell, 1975.

Bataille, Georges. *Histoire de l'oeil*. 1928. Paris: Pauvert, 1979.

———. *Visions of Excess*. Trans. Allan Stoekl. Minneapolis: University of Minnesota Press, 1985.

Bates, Robert H., and V. Y. Mudimbe, eds. *Africa and the Disciplines*. Chicago: University of Chicago Press, 1993.

Beier, Ulli, ed. *Introduction to African Literature*. Evanston, Ill.: Northwestern University Press, 1967.

Benjamin, Walter. "The Work of Art in the Age of Mechanical Reproduction." In Harry Zohn, trans., *Illuminations*, pp. 217–51. New York: Schocken Books, 1969.

Beti, Mongo, and Odile Tobner. *Dictionnaire de la négritude*. Paris: L'Harmattan, 1989.

Bhabha, Homi. "DissemiNation: Time, Narrative, and the Margins of the Modern Nation." In Bhabha, ed., *Nation and Narration*, pp. 291–322.

———. *The Location of Culture*. London and New York: Routledge, 1994. Chicago: University of Chicago Press, 1993.

———, ed. *Nation and Narration*. London: Routledge, 1990.

Blair, Dorothy. *African Literature in French*. Cambridge, England: Cambridge University Press, 1976.

Brantlinger, Patrick. *Rule of Darkness: British Literature and Imperialism, 1830–1914*. Ithaca, N.Y.: Cornell University Press, 1988.

Brodie, Fawn M. *The Devil Drives: A Life of Sir Richard Burton*. New York: Norton, 1967.

Brown, Marshall. *The Uses of Literary History*. Durham, N.C.: Duke University Press, 1995.

Brunschwig, Henri. *Noirs et blancs dans l'Afrique noire française ou comment le colonisé devient colonisateur (1870–1914)*. Paris: Flammarion, 1983.

Burton, Richard. *A Mission to Gelele King of Dahome*. 1864. 2 vols. London: Tylston and Edwards, 1893.

Caillois, Roger. "The Collège de Sociologie: Paradox of an Active Sociology." *Substance* 11/12 (1975): 61–4.

Camara Laye. *L'Enfant noir*. 1953. Paris: Plon, 1987.

Cameron, Keith. *René Maran*. Boston: Twayne, 1985.

Canary, Robert H., and Henry Kozicki. *The Writing of History*. Madison: University of Wisconsin Press, 1978.

Certeau, Michel de. *The Writing of History*. Trans. Tom Conley. New York: Columbia University Press, 1988.

Césaire, Aimé. *Discours sur le colonialisme*. 1939. Paris: Présence africaine, 1955.

Chatterjee, Partha. *Nationalist Thought and the Colonial World*. Minneapolis: University of Minnesota Press, 1986.

Chemain-Degrange, Arlette. *Emancipation féminine et roman africain*. Dakar: Les Nouvelles Editions Africaines, 1980.

Clifford, James. *The Predicament of Culture*. Cambridge: Harvard University Press, 1988.

———. "On Ethnographic Allegory." In Clifford and Marcus, *Writing Culture*, pp. 98–121.

Clifford, James, and George Marcus. *Writing Culture: The Poetics and Politics of Ethnography*. Berkeley: University of California Press, 1986.

Clowes, William Laird. *The Royal Navy: A History*. London: Sampson Low, Marston and Co., 1901.

Coleman, James S. *Nigeria: Background to Independence*. Berkeley: University of California Press, 1971.

Comaroff, John, and Jean Comaroff. *Ethnography and the Historical Imagination*. Boulder, Colo.: Westview, 1992.

Coombes, Annie. *Reinventing Africa*. New Haven and London: Yale University Press, 1994.

Coundouriotis, Eleni. "Authority and Invention in the Fiction of Bessie Head," *Research in African Literatures* 27.2 (1996): 17–32.

———. "Writing Stories about Tales Told: Anthropology and the Short Story in African Literatures." *NARRATIVE* 6.2 (1998): 140–56.

Crapanzano, Vincent. "Hermes' Dilemma: The Masking of Subversion in Ethnographic Description." In Clifford and Marcus, *Writing Culture*, pp. 51–76.

Crowder, Michael, ed. *The Cambridge History of Africa*. Vol. 8 (1943–1970s). Cambridge, England: Cambridge University Press, 1984.

———. *The Story of Nigeria*. London: Faber and Faber, 1978.

———, ed. *West African Resistance: The Military Response to Colonial Occupation*. New York: Africana, 1971.

Culler, Jonathan. *On Deconstruction: Theory and Criticism after Structuralism*. Ithaca, N.Y.: Cornell University Press, 1982.

Curtin, Philip D. "African History." In Kammen, ed. *The Past Before Us*, pp. 113–30.

———. *The Image of Africa*. Madison: The University of Wisconsin Press, 1964.

Dalzel, Archibald. *The History of Dahomy, An Inland Kingdom of Africa*. 1793. London: Frank Cass, 1967.

Davidson, Basil. *The Black Man's Burden: Africa and the Curse of the Nation-State*. New York: Times Books, 1992.

Delafosse, Maurice. *Broussard, ou les états d'âme d'un colonial*. Paris: Emile Larose, 1923.

———. *Manuel dahoméen*. Paris: Ernest Laroux, 1894.

Derrida, Jacques. *Given Time*. Trans. Peggy Kamuf. Chicago and London: The University of Chicago Press, 1992.

———. *Of Grammatology*. 1967. Trans. Gayatri Chakravorty Spivak. Baltimore and London: The Johns Hopkins University Press, 1974.

Deschamps, Hubert. *Roi de la brousse: Mémoires d'autres mondes*. Paris: Berger-Levrault, 1975.

Diagne, Ahmadou Mapaté. *Les Trois Volontés de Malic*. 1920. Nendeln: Krauss Reprint, 1973.

Djebar, Assia. *L'Amour, la fantasia*. Paris: Jean-Claude Lattès, 1985.

Duncan, John. *Travels in Western Africa* (1847). Johnson Reprint Corporation, 1967.

Eagleton, Terry, Fredric Jameson, and Edward W. Said. *Nationalism, Colonialism, and Literature*. Minneapolis: University of Minnesota Press, 1990.

Egonu, Iheanacho. "Le Prix Goncourt de 1921 et la 'Querelle de *Batouala*.'" *Research in African Literatures* 11.4 (1980): 529–45.

Emecheta, Buchi. *The Bride Price*. New York: George Braziller, 1976.

———. *The Joys of Motherhood*. New York: George Braziller, 1979.

Erikson, John D. *Nommo: African Fiction in French South of the Sahara*. York, S.C.: French Literature Publications, 1979.

Ezenwa-Ohaeto. *Chinua Achebe: The Author of* Things Fall Apart. Bloomington: Indiana University Press, 1997.

Fabian, Johannes. *Time and the Other: How Anthropology Makes Its Object*. New York: Columbia University Press, 1983.

———. "White Humor." *Transition* 55 (1992): 56–61.

Fabre, Michel. "De *Batouala* à *Doguicimi*: René Maran et les premiers romans africains." In Riesz and Ricard, eds., *Semper aliquid novi*, pp. 239–49.

——. *From Harlem to Paris: Black American Writers in France, 1840–1980.* Urbana: University of Illinois Press, 1991.

Fanon, Frantz. *Black Skin, White Masks.* Trans. Charles Lamb Markmann. New York: Grove, 1967.

——. *The Wretched of the Earth.* Trans. Constance Farrington. New York: Grove, 1963.

Feierman, Steven. "African Histories and the Dissolution of World History." In Bates and Mudimbe, *Africa and the Disciplines*, pp. 167–212.

Fish, Stanley. *Is There a Text in This Class?* Cambridge: Harvard University Press, 1980.

Flint, John E., ed. *The Cambridge History of Africa.* Vol. 5 (1790–1870). Cambridge, England: Cambridge University Press, 1976.

Forbes, F. E. *Dahomey and the Dahomans.* London: Longman, Brown, Green and Longmans, 1851.

——. *Six Months' Service in the African Blockade From April to October 1848 in Command of the H.M.S. Bonetta.* London: Richard Bentley, 1849.

Foucault, Michel. *Language, Counter-Memory, Practice.* Trans. Donald F. Bouchard and Sherry Simon. Ithaca and London: Cornell University Press, 1977.

——. "A Preface to Transgression." In Foucault, *Language, Counter-Memory, Practice*, pp. 29–52.

La Foule. Paris: Librairie Félix Alcan, 1934.

Fournier, Marcel. *Marcel Mauss.* Paris: Fayard, 1994.

Fraser, Robert. *The Novels of Ayi Kwei Armah.* London: Heinemann, 1980.

Frobenius, Leo, *Histoire de la civilisation africaine.* Trans. H. Black and D. Ermont. Paris: Gallimard, 1936.

Frobenius, Leo, and Douglas C. Fox. *Prehistoric Rock Pictures in Europe and Africa.* New York: The Museum of Modern Art, 1937.

——. *African Genesis.* New York: Stackpole Sons, 1937.

Furst, Lilian R. *All Is True: The Claims and Strategies of Realist Fiction.* Durham, N.C.: Duke University Press, 1995.

Gahisto, Manoel. "La Genèse de *Batouala*."In *Hommage à René Maran*, pp. 93–155.

Galey, Matthieu. "Un Grand Roman africain." *Le Monde.* October 12, 1968.

Gates, Henry Louis, Jr. "Between the Living and the Unborn." *New York Times Book Review.* June 28, 1992, p. 3.

——. *The Signifying Monkey.* New York: Oxford University Press, 1988.

Genette, Gérard. *Narrative Discourse.* Trans. Jane E. Lewin. Ithaca, N.Y.: Cornell University Press, 1980.

"Genital Reminders." *Times Literary Supplement.* December 19, 1968, p. 1425.

Gérard, Albert S. *European Language Writing in Sub-Saharan Africa*. 2 vols. Budapest: Akademai Kiado, 1986.

Gikandi, Simon. *Maps of Englishness: Writing Identity in the Culture of Colonialism*. New York: Columbia University Press, 1996.

——. *Reading Chinua Achebe*. Portsmouth, N.H.: Heinemann, 1991.

Greene, Graham. *It's a Battlefield*. 1934. Harmondsworth: Penguin, 1977.

Greenwood, James. *Prince Dick of Dahomey; or, Adventures in the Great Dark Land*. London: Ward and Downey, 1890.

Hammond, Dorothy, and Jablow, Alta. *The Africa That Never Was*. New York: Twayne, 1970.

Hardy, Georges. *Une Conquête morale: L'enseignement en A.O.F.* Paris: Armand Cohn, 1917.

——. "La Foule dans les sociétés dites primitives." In *La Foule*. pp. 23–47.

Hartman, Geoffrey. "Public Memory and Its Discontents." In Brown, *Uses of Literary History*, pp. 73–91.

Hazoumé, Paul. *Doguicimi: The First Dahomean Novel*. Paris: Larose, 1938. English trans. Richard Bjornson. Washington, D.C.: Three Continents, 1990.

——. "L'Humanisme occidental et l'humanisme africain." *Présence africaine* 14–15 (June/September 1957): 29–45.

——. *Le Pacte de sang au Dahomey*. 1937. Paris: Institut d'Ethnologie, 1956.

Head, Bessie. *The Collector of Treasures*. London: Heinemann, 1977.

——. *A Question of Power*. London: Heinemann, 1974.

——. *Serowe, Village of the Rain Wind*. London: Heinemann, 1981.

Herskovits, Melville J. *Dahomey, An Ancient West African Kingdom*. 2 vols. New York: J. J. Augustin, 1938.

Herskovits, Melville J., and Frances S. Herskovits. *Dahomean Narrative: A Cross-Cultural Analysis*. Evanston, Ill.: Northwestern University Press, 1958.

Higgins, Lynn A., and Brenda R. Silver, eds. *Rape and Representation*. New York: Columbia University Press, 1991.

Hobsbawm, Eric, and Terence Ranger. *The Invention of Tradition*. Cambridge, England: Cambridge University Press, 1984.

Hollier, Denis, ed. *The College of Sociology 1937–1939*. 1979. Trans. Betsy Wing. Minneapolis: University of Minnesota Press, 1988.

Hommage à René Maran. Paris: Présence africaine, 1965.

Hountondji, Paulin J. *African Philosophy: Myth and Reality*. Trans. Henri Evans with Jonathan Rée. Bloomington: Indiana University Press, 1983.

Huannou, Adrien. "Hommage à un grand écrivain: Paul Hazoumé." *Présence africaine* 114 (1980): 204–8.

Hubert, Henri. *Mission scientifique au Dahomey*. Paris: Larose, 1908.

Hubert, Henri, and Marcel Mauss. "Essai sur la nature et fonction du sacrifice." *L'Année Sociologique* (1898): 29–138. Trans. W. D. Halls. *Sacrifice: Its Nature and*

Function. Foreword E. E. Evans-Pritchard. Chicago: The University of Chicago Press, 1964.

Huggan, Graham. "Anthropologists and Other Frauds." *Comparative Literature* 46.2 (1994): 113–28.

Hymans, Jacques Louis. *Léopold Sédar Senghor: An Intellectual Biography*. Edinburgh: Edinburgh University Press, 1971.

Iliffe, John. *Africans: The History of a Continent*. New York: Cambridge University Press, 1995.

Innes, Catherine L. "Chinua Achebe." In Gérard 2: 698–704.

Irele, Abiola. *The African Experience in Literature and Ideology*. 1981. Bloomington: Indiana University Press, 1990.

———. "The Negritude Debate." In Gérard 1: 379–93.

Isichei, Elizabeth. *A History of the Igbo People*. London: Macmillan Press, 1976.

JanMohamed, Abdul. *Manichean Aesthetics*. Amherst: University of Massachusetts Press, 1983.

Johnson, Charles. "Fighting the Spirits." *Times Literary Supplement*. April 19, 1991. 22.

Julien, Eileen. "Rape, Repression, and Narrative Form in *Le Devoir de violence* and *La Vie et demie*." In Higgins, *Rape and Representation*, pp. 160–81.

Kammen, Michael. *The Past Before Us: Contemporary Historical Writing in the United States*. Ithaca and London: Cornell University Press, 1980.

Kane, Hamidou. *L'Aventure ambiguë*. Paris: René Juillard, 1961.

Kenyatta, Jomo. *Facing Mount Kenya*. London: Secker and Warburg, 1938.

Kesteloot, Lilyan. *Black Writers in French*. 1963. Trans. Ellen Conroy Kennedy. Philadelphia: Temple University Press, 1974.

Kortenaar, Neil Ten. "How the Centre Is Made to Hold in *Things Fall Apart*." *English Studies in Canada* 17.3 (1991): 319–36.

———. "'Only Connect': *Anthills of the Savannah* and Achebe's Trouble with Nigeria." *Research in African Literatures* 24.3 (1993): 59–72.

Kourouma, Ahmadou. *Les Soleils des indépendances*. Paris: Seuil, 1970.

Kristeva, Julia. *Revolution in Poetic Language*. Trans. Margaret Waller. New York: Columbia University Press, 1984.

Lane, Christopher. *The Ruling Passion: British Colonial Allegory and The Paradox of Homosexual Desire*. Durham and London: Duke University Press, 1995.

Lang, George. "Text, Identity, and Difference: Yambo Ouologuem's *Le Devoir de violence* and Ayi Kwei Armah's *Two Thousand Seasons*." *Comparative Literature Studies* 24.4 (1987): 387–402.

Larson, Ruth. "Ethnography, Thievery, and Cultural Identity: A Rereading of Michel Leiris's *L'Afrique fantôme*." *PMLA* 112.2 (1997): 229–42.

Lazarus, Neil. *Resistance in Postcolonial African Fiction*. New Haven: Yale University Press, 1990.

Lefebvre, Georges. "Foules historiques: les foules révolutionnaires." In *La Foule*, pp. 70–107.

Le Herissé, A. *L'Ancien royaume du Dahomey: Moeurs, religion, histoire*. Paris: Emile Larose, 1911.

Leiris, Michel. *L'Afrique fantôme*. Paris: Gallimard, 1934.

———. *Brisées*. Paris: Mercure de France, 1966.

Lévi-Strauss, Claude. *The Savage Mind*. 1962. Chicago: University of Chicago Press, 1966.

———. *Tristes Tropiques*. 1955. Trans. John and Doreen Weightman. New York: Atheneum, 1974.

Lévy-Bruhl, Lucien. "Préface." In Waterlot, *Les Bas-Reliefs*.

———. *Primitive Mentality*. Trans. Lilian A. Clare. New York: Macmillan, 1923.

Lukacs, Georg. *History and Class Consciousness*. 1923. Trans. Rodney Livingstone. Cambridge: MIT Press, 1967.

———. *The Theory of the Novel*. 1920. Trans. Anna Bostok. Cambridge: M.I.T. Press, 1971.

Mane, Robert, and Adrien Huannou, eds. *Doguicimi de Paul Hazoumé*. Paris: L'Harmattan, 1987.

Manning, Patrick. *Francophone Sub-Saharan Africa, 1880–1985*. Cambridge and New York: Cambridge University Press, 1988.

———. *Slavery, Colonialism, and Economic Growth in Dahomey, 1640–1960*. Cambridge, England: Cambridge University Press, 1982.

Maran, René. *Batouala*. Paris: Albin Michel, 1921. Trans. Adele Szold-Seltzer. New York: Selzer, 1922.

———. *Djogoni*. In *Hommage à René Maran*, pp. 157–98.

———. *Un homme pareil aux autres*. Paris: Arc-en-Ciel, 1947.

———. *Livingstone et l'exploration de l'Afrique*. Paris: Gallimard, 1938.

———. *La maison du bonheur*. Paris: Edition du Beffroi, 1909.

Marcus, George E., and Michael M. J. Fischer. *Anthropology as Cultural Critique*. Chicago: University of Chicago Press, 1986.

Mauss, Marcel. *Manuel d'ethnographie*. Paris: Payot, 1967.

Mbembe, Achille. *Afriques indociles: Christianisme, pouvoir et Etat en société postcoloniale*. Paris: Editions Karthala, 1988.

Michelet, Jules. *Histoire de la Révolution française*. 2 vols. Paris: Gallimard, 1939.

———. *Jeanne d'Arque*. Paris: Hachette, 1888.

Midiohouan, Guy Ossito. *L'Idéologie dans la littérature négro-africaine d'expression française*. Paris: L'Harmattan, 1986.

Miller, Christopher. *Blank Darkness: Africanist Discourse in French*. Chicago: University of Chicago Press, 1985.

———. "Literary Studies and African Literature: The Challenge of Intercultural Literacy." In Bates and Mudimbe, *Africa and the Disciplines*, pp. 213–31.

———. *Theories of Africans: Francophone Literature and Anthropology in Africa*. Chicago: University of Chicago Press, 1990.

Moore, Gerald. "Amos Tutuola." In Beier, *Introduction to African Literature*, pp. 179–87.

Morson, Gary Saul, and Caryl Emerson. *Mikhail Bakhtin: Creation of a Prosaics*. Stanford, Calif.: Stanford University Press, 1990.

Moukoko, Gobina. "Les Prises de parole et la mort de Doguicimi." In Mane and Huannou, *Doguicimi de Paul Hazoumé*, pp. 69–76.

Mudimbe, V. Y. *The Invention of Africa: Gnosis, Philosophy, and the Order of Knowledge*. Bloomington: University of Indiana Press, 1988.

———, ed. *The Surreptitious Speech: Présence Africaine and the Politics of Otherness 1947–1987*. Chicago: The University of Chicago Press, 1992.

Mulvey, Laura. *Visual and Other Pleasures*. Bloomington: Indiana University Press, 1989.

Nichols, J. A. "Towards a Camusian Reading of *Le Devoir de violence*." *Australian Journal of French Studies* 28.2 (1991): 211–19.

Nwezeh, E. C. "René Maran: Myth and Reality." *Odu* 18 July 1978. 91–105.

Oe, Kenzaburo. *A Personal Matter*. 1964. Trans. John Nathan. New York: Grove, 1969.

Ogunsanwo, Olatubosun. "Transcending History: Achebe's Trilogy." *Neohelicon* 14.2 (1987): 127–37.

Ojo-Ade, Femi. *René Maran, The Black Frenchman: A Bio-Critical Study*. Washington, D.C.: Three Continents, 1984.

Okri, Ben. *The Famished Road*. 1991. New York: Anchor, Doubleday 1993.

———. *Songs of Enchantment*. New York: Nan A. Talese, 1993.

Olukoshi, Adebayo O., and Osita Agbu. "The Deepening Crisis of Nigerian Federalism and the Future of the Nation-State." In Olukoshi and Laasko, *Challenges*, pp. 74–101.

Olukoshi, Adebayo O., and Liisa Laasko, eds. *Challenges to the Nation-State in Africa*. Uppsala: Nordiska Afrikainstitutet, 1996.

Ouologuem, Yambo. *Le Devoir de violence*. Paris: Seuil, 1968. Trans. Ralph Manheim. *Bound to Violence*. Oxford: Heinemann, 1971.

Owomoyela, Oyekan. *African Literatures: An Introduction*. Waltham, Mass.: Crossroads, 1979.

Ozouf, Mona. *Festivals of the French Revolution*. Trans. Alan Sheridan. Cambridge: Harvard University Press, 1988.

Parini, Jay. "In the Land of the Spirits." *The Boston Sunday Globe*. June 7, 1992, pp. 100, 103.

Parry, Benita. "Resistance Theory/Theorising Resistance, or Two Cheers for Nativism." In Barker, Hulme, Iversen, *Colonial Discourse/Postcolonial Theory*, pp. 172–96.

Perham, Margery. "Foreword." In Awolowo, *Path to Nigerian Freedom.*

Philipson, Robert. "Chess and Sex in *Le Devoir de violence.*" *Callaloo* 12.1 (1989): 216–32.

Polan, Dana. "Fables of Transgression: The Reading of Politics and the Politics of Reading in Foucauldian Discourse." *Boundary 2* 10.3 (1982): 361–81.

Polanyi, Karl. *Dahomey and the Slave Trade.* Seattle and London: University of Washington Press, 1966.

Poulet, Georges. "Criticism and the Experience of Interiority." In Tompkins, *Reader Response Criticism*, pp. 41–9.

Pratt, Mary Louise. "Fieldwork in Common Places." In Clifford and Marcus, *Writing Culture*, pp. 27–50.

———. *Imperial Eyes: Travel Writing and Transculturation.* London and New York: Routledge, 1992.

Randall, Marilyn. "Appropriate(d) Discourse: Plagiarism and Decolonization." *New Literary History* 22 (1991): 525–41.

Renan, Ernest. "What Is a Nation?" In Bhabha, *Nation and Narration*, pp. 1–7.

Riesz, Janos, and Alain Ricard. *Semper aliquid novi: Littérature comparée et littératures d'Afrique.* Tubingen: Gunter Narr, 1990.

Roseberry, William. *Anthropologies and Histories: Essays in Culture, History, and Political Economy.* New Brunswick and London: Rutgers University Press, 1989.

Ross, David. "Dahomey." In Crowder, ed., *West African Resistance*, pp. 144–69.

Said, Edward W. *Culture and Imperialism.* New York: Knopf, 1993.

———. "Respresenting the Colonized: Anthropology's Interlocutors." *Critical Inquiry* 15 (1989): 205–25.

———. "Yeats and Decolonization." In Eagleton et al., *Nationalism, Colonialism, and Literature*, pp. 69–95.

Saro-Wiwa, Ken. *Sozaboy: A Novel in Rotten English.* 1985. Essex, England: Longman, 1994.

Schikora, Rosemary G. "Outfoxing the Fox: Game Strategy in *Le Devoir de violence.*" *Perspectives on Contemporary Literature* 6 (1980): 72–79.

Sellin, Eric. "The Unknown Voice of Yambo Ouologuem." *Yale French Studies* 53 (1976): 137–62.

Sembène Ousmane. *Gods Bits of Wood. (Les Bouts de bois de dieu,* 1960). Trans. Francis Price. Hanover and Oxford: Heinemann, 1986.

———. *Vehi Ciosane.* Paris: Présence africaine, 1965.

Senghor, Léopold. *Liberté I: Négritude et humanisme.* Paris: Seuil, 1964.

———. "René Maran, Précurseur de la négritude." In *Hommage à René Maran*, pp. 9–13.

Simpson, George Eaton. *Melville J. Herskovits*. New York: Columbia University Press, 1973.

Skertchly, J. A. *Dahomey As It Is*. London: Chapman and Hall, 1874.

Songolo, Aliko. "Fiction et subversion: *Le Devoir de violence*." *Présence africaine* 120 (1981): 17–34.

Soyinka, Wole. *Myth, Literature, and the African World*. 1976. Cambridge: Cambridge University Press, 1992.

Spurr, David. *The Rhetoric of Empire*. Durham, N.C.: Duke University Press, 1993.

Steins, Martin. "Black Migrants in Paris." In Gérard 1: 354–78.

Stevenson, W. H. "The Horn." In Gerard 2: 659–68.

Stocking, George W. *Victorian Anthropology*. New York: The Free Press, 1987.

Temperley, Howard. *White Dreams, Black Africa: The Antislavery Expedition to the Niger River 1841–1842*. New Haven and London: Yale University Press, 1991.

Thomas, Nicholas. *Colonialism's Culture: Anthropology, Travel, and Government*. Princeton: Princeton University Press, 1994.

Todorov, Tzvetan. *Mikhail Bakhtin: The Dialogic Principle*. Trans. Wlad Godzich. Minneapolis: University of Minnesota Press, 1984.

Tompkins, Jane, ed. *Reader-Response Criticism*. Baltimore: Johns Hopkins University Press, 1980.

Torgovnik, Marianna. *Gone Primitive: Savage Intellects, Modern Lives*. Chicago and London: University of Chicago Press, 1990.

Trautmann, René. *Au Pays de Batouala: noirs et blancs en Afrique*. Paris: Payot, 1922.

Tutuola, Amos. *The Palm-Wine Drinkard*. London: Faber, 1952.

Udumukwu, Onyemaechi. "The Antinomy of Anti-colonial Discourse: A Revisionist Marxist Study of Achebe's *Things Fall Apart*." *Neohelicon* 18.2 (1991): 317–36.

Veyne, Paul. *Writing History: Essay on Epistemology*. Trans. Mina Moore-Rinvolucri. Middletown, Conn.: Wesleyan University Press, 1984.

Vignonde, Jean-Norbert. "Les Précurseurs: Félix Couchoro, Paul Hazoumé." *Notre Librairie* 69 (1983): 33–40.

Waterlot, E. G. *Les Bas-Reliefs des bâtiments royaux d'Abomey*. Paris: L'Institut d'Ethnologie, 1926.

White, Hayden. "The Historical Text as Literary Artifact." In Canary and Kozicki, eds. *The Writing of History*, pp. 41–62.

Williams, David. "English Speaking West Africa." In Crowder, ed., *The Cambridge History of Africa*. Vol. 8 (1943–1970s).

Wilmot, Arthur Parry Eardley. "A Copy of Commodore Wilmot's Report of His Recent Visit to the King of Dahomey." 1863. In Burton, *Mission to Gelele*, II: 227–64.

Wolf, Eric. *Europe and the People without History*. Berkeley: University of California Press, 1982.

Wolitz, Seth. "L'Art du plagiat, ou, une brève défense de Ouologuem." *Research in African Literatures* 4.1 (1973): 130–34.

Wren, Robert M. *Those Magical Years: The Making of Nigerian Literature at Ibadan 1948–1966.* Washington, D.C.: Three Continents, 1980.

Wright, Derek. "Orality in the African Historical Novel: Yambo Ouologuem's *Bound to Violence* and Ayi Kwei Armah's *Two Thousand Seasons.*" *Journal of Commonwealth Literature* 23.1 (1988): 91–101.

Young, Crawford. *The African Colonial State in Comparative Perspective.* New Haven: Yale University Press, 1994.

INDEX

■■

Abam, the, 42, 177n. 19
Absent witness, 49–50, 56–57, 59–61
Achebe, Chinua, 5, 7–10, 15–16, 19, 21–
    23, 37–38, 40–42, 44, 141–143, 165–
    166, 168, 176nn. 14–15, 177nn. 16–
    18, 190n. 2; and *Anthills of the Savan-*
    nah, 141–145, 164; and *Arrow of God*,
    9, 15, 22–23, 37, 39–44, 142, 157; and
    Things Fall Apart, 8–9, 14, 22, 37–42,
    45, 142
Agbu, Osita, 146
Aizenberg, Edna, 119, 188n. 9
Akinjogbin, J. A., 110
Ajayi, J. F. Ade, 51
Allochronic discourse, 11–12, 18, 42, 76,
    89, 91, 115
Anderson, Benedict, 147, 150–151
Anticolonialism, 5, 21–22, 24, 29, 34,
    41, 95. *See also* Resistance
Appiah, K. Anthony, 2, 190n. 3, 190n. 5
Arac, Jonathan, 169, 191n. 2
Armah, Ayi Kwei, 118–119, 186n. 4,
    187nn. 5–7

Asad, Talal, 175n. 8
Ashanti, 50
Authenticity, 1–5, 7, 15–17, 22–24, 33,
    36, 86–87, 107, 120, 122, 125–126,
    136, 159, 165, 173n. 1, 187n. 6
Awolowo, Obafemi, 146, 164
Azikiwe, Nnamdi, 146

Bakhtin, M. M., 4, 6, 39, 43, 148, 151,
    154, 157, 177, 177n. 20, 191n. 9
Balzac, Honoré de, 154
Barr, Alfred, 90
Barthes, Roland, 180n. 14
Bataille, Georges, 11, 65–66, 109, 127,
    174
Behanzin, King, 74–75, 181n. 2
Benin, 9, 50
Benjamin, Walter, 87
Bernasko, Peter W., 50, 59, 181n. 18
Beti, Mongo, 82
Bhabha, Homi, 19–20, 148, 150–153,
    191nn. 7–8
Biafra, 44, 144–146

Black Orpheus, 8
Blood oath, 11, 16–17, 91–94
Bonetta, 55, 63, 180n. 15
Booker Prize, 2, 145, 190n. 3
Brantlinger, Patrick, 16, 51, 178n. 4
Britain, 7, 46–48, 50–51, 71, 112, 146, 163–164; in Achebe's fiction, 38, 40–42, 143, 157; in *Doguicimi*, 100, 103–106
Brodie, Fawn, 46, 59, 60, 68, 181n. 21
Burton, Richard, 16, 46, 50, 54–55, 57–61, 63, 66–72, 73, 77, 178n. 2, 181n. 1

Caillois, Roger, 174n. 6
Camara Laye, 7
Cary, Joyce, 177nn. 15–16
Césaire, Aimé, 5, 14, 30, 82, 182n. 7
Chanson de Roland, 111
Chatterjee, Partha, 147, 190n. 4
Chronotope, 10, 19, 148, 151, 154, 157, 191n. 9
Civilizing mission, 17, 21, 30, 76, 120
Claiming history, 4, 19–20, 145, 148, 162, 165, 168
Clifford, James, 4–5, 12–13, 24–25, 27, 38, 72, 175n. 2
Clowes, William Laird, 55, 57
Collège de Sociologie, 11, 174n. 6
Colonialism: critiques of, 5, 12, 29–32, 39, 103, 136, 138; culture of, 36, 50, 70, 91, 165, 167–168; and geography, 143, 153, 156; as historical period, 38, 40, 94–95, 116, 120–121, 123, 145, 162; and invented tradition, 15, 22, 75, 159
Comaroff, John and Jean Comaroff, 82, 84, 185n. 15
Coombes, Annie, 70, 78, 181n. 20
Counterhistory, 16, 17, 163

Crapanzano, Vincent, 71–72
Culler, Jonathan, 123, 125, 188n. 14
Curtin, Philip, 13–14, 182n. 6

Dahomey, 9–11, 15–18, 24, 30, 112, 114, 120, 125, 178n. 1, 179n. 6; and blood oath, 91–94; and Herskovits, 73–75; and monarchy, 64–65, 68–69, 109–110; and oral history, 84–89, 102, 120; relations with the British, 50–1, 57, 179nn. 6–7, 180n. 16; and Victorian travel writing, 45–51, 58, 63–64, 66, 72, 178n. 4, 178n. 5. *See also* Human sacrifice, Slave trade
Dakar-Djibouti Expedition, 26, 73
Dalzel, Archibald, 11, 47–49, 178n. 4
Davidson, Basil, 145
Delafosse, Maurice, 24–26, 81, 88, 175n. 3
Derrida, Jacques, 3, 54, 64–65, 150, 157, 180n. 14
Deschamps, Hubert, 26
Diagne, Ahmadou Mapaté, 6
Dissent, 20–21, 23, 28, 142, 164, 167
Duncan, John, 50–56, 58–59, 61, 70, 179nn. 9-10, 180nn. 11–13, 180n. 16

Ecole coloniale, 6, 77, 112
Ecole des langues orientales, 24
Egonu, Iheanacho, 31, 176n. 10
Ekwensi, Cyprian, 142
Emecheta, Buchi, 141
Emerson, Caryl, 39, 43
Ethnography, 4, 24–6, 28, 83–84, 89, 114–115, 119, 176nn. 13–14, 177n. 20; and biogeography, 77–81; and catalogues, 11, 13, 52, 68–70, 77–79; and ethnographic impulse, 23, 38, 40, 42; and history, 12–13, 15, 17, 32–33, 36–37, 40, 75, 80–82, 95–96,

114–115, 187n. 7; and nationalism, 81, 117, 182n. 3

Ethnophilosophy, 50

Ezenwa-Ohaeto, 8, 177n. 17

Fabian, Johannes, 11–13, 82, 89–90

Fabre, Michel, 31, 111, 176, 185n. 13

Fagunwa, D.O., 173n. 1, 190n. 5, 191n. 11

Fanon, Franz, 5, 28, 35–36, 117–119, 137–138, 176n. 8, 186n. 5

Feierman, Steven, 14

First Congress of Black Writers, 82, 182n. 7

Flaubert, Gustave, 17, 97, 183n. 1

Forbes, F.E., 47–49, 50, 54–58, 60, 63–64, 69–70, 73, 99, 180n. 11, 180n. 15, 180nn. 16–17

Forgetfulness, 139–140, 148–150, 152, 153–154, 156, 158–163, 168

Foucault, Michel, 117–118, 137, 140

Fox, Douglas C., 90

France: and Maran's attachment to, 27–28, 30–31; relations with Dahomey, 51, 75–76, 92–95; treatment of in *Doguicimi*, 103–108, 111–113

French Revolution, 17–18, 30, 94, 103, 110, 112–114

Frobenius, Leo, 7, 24–25, 89–91, 117, 119, 136, 174n. 3, 175n. 3

Gahisto, Manoel, 25, 28, 174n. 1, 176n. 9

Gates, Henry Louis Jr., 2, 181n. 1, 190n. 2, 190n. 5

Gelele, King, of Dahomey, 61, 70–72, 181n. 18

Genette, Gerard, 52, 121, 133–134, 189n. 21

Gide, André, 103

Gikandi, Simon, 8

Greene, Graham, 2, 129–130, 188n. 15, 188n. 17

Greenwood, James, 178n. 5

Guezo, King, of Dahomey, 17, 51, 58, 88, 97–98, 180n. 16, 181n. 19; fictional treatment of, 100–104, 108–110

Hammond, Dorothy, and Jablow, Alta, 178n. 3

Hardy, Georges, 6, 112–115, 184n. 8, 184n. 10, 185nn. 16–17

Hartman, Geoffrey, 169–171

Hazoumé, Paul, 5, 7, 9–12, 16–19, 31, 46, 72–73, 75–76, 78, 95–96, 131, 165, 167–168, 182n. 3–4, 185n. 16; and *Doguicimi*, 89, 97–112, 114–115, 179n. 9, 183n. 9, 183n. 1, 184n. 2–5, 184nn. 7–11, 185nn. 12–13, 186n. 17, 187n. 18; and "L'Humanisme," 82–85, 88–89; and *Le Pacte*, 75, 81, 83, 89, 91–95, 114, 183n. 9, 184n. 11.

Herskovits, Melville, 9–11, 18, 73–76, 82, 181nn. 1–2

Historicity, of the novel, 2, 20, 23, 28, 32, 37–38, 44, 114–115, 121, 126–127, 129–130, 187–8n. 7

Historicism, 9–10, 13–14, 18–19, 82, 93, 134–135, 139–140, 148, 150–151, 156, 166, 182n. 6; and *Doguicimi*, 101, 104–106, 109; and geography, 143–144, 190n. 4; and transgression, 117–119, 138

Horn, The, 8

Hountondji, Paulin, 50, 63

Hubert, Henri (b. 1879), 10–11, 76–81, 174n. 5

Hubert, Henri (b. 1872, collaborator of Mauss), 45, 174n. 5, 175n. 7

Huggan, Graham, 177n. 14, 189n. 22
Human sacrifice, 10–11, 16–7, 19, 30,
    46–50, 53–58, 63–66, 70, 73–74,
    125, 135, 159, 174, 178n. 3, 179n. 9,
    181n. 21; and Bataille, 11, 109, 174n.
    6; and Hazoumé, 76, 97–102, 107,
    109, 111; as landscape, 55–56, 61–
    62, 72, 162. *See also* sacrifice
Hybridization, 4, 39, 43, 177n. 20

Ibo, the, 37–38, 40–44, 177n. 19
Illustrated London News, The, 66–67
Inaugural gesture, 1, 2, 4–5, 7–8, 17,
    21–22, 168
Independence, 20, 37, 38, 44, 81, 108,
    153, 164; in *Le Devoir,* 116, 118, 123,
    137; in *The Famished Road,* 141–142,
    145, 148–149, 156, 158, 162
Institut d'ethnologie, 24, 25, 81, 84
Irele, Abiola, 5, 12, 173n. 1
Isichei, Elizabeth, 177n. 19

Jan Mohamed, Abdul, 38
Joan of Arc, 17–18, 110–112, 184n. 4
Johnson, Charles, 1
Julien, Eileen, 189n. 18, 189n. 20

Kenyatta, Jomo, 81
Kesteloot, Lilyan, 12, 76
Kortenaar, Neil Ten, 143
Kourouma, Ahmadou, 2, 43
Kristeva, Julia, 45–46

Lamb, Bulfinch, 179n. 7–8
Lane, Christopher, 50, 180n. 12
Lang, George, 119, 186n. 5
Larson, Ruth, 175n. 6
Lazarus, Neil, 119, 164
Lefebvre, Georges, 113

Le Herissé, A., 88
Leiris, Michel, 11, 26–28, 73, 175n. 6
Lévi-Strauss, Claude, 3–4
Lévy-Bruhl, Lucien, 24, 86–87
Liminality, 19, 148–149, 152–154, 163
Lindfors, Bernth, 8
Literary history, 10, 12, 16, 76, 165–166,
    169, 191nn. 1–2
Livingstone, David, 175n. 4
Lugard, Frederick, 146
Lukacs, Georg, 31–32, 176n. 12

Malinowski, Bronislaw, 81
Manning, Patrick, 94, 96, 182n. 3,
    183n. 9–10, 185n. 11
Maran, René, 9–10, 21, 26–27, 15, 28,
    137, 165, 168, 175n. 1, 175n. 4, 176n.
    7–13, 182n. 7, 185n. 13; and *Batouala*
    5–8, 12, 15, 22–25, 28, 31–37, 43–45,
    174n. 4, 184n. 6, 186n. 18; com-
    pared to Achebe, 21–23, 43–44,
    166; correspondence with Gahisto,
    26–28, 174n. 1, 176n. 9; preface to
    Batouala, 28–31, 114; his review of
    Doguicimi, 111
Mauss, Marcel, 11, 24–26, 45, 64,
    174n. 5, 175n. 5
Mbembe, Achille, 161
Memory, 45, 91, 122, 136–137, 150, 152,
    157, 160–162; and place, 19, 148,
    154, 190n. 2; and oral history, 88,
    134; and to memorialize, 169–171.
    See also forgetfullness.
Michelet, Jules, 17–18, 110–114, 167,
    185n. 14
Midiohouan, Guy Ossito, 6, 31, 185n. 16
Miller, Christopher, 1, 2, 6–7, 24, 43,
    89, 129–130, 136, 174n. 3, 175n. 3,
    188n. 17, 189n. 19

Molestation, as narrative technique, 117, 122, 123, 128, 131–2, 139

Moore, Gerald, 173n. 1

Morrison, Toni, 170

Morson, Gary Saul, 39, 43

Mudimbe, V.Y., 13–14, 82–83, 173n. 2

Musée d'ethnologie du Trocadéro, 87

Musée de l'homme, 11, 81

Museum of Modern Art, New York, 90

Narrative space, 11, 117, 120, 144–5; and contact zone, 95–96; and hybridization, 43

Nation, 2, 10, 17–18, 19, 40, 77, 97, 106–7, 109, 116, 138, 156, 159–160; and emergence of new, 142–144, 148–149, 150, 163–164; and reinscription, 111–115

Nationalism, 31, 81, 140, 164, 168; and Hazoumé, 94, 98, 102–103, 108, 110; and Nigeria, 141–142, 145–146, 148, 153, 190n. 2; theories of, 19, 147–148, 150–152. *See also* Independence

Native point of view, 16, 19, 84, 107, 117, 130, 138–139, 184n. 4; and *négraille*, 119–122

Negritude, 5, 8, 14, 16–17, 24–25, 32, 76, 82–83, 89, 136, 175n. 3, 182n. 4, 183n. 7–8

Niger Expedition, 51

Nigeria, 8, 19, 145–146, 163–164, 170; and civil war, 44, 141–142, 146; treatment of in *The Famished Road*, 150, 153–154, 158–159. *See also* Biafra.

Objectivity: and ethnographic authority, 25, 27, 29, 43, 99; and Ouo-

loguem's attack on, 119, 125, 128, 134

Oe, Kenzaburo, 169

Oje-Ade, Femi, 31, 176n. 11

Okri, Ben: compared to Ouologuem, 10, 116–117, 121–122, 136–137, 140, 168; and *Famished Road*, 18–19, 56, 141–142, 148–150, 152–164, 170, 190n. 3, 191; and idea of nation, 146–148, 152–154; and reviews of, 1–2, 4–5, 145

Oloruntimehin, B.O., 51

Olukushi, Adebayo, 146

Ouologuem, Yambo: *Le Devoir de violence*, 18–19, 75, 116–140, 165, 186nn. 1–6, 187n. 7, 188nn. 8–15, 189n. 19, 189n. 22; reception of, 1–2, 4–5, 125–127, 129, 131, 139. *See also* Ben Okri, Plagiarism

Ozouf, Mona, 114

Parini, Jay, 2

Parry, Benita, 186n. 3

Perham, Margery, 164

Place: and claiming history, 44, 167; as fantastic landscape, 149–150; as narrative paradigm for nation, 19, 81, 143–144, 147–148, 151–153

Plagiarism, 2–3, 125, 129–130, 188n. 10, 188n. 17

Polanyi, Karl, 178n. 1, 179n. 7

Postcoloniality, as future, 15, 19, 40, 115, 118, 134, 145, 150

Postcolonial literature, 22, 56, 138, 156, 165

Postcolonial period. See Independence

Postcolonial studies, 14, 19, 20, 118, 148

Poulet, Georges, 124–125, 128

Pratt, Mary Louise, 55, 58, 95–96, 174n. 3, 179n. 10

Présence africaine, 17, 76, 82–83, 182n. 6

Prix Goncourt, 5, 24, 31

Prix Rénaudot, 125–126

Ranger, Terence, 22–23

Realism, 17, 23, 25, 27–28, 31, 117, 119, 142, 154, 190n. 3

Reinscription, 17–18, 44, 95, 103, 106, 108, 110–112, 114

Renan, Ernest, 152

Resistance, 51, 94–96, 112, 120, 138–9, 157, 160, 165, 174n. 3, 183n. 11, 186n. 3; v. dissidence, 19–20; to human sacrifices, 53, 100; novel of, 38–39, 41, 42. *See also* Anticolonialism

Resistant history, 4, 116. *See also* Counterhistory

Rousseau, Jean-Jacques, 54

Royal Geographic Society, 51

Sacrifice: and history, 16, 18; and Doguicimi's self-sacrifice, 97, 111–112; and Kristeva, 45; and Mauss, 45, 175n. 7. *See also* Human sacrifice, Violence.

Said, Edward W., 10, 18, 20, 38, 95, 138–139, 183n. 11

Salvage ethnography, 38, 175, 189n. 22

Saro-Wiwa, Ken, 141, 144–145, 164

Sartre, Jean Paul, 83

Schwartz-Bart, André, 2, 186n. 4, 188n. 10

Scott, Walter, 141

Sembène Ousmane, 156–157

Senghor, Léopold, 5–7, 17, 24, 32, 36, 44, 82–84, 89, 174n. 3, 175n. 3, 182n. 7, 183n. 8, 185n. 16

Skertchly, J.A., 49–50, 54, 61–62, 73, 99, 179n. 8, 181n. 2, 181n. 21

Slave trade, 51, 52, 55, 63–65, 68, 70–1, 76, 94–95, 101, 110, 135–136, 170, 178n. 1, 178n. 3; and Doguicimi's critique of, 103, 104–105, 107

Songolo, Aliko, 188n. 11–12, 188n. 17

Soyinka, Wole, 8, 118, 141, 157, 186n. 2, 189n. 1, 190n. 5, 191n. 12

Spectacle, 46, 66, 98, 100, 117–118, 127

Speke, 59

Spurr, David, 14–15, 68–69, 103, 184n. 8, 184n. 10

Stevenson, W.H., 8

Temperley, Howard, 52

Thomas, Nicholas, 77

Torgovnik, Marianna, 174n. 6

Tradition, 8, 46, 93, 107–109, 117, 161; and Achebe, 15, 40–41; and anticolonialism, 21–23; and invention of tradition, 22, 31, 75, 159, 166; and Maran, 33–36; v. humanism, 83–84, 108

Transgression, 19, 137–140, 148–149, 154, 156, 165, 186n. 1; v. resistance, 116–117, 123–124

Trautmann, René, 176n. 13

Tutuola, Amos, 8, 142, 173n. 1, 190n. 5, 191n. 11

Veyne, Paul, 139–140, 166–168

Vignonde, Jean-Norbet, 182n. 4

Violence, 20, 118–119, 144; and authenticity, 3, 107, 125, 129; and representation, 45–46, 52–53, 122, 127–128, 131, 135–136, 180n. 12; as sexual violence, 126, 130, 132–133. *See also*

Human sacrifice, Sacrifice, and
Transgression
Voyeur, 124–125, 127, 133

Walcott, Derek, 171
Waterlot, E.G., 76, 84–88
Wilmot, A.P., 50, 54–55, 57–59, 65–66
Witness, 46, 59, 99–100, 137, 162,

179n. 10; reader as, 124–125. *See
also* Absent witness
Wolf, Eric, 174n. 8
Wolitz, Seth, 188n. 15, 188n. 17
Wright, Derek, 186n. 6, 188n. 9

Yeats, William Butler, 38
Young, Crawford, 145–147